Cockleshell Journey

JOHN RIDGWAY

Cockleshell Journey

The Adventures of Three Men and a Girl

HODDER AND STOUGHTON
LONDON SYDNEY AUCKLAND TORONTO

To all those at home who
made it possible,
Mr. and Mrs. Bell, Mrs. Price
and Lady D'Albiac

Contents

Illustrations

I

We Sure Hate to Lose Good Men

AT 580 M.P.H. LIFE was cosy. Schmaltzy music drifted nostalgically over 103 empty seats, leaving the three stewardesses in their heavy coats with little to do. The ten passengers gazed out of the windows; they were on one of the last Boeing 737 flights from Buenos Aires to Punta Arenas at the southern tip of communist Chile. For four passengers the view, just ten minutes from their destination, was rather important, because for them the air-conditioned comfort and canned music soon had to stop.

For the next three months, October–December 1972, Richard Shuff (twenty-eight), Krister Nylund (twenty-three and Swedish), were going to attempt the first crossing of the Gran Campo Nevado Ice-Cap with my wife, Marie Christine, and me. Below us the land looked forbidding, still in the grip of southern winter. Grassland burned brown by icy gales that whirl clear round the world, hindered only by this god-forsaken fingertip of South America. We passed over an assortment of bleak lakes coloured black, green and café-au-lait, there were a few scattered sheep farms but no trees. Slate-grey fiords probed spikey fingers into the flat lands below, as if to squeeze up against the snow-covered peaks of the cordillera Andes, which marched down the western rim of our horizon.

"This doesn't look much like a summer hol to me," muttered my wife.

"You're lucky to be asked to join the expedition," I sniffed importantly, while secretly trying to reassure myself that three months' camping in snow could be fun.

"There's Skyring – that long one leading into the mountains," Richard jabbed his finger at the window as the plane banked for its approach to the runway.

"It looks pretty cold up there," replied Krister, and no one answered.

Suddenly we were much lower, the ground speeding past showed there were trees after all, dead-looking woods along snow-topped hills. The wheels bumped tarmac. Engines reversed thrust, screaming power. The plane taxied up to the unpretentious airport building and the doors opened. We followed the other half-dozen passengers to the tail-end of the plane, anxious to feel just how cold it was.

"Captain Reedgway?" I hate being called 'Captain'. I groaned inwardly, there was an official-looking reception party. It only needed a couple of sentences from the burly agency man for me to guess it was going to be expensive in Punta Arenas unless we were very careful. Luckily for us the British Consul had kindly arranged for his son, Charles King, and his assistant Señor Barrientos to meet us as well, and in the car on the way into town they gave us advice on where we could find reasonably priced accommodation. While it is always nice to be met at an airport, it is a pity that such greetings so often end up in the most expensive hotel in town; and it's particularly incongruous when such a hotel is succeeded by a tent for three months.

Punta Arenas (Sandy Point) southernmost city in the world. The sprawling, untidy home of eighty thousand people, mostly impoverished immigrants from the island of Chiloe, seven hundred miles farther north up the rugged west coast of Chile, shanty-town dwellers. Constant raw winds send dust swirling into your eyes at every bleak street corner. From the ugly waterfront you look across the storm-lashed Magellan Straits to the snowy peaks of Tierra del Fuego. Grim leafless trees rise, wind-burned, up snow-topped hills to the back of town. People queue resentful-eyed outside empty shop windows, waiting restlessly for the fundamentals of life. The communist government, American economic pressure, and lack of foreign exchange all conspire to produce what is probably the most un-swinging free port on earth. Shortage of toothpaste because Chile hasn't the machinery for making the tubes to fill with the stuff, a three-month absence of loo paper; much worse, no money to buy drugs for the hospitals. A country embattled, yet strangely a country trying proudly to find its feet and stand alone on its own resources. Not really the place for 'a summer hol' as Marie Christine had said; thank goodness we had brought our equipment and supplies with us.

"There's an American research ship in the docks, they've asked us down to look over their charts tonight," said Richard on the morning of our second day in town. We were having a lot of trouble buying simple bulk supplies of things like sugar and oats; but a visit to the ship seemed a priority. And so, shortly after dark, we splashed our way through the dockyard puddles, leaving Krister behind in bed with an upset stomach.

The Antarctic research ship *Hero* is a diesel-powered but sail-equipped wooden ship. Wood provides resilience in ice and acoustic quiet. Sails assure steadiness, safety and again silence. Her oak hull is sheathed in greenheart to protect against abrasion by floating ice. She has a normal crew of ten men and ten scientists. Although primarily designed for trawling and other biological collecting, *Hero* has four laboratories and an acoustically quiet work boat to support such diverse activities as physical oceanography, bio-acoustic studies, onshore geology and biological investigations.

On this dismal October night she lay alongside the dock between a Norwegian freighter and a Chilean Navy patrol boat. A mile or two offshore on the other side of the dock we could see the old four-master coal hulk silhouetted against the last rays of sunset, a reminder of braver days. Bob Riseborough, a marine biologist, was our host, and he greeted us with typical American warmth as we came up the gangplank to board the 125-foot vessel, which throbbed quietly with all the little noises involved in replenishment.

When we reached the tiny chart-room, we found Captain Lenie already poring over charts of the area in which we proposed to operate. A short, dynamic Flemish American in khaki fatigues, he cut through the introductions and waved the three of us forward to join him round the table, while Bob looked on from the doorway.

"You wanna go up here, in two ten-foot rubber boats?" he asked, the insanity of the idea filtering through the gutteral tone of his voice.

"Look – I tried to get through these narrows only a few days ago." His finger stabbed the chart where it showed a narrow channel running between the mountains at the southern end of the ice-cap.

"This ship is a goddamn ice-breaker, but I had to turn

back." He gestured with his hands to emphasise the futility of our project. Out of the corner of my eye I could see a film of worry cover Richard's face. Ever respectful of authority this message was getting to him, hard.

"That's a helluva piece of country. These glaciers on the sides of the mountains – they're just stuck on, waiting to come crashing thousands of feet down into the sea."

I felt Marie Christine stiffen with anxiety. The captain was used to making the running in conversation aboard his ship, now he hardly paused for breath in his prophecy of disaster.

"There are rapids here in the narrows, it's not much over twenty yards wide and the icebergs are grounded by the tide. The cliffs are so high they blot out the radio," he went on, but at least the last part wouldn't bother us – we had no radio!

"Apart from the icebergs grinding about in the channel, the glaciers will be calving now with the onset of spring. That will mean avalanches and tidal waves as a result. Out here on the Pacific coast there's a terrific swell, and here, there's a Tide Race." I made a note of the place, Punta Quidora, we'd have to watch out for that.

The captain continued with his gloomy forecasts; showing utter amazement when he learned that Marie Christine was actually coming with us. I listened carefully, not having to say much helps concentration; I'd been involved in this kind of conversation more than once before about other projects. Eventually we reached a point where there really weren't many more disasters to be imagined: it was time to leave the ship.

"We sure hate to lose good men," said the captain as he shook my hand at the door. I smiled and thanked him for making time to see us.

Bob was coming ashore too, and the four of us walked along the pier in silence. No one was really sure what to say. I began to wonder what on earth I was doing here anyway, surely I should be at home toasting my feet in front of the peat fire?

I suppose the original cause of my wish to explore the west coast of southern Chile sprang from a collision between my yacht and a trawler, hired by a T.V. crew off the west coast of Ireland. It was the start of the 1968 race to be the first person to sail alone non-stop round the world. As a result of the accident I had to abandon my attempt at Recife in Brazil, and so I didn't sail round Cape Horn. From then on I was always hoping to find a way to get down and explore the area. In 1970/1 I led the first expedition to follow the complete course of the Amazon from its farthest source to the sea. One of the aims of that expedition had been personal; I had arranged it so that the four members of the team knew each other hardly at all. I had hoped to prove to myself that I was able to persuade the three men and one girl to come together and part good friends at the end of what was certain to be a testing experience. It was not unlike a party of four strangers thrown together after their plane had crashed in the jungle: an interesting situation. In the event, although technically the expedition worked well and we achieved our main aim of following the entire length of the river, I was unhappy at my inability to lead the four strangers into friendship. Now in a similar situation in Chile I hoped to do rather better with four people who knew each other very well and were already good friends.

First practical steps towards Patagonia were taken in March 1971 when Eric Shipton paid a brief weekend visit to our School of Adventure at Ardmore on the north-west coast of Sutherland in Scotland. I knew Eric had been to the thousand-mile-long jigsaw of unexplored islands and mountains, and so I asked him if he could recommend a place where I might go. As we strode together across the high ground at the back of our croft, four miles off the coast road, he said that Ardmore reminded him of the west coast of Chile and that the best thing would be to get out the maps in the Royal Geographical Society with him next time I was in London.

And so it began. One of the first things I found out was that Patagonia is not a country at all but that the name refers to the whole of South America south of the latitude 40° S, and so in fact Patagonia is partly Argentina and partly Chile. It was the Chilean part that interested me, wild, rugged and un-inhabited, a region of storm and torrential rain. The climate is sub-antarctic, and the glaciation so extensive that, although the mountains are not particularly high, they are as spectacular as any in the entire Andean range. Although most of the channels had been charted since the voyage of the *Beagle* in

1831, for hundreds of miles along this tortuous, uninhabited coast, no one had penetrated inland.

That so much of the region still remains unexplored is due to the physical difficulties of travel there. The chief problem is the weather, reputed to be the worst in the world; heavy rain with rare brief spells of sun and above all else the awful wind. Storms rage for weeks at a stretch, with gusts up to 130 m.p.h. The terrain is unusually difficult, with access limited to small waterborne craft, which are of course especially vulnerable to bad weather. The glaciers are so crevassed in their lower reaches as to be impassable. In the foothills, the forest has been rendered virtually impenetrable, by the action of the endless wind on belts of stunted trees; there exists what is really a mammoth hedge of tangled trunks and branches.

In the R.G.S. with Eric Shipton it was a question of deciding on one or many possible objectives. I had done a bit of rowing, and sailing, and seen a bit of jungle, now I wanted to do a bit of mountaineering.

"There's an interesting spot, a small ice-cap, no one's ever been there," murmured Eric in passing, as we flipped through a whole atlas of fascinating places down the west coast of Chile. "It would also need all your boating experience," he added, and I looked at it with renewed interest.

"Gran Campo Nevado – that just means 'Big Snow Field' doesn't it?" I translated from the Spanish, and Eric nodded.

"I've got to go to a meeting soon, so I'll tell you what I can about the ice-cap and then leave you to work it out for yourself," he said wisely, knowing well that once the idea has been planted it's best to spend as long as possible alone, making what the Army calls an appreciation of the situation.

After a couple of hours with the map I'd made up my mind. The scheme was on. A small team of four, fly to Punta Arenas, October 1972 to January 1973, two inflatable Avon dinghies, two Seagull outboards, tents, equipment and rations to be shipped out to Punta Arenas for October 1972. Hire a truck to take everything out 115 miles to Base 1 at Estancia Skyring (*estancia* means sheep farm) at the end of the track on the north shores of Seno Skyring (*seno* means sound). From there everything would be up to us: eighty miles by boat to Base 2 on the southern side of the ice-cap at Punta (point) Rengo on Canal (channel) Gajardo. From there eighty-eight miles by boat, out and along the Pacific Coast to Base 3 at the foot of the northern glacier, if we were unable to climb up the steep southern side of the ice-cap. One way or another, the main aim was to make the first crossing of the Gran Campo Nevado Ice-Cap, in fact we should almost certainly be the first people to set foot on 'The Big Snow Field'.

It was an exciting prospect. The challenge was to turn the dream to reality.

The team was not difficult to select. Apart from myself, there would be my wife, Marie Christine, who had so unexpectedly enjoyed the discomfort of the latter part of the Amazon expedition. Richard Shuff had been the Chief Instructor at our School of Adventure at Ardmore for the past three years. Each winter when the school is closed he tries to do something unusual. He has, for example, been to work on a kibbutz in Israel, and he has served in the Malaysian jungles doing two winters with the Special Air Service Volunteer Reserve. An expedition in Chile would be just his style for a winter trip, and he would provide the climbing expertise we needed. The fourth member was often in doubt, various people hoped to come but various circumstances prevented them all. For a long period there were only going to be the three of us; then in early September our old friend, Krister Nylund, aged twenty-three, came over from Sweden. Krister had worked at Ardmore as a voluntary instructor during the summer of 1971 and we were all three delighted when he agreed to come on with us to Chile.

Planning and executing expeditions to distant parts of the world is a tricky hobby. To illustrate the administrative and logistic problems I will simply give one example and then go on with the story of the expedition itself.

After some trouble with delivery dates, we assembled the stores for shipment at Ardmore in June 1972. Lance Bell then crated everything into a 'coffin' with dimensions of seven feet by two feet eleven inches by two feet four inches. We made firm arrangements for the 'coffin' to be shipped from London to Punta Arenas via Antwerp on 4th August. The journey got off to a bad start when our ancient Land-Rover pick-up broke down on its way to Inverness. Sinclair Mackintosh, Factor to the Westminster Estate, came to the rescue with a Volkswagen pick-up, but John Strachan's gallant attempt to do the hundred-mile journey in just over two hours, to catch the train, failed, and he arrived at the station just in time to hear the guard's parting whistle.

Next night the coffin was on the train to Euston, it was met by Richard's friend Frank Poppleton and his wife Jean. They were told the porters could deliver the coffin 'to' their waiting transit van but not 'on to' it, but after some good-natured banter with three tiny West Indians (whose names were Rastus, Napoleon and something unprintable) Frank and Jean were given exceptionally good service when money changed hands. Once at the docks the tallyman told them to wait until later, so Frank approached another tallyman and told him that they only had one box and Jean was feeling unwell so could they speed it up? Within twenty minutes another docker arrived and the transit was backed up to a bay with doors open. The tally-man told Frank that he'd told his mate "The missus is a bit dicky so he'd do the job straight away."

Matey arrived with a fork-lift truck and Frank was asked "Got your union card, mate?" On being told 'no' they refused to unload the transit. Resourceful Frank tipped Jean the wink to do 'unwell female gestures'. It worked, and fifteen minutes later they were unloaded and away to a cheerful "Stay off the vodka next time, Luv."

Dock strike. The whole expedition looked in jeopardy. The coffin could neither be taken on a ship, nor out of the docks for flight to Antwerp. The ship was missed, no more ships to Punta Arenas until November. Hopeless. Michael Ackerley, chairman of the Ackerley Group, which includes two shipping agencies, rushed to our aid. Wits and physique honed to a perfect edge by businessman's courses at Ardmore for two successive years Michael was the right St. George to slay the Dragon.

Dock strike ends. J. D. Hewett & Co. Ltd., secure the coffin from the docks and place it on a ship to Buenos Aires in the nick of time. They arrange onward flight to Punta Arenas, there being no suitable ship. The coffin flies to Santiago and arrives just in time for an air strike on that foreign strand. Much urgency. We fly to Punta Arenas. Santiago air strike ends, coffin flies to Punta Arenas. We arrive at Punta Arenas just in

John Ridgway

Marie Christine

Richard Shuff

Krister Nylund

time for a transport strike to prevent the coffin from being taken to the town and released to us. Transport strike ends, and we are reunited with the wherewithal for our expedition. Expeditionaries have to be keen.

Marie Christine and I said goodbye to Richard and Bob Riseborough as we neared the centre of town after our short and silent walk back from the *Hero*. We had arranged to meet the Honorary Consul, Denley King, at the British Club, and they were going on to join some of the research ship's crew at the Cabo de Hornos Hotel. As well as our thoughts, there was another reason why there had been little or no conversation during the walk from the docks: many of the vehicles on the streets were without silencers, it seems Chile doesn't make those either. Punta Arenas was not a relaxed place to be; there was a general air of uncertainty, both political and economic. The ridiculous inflation had caused a great spate of rumour-mongering; walking the streets we could sense the wariness of everyone about us.

The atmosphere in the British Club was that of a museum. It was a curious feeling to walk up the bare stone steps which had felt the tread of great men like Sir Ernest Shackleton, and to emerge into the distant past the moment we entered the club itself on the top storey of the dilapidated building. Everything was dark and gloomy. The barman came every night at six, but there were practically never any customers because the British colony was finished, either dead or gone away. Crazed glass, a leaky roof and wooden lathes sticking like broken ribs through the plaster on the walls, gazed down on the dusty billiard tables. The library was filled with old books like *Three Years of Slavery Among the Patagonians* and magnificent leather armchairs whose anti-macassars had long since been thrown away. In the bar we were surrounded by rows of presentation photographs of British warships which had visited Punta Arenas; these were notable for their diminishing size over the years. It was a creepy place to be in and perhaps it was no bad thing that it was to close at the end of 1972.

Next day we visited Señor Amerigo Fontana who was head of the Magellan Agrarian Reform, and a most powerful man in the communist government. Short and slight with dark hair

and a pale intense face, it was the tiredness of his eyes that
struck me most. Even his bitter critics grudgingly admitted that
he had carried out the plan he had outlined on the local radio,
when his government had come to power by democratic vote
in 1971. He had the clear desk of efficiency, although he spoke
no English he was quick and to the point. Our childish imagina-
tions read a sort of Zhivagoesque situation into the meeting,
and we were not at all surprised when his secretary appeared
wearing a pullover and jeans. Personally I took an immediate
liking to him and I felt he was 'a good man to have on your
side'. Although clearly very busy with the work of expropriating
sheep farms he found time to make arrangements for our
accommodation at Estancia Skyring which was in fact a place
he had recently taken over.

Apart from Mr. King and Señor Barrientos, perhaps the
most enthusiastic supporter of the expedition in Punta Arenas
was Hugh Macleay. A naturalised Chilean of New Zealand
farming stock, Hugh was loved by all and sundry. A big burly
man in his mid-thirties, with pale ginger hair and blue eyes in
an open face, he had the kind of mouth that is always curved
upwards in a smile. He too had just lost a battle with Señor
Fontana but seemed to bear him no grudge for doing his job.
He had the kind of hard-driving, hell-raising colonial leader-
ship that Chile was desperately in need of; and he put a bit of
it to work for us with the result that we were on our way to
Skyring with everything we needed after only four days in
Punta Arenas.

The four-and-a-half-ton red Dodge Fargo truck was Hugh's
and we were driven by one of his men, Señor Lopes. Most of
the 115-mile journey was through flat brown grassland. The
wind blew chill, even with five of us in the cab. Several times
we saw the South American ostrich, the rhea, close to the wire
fences bordering the road. There were plenty of sheep, which
looked quite different from their Scottish cousins, for their wool
almost covered their heads giving them a leonine appearance;
also their legs were surprisingly long. When we turned to the
west the land became gently undulating, the first ripples of the
grim-looking Andes which now lined the distant horizon.

Ibis, geese and duck, all became much more abundant as we
drove along the northern shores of Seno Skyring. The water

was rough, with spume blown before a fresh westerly gale. Cold fear mingled with cold lunch, when we stopped by the sound and looked up ahead into the teeth of the wind, with the truck windows firmly wound up. From now on it was up to us. We would hear no more English spoken, and soon we would be alone.

We stopped at a sawmill called Las Colas, and agreed to return on the following day with the two rubber dinghies for their wooden runners to be fitted, to prevent undue wear from rocky beaches in the weeks ahead. Then we drove the remaining dozen miles to Estancia Skyring.

2

Skyring Life

ESTANCIA SKYRING WAS A picture of efficiency, smart low red buildings all laid out just so. Our kit was all off-loaded into a wool shed the size of an aircraft hangar, with fifteen shearing points each immaculately maintained. The roof was hanging with fleeces from the many sheep that had not survived the fierce winter. Arturo, the fat black-haired young foreman, was very friendly, and language was no barrier to us. Among the scrubbed whitewood tables of the cookhouse, the tiny cook greeted us with what seemed to be a universal greeting along the Skyring shores, "*Pocito café?*" Our accommodation was a small bungalow, formerly perhaps the home of a European foreman. There were pathetic reminders of now vanished children, a broken swing, a few toys. Times were changed. In the garden the primulas and daffodils ran wild among lupins and polyanthus, gardening was now a thing of the past.

In the evening the four of us walked up the track along the shore to the Rio Perez, reputed to be a fine trout river. On the way we practised with our catapults brought out from Piccadilly as our means of defence against marauding animals, and for hunting duck for the pot.

"Enemy left," shouted Richard, diving for the cover of a fence post and firing wild pebbles at Krister who shook with laughter like a shaggy lion. The standard of marksmanship indicated a great victory for slimmers in the days ahead.

To our surprise the river was as cluttered with fishing line and litter as the Grand Union Canal at Slough.

"This whole place might just turn out to be another grubby national park," I muttered sorrowfully to myself, tired by the journey from Punta Arenas.

Mutton was the only food at Skyring, three meals every day, and so we were rather relieved when Marie Christine and I got the chance to go down to Las Colas to fit out the two dinghies. Marciel ran the office there sitting at a simple desk surrounded by posters of nudes and communist propaganda. The bathing beauties contrasted rather favourably with Mao, Castro and Allende. Two keen Chilean carpenters, in grey overalls and old trilby hats, worked with bewildering speed on the wooden runners and slatted floorboards of my design. They finished the job in a day and we returned to Estancia Skyring to find Richard and Krister had sorted the stores and equipment in readiness for a move on the next day.

Fortune began to smile on us. First there was a near miracle, when the black grip containing all our film, maps and reference books came in on a mail bus after being lost at Buenos Aires airport. The taxi-driver who had dropped us at the airport before dawn, had gone off with the grip still in the boot of his taxi; we had gnashed our teeth and tried to think of other things. To the eternal credit of Buenos Aires, the driver returned the grip to Aerolinas Argentinas and Special Investigator Señor Oscar Montiel put it on the next plane to Punta Arenas, from where Señor Barrientos put it on the mail bus for Skyring. Anyone with experience of South America would describe this incident as miraculous. The next stroke of luck was the discovery of five hundred rounds of ·22 ammunition in the crate of stores, the ·22 rifle had had to be removed back in the United Kingdom, but the ammunition had been overlooked. This ammunition was a powerful bargaining tool in the sheep farm bunkhouse, many of the horsemen had ·22 rifles but ammunition was unobtainable in Chile. For a down payment of two hundred rounds Arturo lent us his own rifle for the expedition, and our catapults became obsolete at one stroke.

Our biggest slice of good fortune arrived in the form of three men who arrived in two hand-built boats from the western end of Skyring. After minimal bargaining they agreed to take us, our stores and our deflated boats back with them in their boats on the following day. We now had local guides who would take us right to the edge of the unknown in one day if the weather stayed fine. As is the way in remote places, each of these men was a clearly defined character in his own right.

Francisco Llanllan left his native island of Chiloe, some seven hundred miles to the north when he was twenty-five years old; now twenty years later, he is the father of seven children and his wife and family live on the Estancia Las Colas. He is essentially a woodcutter living for much of the year on the tiny island of Rucas at the western end of Skyring. Short and square, with black hair and friendly brown eyes that are always smiling Francisco quickly became a firm friend. He loves the sea and boats, and is never happier than when battling alone through the stormy waters of his beloved Skyring. A badly scarred nose and prominent jaw muscles testify to a hard simple life in the open air.

Calisto is more Spanish in appearance than Francisco. He is really only a complete person when astride a horse. Enthroned on a massive sheepskin saddle, white teeth flashing his radiant smile through an enormous black beard, Calisto infects everyone with his buoyant personality. The red and white spotted handkerchief at his throat gives him the style for which city-dwellers spend hundreds of pounds, trying to capture in vain. His high-pitched laugh is known and loved all along the northern shores of Skyring.

Alexandro is different again. Well under five feet in height he looks like a child beside his 'amigo Calisto'. He lives on a small island called Unicornio with his sister Fresia, they are two of only forty-six surviving pure Alacalufe Indians. His face wears a permanently embittered expression, and no smile ever interrupts his short bursts of bitter speech. Perhaps it is the expression of the Indians all over the world, the unfortunate losers in a battle between races for existence. Dressed in patched wellington boots, tattered green baize trousers worn over torn jeans, supported by ancient braces over a check shirt glazed with dirt, poor Alexandro conveys an impression of rock-bottom poverty. His proudest possession is the old blue double-ended boat he built for himself on Unicornio.

After our last mutton breakfast we loaded up the two wooden boats on a startling flat calm morning, under blue skies. Arturo gave us half a sheep and shook our hands as if doubting we would return. Francisco's ancient Archimedes outboard started somewhat reluctantly and we were off, the bigger grey boat towing Alexandro and Calisto in their blue one. We were full of optimism, tomorrow we should be at the foot of the ice-cap and the expedition properly under way. Around us we saw plenty of life, porpoises gambolled close to, and geese flew overhead. Strange flightless steamer ducks ploughed their way across the calm water, hundreds panicking at our approach and lashing the water to white. Spring and the expedition were on their way, it was grand to be alive.

All morning we motored along without incident, the snow-capped mountains seeming to draw no nearer in spite of the hours of travel. The three locals must have thought us queer in our new orange waterproofs worn on top of bulky duvet jackets. In the early afternoon our affairs took a turn for the worse. We dropped off a sack of potatoes at a smallholding and the wind began to get up. The outboard failed to restart and in fact it never started again for the rest of the time we were with Francisco. There was nothing for it but to stop for the night. Calisto and Alexandro put up a shelter in the forest by the shore and the rest of us made our way back to the smallholding at Rio Pinto.

Sergeo, who had been pleased to get his potatoes, was rather stunned to have five visitors come to stay. A small dark man with almost no shoulders, dressed in old Wrangler jeans a Norwegian pullover and patched gumboots, his round bland face wore an expression of almost constant embarrassment at our presence. A solitary bachelor in his early thirties Sergeo could not speak one word of English and it needed all Francisco's charm to smooth our stay. The little hut was apparently a hundred years old, certainly the white-enamelled range with its blue motif looked this age. Thick timber walls were lined with hardboard from Hayter of Bournemouth. A pin-up of Ava Gardner, and an American ranch calendar with each day crossed off completed the décor. From nowhere Francisco produced a good hot stew of mutton, garlic, lentils and spaghetti which we ate with a feeling of embarrassment that Sergeo might be left to starve as a result, on our departure. Marie Christine and I were given the *matrimonio* room which was normally poor Sergeo's, and he and Francisco moved out to a hut near by.

The weather kept us holed up at Sergeo's place for two days. Vicious williwaw squalls shrieked down from the four thousand-foot snow-covered mountain at the back of the hut, their strength absorbed by a row of tree trunks stuck vertically in the

ground to act as a windbreak to windward of the little homestead. Francisco and Sergeo sucked herbal tea called *yerba maté*
and watched the weather philosophically. In between squalls
the four of us zeroed Arturo's ·22 rifle on a twenty-five-yard
range we built on the beach. We all fired good groups and looked
forward to roast duck in the future.

Eventually the weather improved, and we rejoined Calisto
and Francisco, somewhat shamefacedly, at their shelter on the
shore. Before setting off in the boats I managed to shoot an
ashy-headed goose which Francisco pot-boiled on the beach to
everyone's delight. The journey on to Calisto's home at
Chinchorro, beneath the jagged white tooth of Cerro Dynover,
was rough. We had to use one of our new Seagull engines on
Francisco's boat, and the see-sawing effect of the waves caused
the motor to dip deep in the water one moment and then as
the stern lifted so the propeller would come clear of the water
in a scream of wasted power, which did nothing but harm to
the machine – as we were to find out later.

It was early evening when we arrived at Chinchorro to be
greeted by the owner Paulino Vasquez. A tall, lean, stooping
fellow dressed in faded blue jeans and jacket; with his short fair
hair he didn't look his forty-five years. He owned two hundred
cattle and had been born at Chinchorro, which is a five-hour
ride on horseback from Estancia Skyring. He and Calisto made
us very welcome in the strong timber bungalow, up on a ridge
between the sea and a chain of freshwater lakes. Here again
the building was sheltered by a massive log windbreak. Luckily
Richard was able to give some medical attention to a third
member of the work-force who was ill in bed with bronchitis.

The weather clamped down for another three days and we
made ourselves comfortable in the outpost. From the windows
of the sixty-year-old house, we were looking directly at unexplored country; in one way we were keen to get started, but
the old Carron stove from Dover burned warm, and the sleet
thumped the house in a way unconducive to happy camping.
The wooden lining of the outside log walls was lined again with
brown parquet linoleum, as was the floor and even the kitchen
table. Small Lufthansa posters from the 1950s decorated the
room with views of Constellation aircraft in different parts of
the world. The rickety shelves were lined with the essentials of

life: outboard oil, shotgun pellets, yeast and cooking oil – not a sign of chrome; but it was home.

Our time at Chinchorro was interesting, but we were restive and so we were glad to be on our way as soon as the wind dropped. All the same we were sad to say goodbye to Calisto and Señor Vasquez.

An hour and a half in grey mist-shrouded calm, towing Alexandro's boat and we arrived at Isla Unicornio. Heavy rain started to fall and Francisco warned us we should have to stay the night.

The island, which is named after a contemporary of Magellan, is overshadowed by the great snowy eastern flank of Cerro Dynover a couple of miles away across the water. Alexandro and his sister Fresia proudly showed us the certificate which allowed them to live away from the official Alacalufe colony at Puerto Eden. They live in a dilapidated corrugated iron shack lined with smoke-blackened wood and newspapers; the rain leaked through a thousand nail-holes made by previous owners of the tin sheets.

The two Indians had about ten dogs in various states of disrepair; they were sort of Airedale mongrel Alsatians and they smelt disgusting. We spent the night in the hut, Richard and Krister were condemned to the floor in the main room along with two wet dogs and a cat; Marie Christine and I were a little luckier with a small spider-infested room, outside which the dogs howled mournfully. Before blowing out the little lamp of string dipped in mutton fat, I read the newspaper lining on the wall which gave faded news of trouble in Costa Rica.

Next morning we were away, just as soon as we could load the boat. The two Indians waved us a cheery farewell and returned to their life of empty poverty: to paraffin-tainted sugar in an old Mazawattee tea tin, and dead batteries that had to be heated over a stove made out of a half a forty-gallon oil drum, before they could be persuaded to squeak a little honky-tonk music to enliven days that were but crayon crosses on a grubby calendar.

It took us a little under an hour to reach the small creek on Punta Laura at the head of which Francisco assured us we would find the hot sulphur springs. We moored the heavy wooden boat to a tree and set up our camp for the first time, using a couple of our four mountain tents; Francisco preferred to build his own shelter, draping his heavy canvas sail around a frame of branches like a tepee. The weather was closing in again and our visit to the sulphur springs was not the inspiring occasion we had expected; true, the vegetation was luxuriantly semi-tropical, but the springs were bubbling up through thick mud and leaf mould, and they smelt none too pleasant. We returned to the camp to wait for a break in the weather; we were at the entrance to the western end of Skyring, but the dream of a one-day trip to the foot of the ice-cap was now far from a reality.

The morning of our fourth day at Punta Laura dawned with clear blue skies that were to hold throughout the day. After a brief foray from the tent to answer the call of nature, and the usual short conversation with Francisco when we both agreed there was '*mucho viento*', I returned to doze for another couple of hours in the comfort of my blue down sleeping-bag. Outside, beyond the harsh light of our orange tent world, Marie Christine and I could hear the rush of wind through the tops of the beech trees above, where the westerly gale funnelled through the defile at the back of the camp site.

"Might as well sleep in – we're not going to move today," I said, feeling the anxiety beginning to depress me.

"Well, we don't want to open another ration pack . . . I know, why don't we go on survival today," smiled Marie Christine, bright and cheerful as ever. "You might be able to shoot a duck and in any case there are plenty of mussels now the water level is falling."

"Okay," I replied, with little conviction. "We'll see what the others think when they surface later on." This wasn't really fair because Richard was usually first up in the mornings, in search of 'Rosy Lee' (tea) or even '*Pocito café*' with Francisco who always seemed to be awake in his tepee-like shelter. This shelter contrasted strongly with our two new orange mountain tents which looked rather out of place in their sylvan setting by the creek, as did the pair of shiny Seagull outboards mounted on the stern of Francisco's rough old hand-built boat as it lay moored by the bow to a fallen tree on the grey pebble beach. All our kit was still new and we felt Francisco must be laughing up his sleeve at the four dudes who had come to challenge the

Gran Campo Nevado. All his gear was old and in tatters, yet he moulded into the wood so well that unless he moved he was scarcely visible. He'd been coming this way regularly for fifteen years, since he settled on Isla Rucas in 1957. Punta Laura was always a problem on his route home, because the point jutted far out from the northern shores of the fifty-mile-long sound towards Isla Grande, thus causing a bottleneck little more than three miles wide through which the westerly gales roared almost incessantly from November to February. The short savage seas frequently forcing him to hole up in the creek. Now, with his own ancient outboard out of action, we were relying on our short-shaft Seagull motors to get us home to Isla Rucas. Conditions would need to be extra calm for very little swell was needed to set the boat see-sawing and our engines screaming protest as their propellers alternately plunged too deep or were lifted clear of the surface.

When we finally emerged from our tent at eight-thirty, Marie Christine and I found the problem of a survival day was eased, if not completely solved, by Francisco who was busy making sort of dumpling pancakes from materials contained in the many sacks he carried aboard the boat. Along with Richard's cup of tea we were soon sitting round the fire eating what was really a dreadful-tasting concoction: boiled flapjacks of flour, water and a little salt.

"Try them with a little sugar," said Krister, dipping into the tin. "I think they'll be all right so long as they're hot. Say it this way . . . there isn't anything else."

We all grinned at the cheerful Swede, but he was wrong, for Francisco had left the fire and was already picking mussels, only elbow deep out along the black finger of rock which split our part of the creek from the other slightly larger bay. This was the bay which received the warm waters from the hot sulphur springs which bubbled to the surface some fifty yards inland among almost tropical vegetation.

Marie Christine gingerly made her way out to help Francisco, while the rest of us kept on choking down the flour and water pasties. Pretty soon the black pot Arturo had lent us back at Skyring was hanging over the fire filled to the brim with shellfish each a couple of inches long.

"Just like a survival day back at Ardmore," laughed Richard.

"Only this time it's for real," replied Marie Christine, and Francisco murmured "*Mucho Bueno*" as the black shells began to open in the steaming pot.

After we had all eaten our fill, Francisco began to make his usual preparations for going on a walk, and as Marie Christine wanted to stay behind and wash her hair I suggested to Richard and Krister that we three might go with him to see if we could get a sight of Canal Gajardo where it opened into the other side of Seno Skyring, some distance farther to the west.

"We'd better take the rifle," Krister said hopefully, and I went back to the tent to collect it together with half a dozen rounds of ·22 ammunition. At first Francisco followed the steaming course of the stream leading to the hot springs, then he climbed up the valley wall, moving too swiftly for my bulky frame through a tangled mass of slippery fallen trees and thorny undergrowth which seemed to catch my clothing at every step. Last in the file of four, I also carried the rifle, which, although light, was unwieldy in a situation where most of the walking was done in a doubled-up attitude.

'I'm getting old,' I thought, as I struggled to catch up with the others.

When we finally emerged from the thick undergrowth and clambered the remaining hundred feet or so to the top of the hill, the first things we noticed were the white mountains and the wind. On our way up the lee-side of the hill the sun had warmed our backs from a cloudless blue sky and there was scarcely enough breeze to cool us, dressed as we were in our polar sweaters. From the summit we looked for the first time into the western end of Seno Skyring; it stretched for some twenty miles in length and roughly four miles in width, north-west into the Andes. The whole area in front of us, and on up and across the dazzling snow-covered mountains to the Pacific, was completely uninhabited save for Francisco and three other men. They lived on Isla Rucas, a tiny island in the Archipelago Senoret, a dozen miles up close to the north shore of the sound.

We were completely surrounded by snow-covered mountains of all shapes and sizes, except to the south-east. There the sound ran away into the distance ultimately presenting an horizon as clear and straight as if it led directly to the Atlantic ocean instead of bending to the south as it does through a narrow channel into Seno Otway. Down there it is bordered all along its eastern shores by the flat sheep-farming lands which lead it to the Straits of Magellan.

We couldn't look for long, because the chill of a fresh gale from the north-west made our eyes run. But across the rough water, just twelve miles west-south-west, the sharp tower of Cerro Atalaya rose six thousand feet sheer from the sea, where it guarded the narrow north-eastern entrance to Canal Gajardo. Beyond Atalaya we could just make out the jumble of glaciers fringing the massive white plateau of the Gran Campo Nevado.

"Pretty chilly, isn't it," muttered Richard, and he turned to look for a bit of shelter below where we were standing. We all followed him. Just a few yards down we sat on rock warmed by the sun and free from the chill wind. Richard rolled yet another, of what he kept protesting, were the very last of his cigarettes. Krister and I looked about us in comfort, while Francisco nipped off and set fire to the brush.

"If I did that at home in the Swedish forests they'd put me in prison," said Krister, "But I suppose he just has no other way of land clearance here," he went on, nodding at the forest which completely surrounded the sound, starting at the water's edge and running right up into the snow.

Three major problems had made themselves quite clear on our brief look up Skyring. The water was going to be rough practically all the time, and if we fell in, no kind of life jacket would sustain us long in the liquid ice. The forest, which I thought Shipton had jokingly called 'impenetrable', back in London, really looked as impenetrable as any jungle I had seen in Malaysia or Amazonas. The mountain snows allied with the vicious wind would show us little pity.

"*Más tardes, posiblimente calme,*" smiled Francisco softly, as he returned gazing up into the sky.

"*Si,*" I replied with a nod – "He says it may get calm later on in the day."

"Let's go on down and have some more mussels," grinned Krister, and we all got up and set off back to our camp. Now that I'd had a look at it all, I couldn't really say I felt much less anxious about it.

Just after seven o'clock that evening, Francisco suggested he and I should take the boat out into the channel and see if we could make any headway. We did and could, and so after a few expressive nods between us, I turned the boat back towards the creek. Just as we passed the sheer cliff, which guarded the western side of the entrance to our camp, a large rock fell from its overhanging face some eighty feet up, making a sizeable splash as it entered the water.

'Spring is in the air,' I thought grimly of the avalanches which Francisco had warned would come with the onset of warmer weather.

A wave of my green woollen lady's golfing hat from the boat signalled the start of our fastest camp breaking to date. With scarcely an hour's daylight left we wanted to be clear of the bottleneck between Punta Laura and the snow-capped Isla Grande before it grew completely dark.

We passed out into the rougher water and a seal surfaced close to the boat as if to wish us well.

It was the same old problem: the dying swell set the boat see-sawing, and for more than half an hour it was touch and go whether we should have to turn back again to the creek. Although both motors were mounted on the transom bracket I could only run one at a time owing to the vibration. Soon my left hand was frozen through having to reach behind me to steer and adjust the throttle every time the bow dipped into a trough, which in turn lifted the propeller clear of the water at the stern. Perhaps it was the four days of waiting that kept us at it, anyway we did keep going, and eventually we rounded the headland. Then, in response to Francisco's insistent waving, I angled across the sea so as to keep close to the shore and thus keep the swell on our port bow. This tactic reduced the see-sawing a bit and instead it introduced a bit of rolling. Looking up forward, over the canvas-shrouded mound of our stores and fuel, I could see the slight figure of my wife; she was well wrapped up in the waterproof suit, which she had on over the bulky warmth of her lifejacket.

'She's going to have to get used to rough water,' I thought, noticing how she kept reaching for the sides of the boat to reassure herself we weren't turning over.

We were in luck. When it became really dark the wind dropped completely, and soon the sea was flat. A tank of fuel on the motor lasted a bit over an hour, so at nine-thirty I cut the engine when we were about three hundred yards clear of an immense cliff, which seemed to descend on the sea from the sky itself.

"What's that noise?" asked Marie Christine from the bow. From right at the foot of the cliffs came honking, grunting sounds, which were only punctuated by the clinking splashing inseparable from refuelling a small outboard motor at sea on a dark night.

"*Mucho lobos*," said Francisco pointing at the cliff, and I remembered him telling us that Alexandro fed his dogs with the seals he shot out on Punta Laura. Francisco went on to explain that this was a permanent colony of more than a hundred seals, some of them very large.

The other engine started again on the third pull. I was very pleased, as this confirmed we had both engines working if there was an emergency.

The surrounding mountains glowed white against the black moonless sky; the foot of this mighty cliff was no place to be stuck with dud motors if the wind should get up again – and it was only a matter of time before it would. While I was reflecting on the bizarre coincidence that the cold white tooth rising six thousand feet from the shore opposite should have the same name, Atalaya, as the first town I had passed on the Apurimac Amazon on my way from the source to the sea, not quite two years previously, I happened to glance back at the engine to check it was running properly.

'Too much steam,' I thought, immediately checking the out-fall from the water-cooling system. To my alarm I saw there was no water at all coming out, only clouds of steam. This was no place to mess around and run the risk of making the engine seize up through overheating, so I cut the motor and raised the propeller clear of the water by tilting the shaft until it engaged the folding bracket on the transom fitting. I was vastly relieved when the other motor, which I had run for the first hour and a bit of the trip, started perfectly on the third pull of the starting cord.

The black-and-white scenery on that dark night was drama-tic.

I was reminded of Captain Hudson, cast adrift to die in a long-boat by his mutinous shipmates; for there were no lights on the shore to guide us and we were in a hostile place where the winds could rise again at any minute to drive us back on a cruel shore. Then as we moved clear of the ominous cliff, we saw a sight I shall remember for the rest of my days. Very slowly, the distance increased between us and the sheer black foreground of the cliff which rose perhaps a thousand feet into the sky. Then the sparkling white jewels of the Diadem Mountains crept up from behind the cliff top against the velvet black cushion of the night sky. Up and up crept the dazzling towers, minarets and all manner of shapes, until the magnificent crown sat perfectly on a dark head nearly three miles long.

Quite suddenly in the darkness, we cleared the western end of the Chinchorro Peninsula and crossed the mouth of the narrow ten-mile-long fiord which winds north-east round the back of the Diadem Mountains to make the western seaboard of the narrow isthmus on which Paulino Vasquez has his homestead.

It was still flat calm and in all the vastness of the night our tiny motor seemed to make little noise. Occasionally the boat vibrated a bit, and Francisco and I exchanged worried glances until we realised it was only Marie Christine thumping her feet up and down to get them warm. We all felt pretty cold, and jammed down in the pointed stern behind the wall of biscuit boxes and two-stroke oil cans, I found my orange waterproof trousers soon stopped the circulation round my permanently bent knees. I was grateful for the calm as I gingerly lifted my legs and laid them straight across the far side of the boat. My mind went back to rough nights on the Atlantic in the rowing-boat. On those nights in the cramped sleeping end of the boat, such an action sometimes resulted in a tricky wave sneaking up and emptying itself down the inside of the waterproof trousers.

"Francisco, *por favor, quentas horas* Isla Rucas?" called Marie Christine from the bow in her stilted Spanish.

"*Solamente media,*" Francisco replied, reassuring us it could only be another half hour before we would be gathered round a fire at his house. The only snag to this was that it was now nearly midnight and surely our three unsuspecting hosts would be asleep?

Marie Christine unloading
equipment on arrival in
Patagonia

Boat trials from the wool shed at Estancia Skyring

3

Isla Rucas

AT LAST WE REACHED the outlying islets of the Archipelago
Senoret and began the hazardous approach, winding in and
out through narrow channels, towards Francisco's own Isla
Rucas. Even at half throttle, the little Seagull motor pushed
the heavy twenty-two-foot boat and its couple of tons of cargo
at a good three knots. If Francisco made a wrong turning in the
dark and we ran up on a reef the expedition might come to a
premature end. He knew none of us spoke much Spanish and
the only English word he knew was 'refoil' which he had written
laboriously into his Diario as the English pronunciation of
'rifle'. All illustrations as to direction and speed came to me
by the waving of one or other of his arms, but in rather more
than three-quarters of an hour we finally headed straight
towards a particularly black piece of coast without any sign of
a channel, and he signalled for me to cut the motor. Just before
the bow nudged gently up on to a pebble beach, I caught a
glimpse of a little hut, silhouetted on the ridge only some forty
yards from the fallen tree pier in the corner of the sheltered bay
which was Francisco's home port.

Within minutes we were crouching numbly round a fire he
had soon got going, while Francisco told us the hut was empty
because his three *amigos* were farther up the island, near the
woodcutting area. He showed us where to put our things and
then went into the other room to sleep among the few odd
fleeces he kept in the hut.

Next morning we got up at eight, still hopeful of a move into
the Canal Gajardo that day, but after a small breakfast of
milkless tea and yesterday's porridge, which had been brought
from Punta Laura in a saucepan, Francisco said to leave our
kit and go with him to meet Amigo Silva up at the other
place.

"Let's take our wash things, it'll probably be more comfortable up there," said Marie Christine, hopefully. We all thought we were at a sort of outpost and that where Silva was there would be the main building; something along the lines of Paulino Vasquez's place back at Chinchorro.

Just before we pushed off in the boat Francisco collected a pailful of mussels from the beach. The journey up the channel, a mile or so south-west through the islets under the lee of Isla Rucas towards Silva's house, was a pleasant introduction to the Archipelago. We saw many steamer ducks, a few pairs of ashy-headed geese and numerous cormorants in the channels among the heavily wooded and steeply hilled islets. Francisco said there were quite a few wandering seals and a lot of otters which were very difficult to shoot but worth a great deal if he could get the skins to Punta Arenas.

We were all rather dismayed when we saw Silva's 'house', for it turned out to be a simple lean-to hut perched on a wooded hillside; it served as no more than a temporary base for the woodmen. Indeed it had only been built a couple of weeks previously, because until then the island had been covered with snow which made felling operations impossible. The floor area was approximately six feet by eight feet, and the construction was no more than a few planks and slim tree trunks thrown together; it had already weathered a uniform silver grey. As we scrambled up the few yards of steep rocky bank it seemed we had arrived at an opportune time, for the few rusty sheets of corrugated iron which served for a roof were weighted down by a couple of twelve-pound steamer ducks all plucked, singed and ready for the big black stewpot we knew we would find inside. There was no door, only a gap in the vertical planks on the leeward side of the hut. Through this we were enthusiastically waved by the three woodcutters who had come down to the shore as soon as they had heard the sound of our motor.

Inside the hut, we found a bare mossy earth floor with rough plank beds along three walls, the bedding itself was made up of sheep skins and old tarpaulins. The interior was in some places lined with bits of cardboard from packing cases, and in other parts the gaps between the planks were plugged with old pieces of rag; it looked a dismal place to spend the night in a westerly sleet storm. There was a crude plank table along the remaining wall, adjacent to the gaping doorway. The centre-piece of the dwelling was the stove, made, as always along the shores of western Skyring, of half a forty-gallon oil drum. It had a five-inch diameter stove pipe, ten feet long, leading from one side of the drum top up and out through the roof of the hut. This pipe was made of several sheets of inter-locking metal curled into shape and held in place at intervals by short lengths of fence wire.

Francisco motioned that we should sit ourselves on the beds. He then emptied the pail of mussels on to the sizzling hot top of the drum, and pushed a few more split lengths of wood through the hole in the side. Outside, Silva set about splitting more wood for the insatiable stove with his mighty axe, which had a handle nearly five feet long. While we sat and warmed ourselves the other two *amigos* stood around the doorway wondering at what strange circumstances had brought these four orange-suited oddities, including the first female in more than a decade, to Isla Rucas. We were equally surprised to see they were only boys; one, Francisco's eighteen-year-old son, José, was a dark-haired, moon-faced youth inclined to fat and with a placid bovine air about him. The other boy was much younger, and he turned out to be the fifteen-year-old son of Riviera, the absentee landowner of the Estancia Pinto, on which Sergeo was the sole resident when we had been stranded there on the previous week.

While we carefully extracted the pink mussels from their shells which had cooked and opened on the stove, Silva came in to join us while the boys embarrassed us by standing outside in the light drizzle. Straightaway the two *amigos* set about a *pocito maté*. The main reason why Francisco had insisted we call at his home first before going on to Canal Gajardo was that Amigo Silva was out of *maté* and this lack of bitter herbal tea was regarded as serious, particularly as *maté* was '*mucho bueno por los organ*'. Francisco insisted on handing the little bowl of tea round and we each took a suck of the acrid stuff through the slender copper pipe sticking out of the top.

Silva was clearly a man who lived by the use of his mighty axe, there was no saw on Isla Rucas. His every day was spent felling *sepre* (cypress), a slim straight tree much favoured for fence posts on the estancias at the eastern end of Skyring where it doesn't grow. Perhaps in his late forties, and already gap-toothed, his short black hair streaked with grey, and grizzled beard made him look older. All the same the knotted sinews of his neck and his great rough hands with their fingers like sausages, each terminating in space-like nails that looked armour-plated, spoke of a man possessed of far greater strength than most. In spite of the cold drizzle, he wore only a grey dirt-glazed flannel shirt and heavily patched grey corduroy trousers over ill concealed and grimy long-johns. Like his great friend Francisco, Silva was from Chiloe, an island far to the north up along the west of Chile. Twenty-five years before, Silva had sailed south to Punta Arenas in an open boat with three friends, along what is probably the most treacherous coast in the world. The journey took them seven hard months. Besides his athletic grace and dynamism, the most remarkable thing about Silva was his barking laugh, it was never silent for long.

Once the mussels were eaten Silva grinned hugely and pro-duced a black pot full of *tortas*, small bread rolls like doughnuts which he made once a week. After he'd passed these round, we all got mugs of hot black coffee straight from the battered kettle which is on the stove all day long. Silva chattered away in Spanish to Francisco and made a fuss of his young, white collie Pellin, while we tried to imagine life in a woodman's hut. There were a few sacks of flour and sugar, an ancient alarm clock which looked permanently stopped on a rough shelf with some tins of chilli paste and pimento; but it wouldn't be much of a place to come home to after a long hard day felling cypress trees in the rain.

"Well, we can hardly sit here all day, should we have a go at shooting a duck?" suggested Krister.

"It would be a gift in return for the one they are obviously cooking for our lunch," I smiled optimistically. The two boys had already put the pot on the stove and we felt ashamed of eating so much of what little food they had.

Richard stayed behind to help with the chopping of wood, and Krister, Marie Christine and I set off in the boat to try our luck. An hour later we returned with one of the steamer ducks, a huge bird weighing more than ten pounds. We were just in time to tuck into steaming tin plates of duck stew which once emptied were quickly refilled by the watchful Silva who seemed to see the whole occasion as the greatest fun. After this Richard made the mistake of agreeing to try a little of the salt beef which hung grotesquely from a rusty hook on the wall. Try as he would he couldn't eat the stuff, and Marie Christine managed to save any embarrassment by gesturing that he was full up to the eyeballs with the excellent duck stew.

"That was the worst meat I've ever tasted," muttered Richard, "it was absolutely rank!"

It was now well into the afternoon and I was keen to get back to Francisco's home to try and get the cooling system to work on the faulty motor. In spite of Francisco's smiling protestations that it was 'no problem', I had a feeling it might be something serious. All the same there was no move to go, so we just fell asleep on the sacks while Silva set to work with his bread box and made a whole new batch of delicious *tortas*. After our nap, and when at last we had dipped most of these in sugar and eaten them still hot, and also washed them down with mugs of sweet tea, only then did Francisco gesture it was time to go home.

No amount of hot or cold water flushed through the pipes would induce the faulty engine's cooling system to work again, and after a snack of biscuits and tea we all turned in. I was left with a feeling of foreboding; with one engine already out of action, what chance had we in the storms ahead?

During the night the wind gathered strength and the corrugated sheeting rattled a protest on the roof as each gust swept up on to the ridge and buffeted the little hut. Marie Christine rolled her sleeping-bag nearer to mine.

Straight after a breakfast of mussels next morning, with the north-westerly gale still battering the hut, we set to on the motor. In a way I felt stimulated by the problem, something unforeseeable which needed fresh thought and ingenuity rather than the straightforward following of a plan. Slowly but surely we checked each possible cause of the fault and then set about dismantling the engine. By removing the propeller unit and silencer we were able to slide out the shaft with the simple rotary pump at its bottom end. The water-entry channel was clear, but the eighteen-inch pipe which takes the cooling water up into the cylinder block had sheared off at the water union with the cylinder, inside the silencer. Gravity jammed the pipe down, so there was a gap of an inch or so at the top, across which the water couldn't possibly pass.

"*Mucho* problem!" intoned Francisco, mournfully shaking his head.

"It looks as if we must plan to use only one motor from here on," Richard said with a resigned note in his voice. But he had reckoned without Francisco's years of experience in making do with little or no resources, save his own ingenuity.

Krister too, was looking at the motor in a way which showed he was going to keep at it.

"If we are prepared to sacrifice one knife, we could cut around where the pipe is broken off; when the small piece falls out we could then jam the pipe back up in the hole," he said in his careful English.

It was like five escaped prisoners of war, holed up on a remote island. We had plenty of time, but the engine was vital for our survival. Squatting on the side of the bed, or on one of the rough little benches, each one of us tried to remedy the problem which could only be solved properly if we could fit a new part. Back at Ardmore, with spares easily obtained from the manufacturers in Poole, Lance Bell would find this job quite simple. Here on a remote islet among the Andes of southern Chile, spares were out of the question.

I picked up the long, thin, round metal file which Arturo had kindly lent me back at Skyring and gestured to scrape the broken piece of aluminium pipe with it.

"*Si*," Francisco nodded enthusiastically at my plan to ream the piece of pipe clean out of the bronze union.

The motor was now standing upside down on the dirty plank floor; it was resting on the top of the flywheel and the fuel tank, and it leaned against the bed. Foolishly flattered by Francisco's confirmation of my engineering prowess, I jammed the pointed end of the file in the broken pipe and set to work. At first it went well and I seemed to be making progress; then suddenly the brittle grey metal of the file snapped close to the point and I was left staring down at the sheared-off pipe hideously blocked by the tip of the file.

"Now you gone and done it, John!" grinned the Swede.

"Lance wouldn't think much of that," Richard added.

I couldn't think of much to say and Francisco just shook his head sadly.

"I think I'll walk up to Silva's place, the Riviera boy had got caught in the eye by a branch when they were out stalking ducks the day before yesterday. These drops should help," said Richard waving a small bottle from the medical kit, and making a diplomatic exit.

"Okay, Richard, but I think we should try and keep Francisco here to help with this business," I said, waving disgustedly at the botched job.

"Yes, I think we go on," confirmed Krister.

The hours went by, filing, chipping, hammering and cursing. Francisco produced half a dozen ancient tools which flaked red rust on to the shiny yellow of the bronze union. From somewhere else he found a couple of inches of battered copper pipe green with age, but just the right gauge – if we could get the broken piece out of the union.

Marie Christine brewed a cup of tea on the fire and this, with a packet of wine biscuits, passed for Sunday lunch.

Later in the afternoon, in spite of great efforts to save it, the piece of the file finally fell through into the water-cooling channels of the inverted cylinder block itself. If we got the system to go again, there was always the chance that the loose fragment of file might sooner or later get washed into a jamming position inside the block where we certainly couldn't get at it. Still we had the entrance clear, and the inch of old copper pipe now reduced in external circumference by hours of careful filing and polishing fitted nicely in both the hole in the block and inside the aluminium water pipe itself. Francisco hammered deftly, and soon he nodded satisfaction, the long water pipe was again firmly projecting from the block.

"What about wiring it all in place, and passing the ends out through the silencer jacket when we fit it, that'll hold it firm," I suggested, hoping this would in some way make up for the awful business of the broken file.

"Yes, and we could put masking tape around the bottom of the pipe to stop it from falling too far down into the channel at the propeller end," Krister added, and he set to with such enthusiasm that within half an hour the motor was reassembled with Francisco nodding his head and muttering, "*Muy industria!*" to himself.

"Now for the trial!" I said.

"Let's go up and pick up Richard – he'll be delighted," Krister suggested.

"Francisco . . . a Silva, *si*?" I grinned.

"*Si,*" he nodded with a laugh.

Marie Christine decided to stay behind because it was still blowing hard and raining a bit as well. We pushed off the boat from the fallen tree pier and started up the motor without any trouble. I gazed down at the small hole through which the warm circulating water must come if the system was working properly. At first nothing happened and I began to fear the piece of file had jammed, but suddenly there was a splutter and a rusty stream of water burst out of the hole. This quickly cleared and the system settled down to work perfectly. We headed the longboat for the open water of the channels and loud cheering from the three of us brought Marie Christine to the window of the hut to wave frantically at my 'thumbs up' sign. A pair of ashy-headed geese took off from the hillside in disgust.

We arrived at Silva's just in time to collect yet another week's supply of delicious *tortas* in the old black pot. Silva was clearly delighted at Richard's attention to the boy's injured eye, and as if to congratulate us, the weather improved as we made our way back to Francisco's hut. He took us up another channel, to show us a favourite haunt of the steamer ducks where perhaps a hundred and fifty of these ten- to fifteen-pound flightless birds took off into open water with their characteristic 'steaming' flapping across the surface. We gave Francisco a go with the rifle, and we were much reassured when he missed with two shots before returning it to its home in the bow with a sad smile.

Marie Christine was quick to get the frying pan on the fire when we got back to the hut, and Richard soon had the billy-can on the boil for his 'Rosy Lee'. The *tortas* dipped in sugar tasted all the sweeter for the knowledge that we had managed to get the motor to go again.

Francisco's island home was not haphazardly sited. It was not until we had been there for several days, pinned down by north-westerly gales, that we were able to discern one or two of the main factors which had influenced him in his choice of position fifteen years before. To begin with we were rather surprised that he should build right on top of the ridge, but the reason was just the same as why the three croft houses at Ardmore are sited a hundred and fifty feet above the sea: to make the most of every scrap of useful soil. The shallow saddle at the eastern end of the island is relatively well protected from the prevailing westerly winds, by the long narrow shape of the island itself, and by a handful of other smaller islets scattered to the west and south. A casual glance down at the saddle from the high ground to the north shows that the stumps of the trees all around the hut are much bigger in diameter than are those elsewhere, this alone says something of the depth and fertility of the soil on the saddle.

From the one remaining window in the front of the hut, the view is across forty yards of gently sloping land, to where the sea laps timelessly on the shallow beach of flat grey pebbles. Farther away, perhaps half a mile in the foreground, a low but heavily wooded island guards the eastern shores of Fiordo Las Rucas which runs away three miles to the north-east. Beyond that a narrow valley runs off into the middle distance, before being blocked by the snow-capped mountains. On the days when the morning sun shone on us, the view from a seat on the three wooden steps of the hut offered everything I have ever wanted from scenery: sea, mountain, forests and peace.

In many ways Francisco's life was like that of the crofters of old, along the west coast of Scotland; indeed many highland shepherds came to Patagonia in the early part of this century to work sheep. The fifty acres he burned, to clear for his small flock of sheep, have not taken to grass as well as he hoped, in spite of the barrel of seed he keeps in his bedroom. Here and there on the hillside we came upon little patches of ground, maybe ten or so yards square, on which he had cultivated vegetables at one time or another. On the forty yards stretch of garden down to the beach on the leeward eastern side of the saddle there lay the most evidence of Francisco's struggle with the land. This band of land ran along the beach for a hundred yards before rising sharply at either end. Behind the house, as on the hillsides the land was a jumble of thick mossy tussocks which had proved nearly useless. The strip along the beach showed green with grass in places cropped short by the sheep;

just as in Scotland, the sheep ate the grass and left the rank clumps of rushes to multiply and creep across the land unless kept in check by man. 'Lazy beds' dominated the cultivated strip, fenced in by six-foot poles of cypress spaced close enough to obstruct the sheep but wide enough to let in the life-giving sunlight.

While we watched him dig in seed potatoes one morning, with a big red bumble bee buzzing around the disturbance, Francisco came across to the log on which Marie Christine and I were sitting in the sun.

"*Mucha plata*," he grinned, holding out three condor dated 1957, the year he had come with his wife to Isla Rucas. The light alloy coins were valueless, but he seemed pleased to have found them, as if they were evidence of the continuity of his work.

We walked back to the hut, past the rough hand windlass Francisco had built from his own trees to haul the long-boat he'd also built himself years before; we paused to watch a white-breasted cormorant flap heavily across the little bay and Marie Christine said, "You know you could do jolly well here if you really got down to it." I smiled to myself thinking that was just what she'd said about Ardmore nearly ten years before; this was the first trip I had ever been on without wishing I was home. The two places were really very similar just as Eric Shipton had promised.

Although it was sunny and quite calm where Francisco was scraping about in the earth by the beach, fifteen feet up above the sea where the hut sat astride the ridge the wind howled as usual.

Before clambering up the three loose plank steps to the door, I had a quick look around the side of the hut through the scattered criss-cross poles which served as a windbreak. Away up at the end of the channel leading beyond Silva's hut, I could see the waves seething in the main sound of Skyring at the feet of the solid white Andean chain of maintains. 'No hope today,' I thought – 'if only we had the *Ada* or the *Rebecca* from Ardmore we'd soon make it, it only needs an hour to get across and into the lee of the mountains.'

The hut was built first, before the boat, the pier or the wind-lass. There had been a couple of other lesser huts nearer the beach, but they were now only a wreckage of twisted planks strewn about one corner of the arable strip. Francisco's home measures twenty-five feet by twelve feet, it is raised about three feet off the ground by an uneven pattern of tree stumps and stark cypress poles driven into the ground. The framework of the house is also of cypress trunks roughly hewn into four inches by four inches and six by six inches. The floorboards and the overlapping planking of the walls look as if Francisco may have bought them ready-cut from the Las Colas sawmill near Estancia Skyring about twenty-five miles eastward along the sound of Skyring. Overhead through the rafters and above a few scattered planks bearing small square bales of dried seaweed, looking just like sheeps intestines, but in fact used to make soup, the roof of rusty corrugated sheeting had also come from service elsewhere. A few pieces of flat tin probably cut from an empty forty-gallon oil drum, cover the spaces where the sheeting has corroded through or just run out. In a couple of places in our room old wooden boxes with part of their lids removed had been nailed to the wall to act as mouse-proof food shelves, but we found to our cost that the mice of Isla Rucas probably grow wings by night and so have no trouble in flying through the letter-box openings of the food shelves.

At the back of the hut behind the windbreak and surrounded by a circular wall of vertical cypress poles was the well. This was simply a hole dug in the moss about three feet across and four feet deep. The water was always stained a dark brown and tasted rather bitter, but we never suffered any ill effects from drinking it. At the front of the hut, as if Francisco doubted the efficiency of any windbreak at the back, he had braced the house with three long slim cypress trunks which each ran at an angle from the eaves down to stout tree stumps. I felt sure it was these braces which kept the hut standing.

To many people, this little hut might represent a squalid deprived existence, but we really enjoyed our stay there even though the bad weather raged on and on out on the sound itself. It's true we were in a hurry to get started on our own but all the same there was a wonderfully secure atmosphere about the tiny island home which I have missed in many infinitely more sophisticated homes in British cities. Neither Francisco nor Silva owned a watch and I only ever saw one clock and that was broken. Sometimes Francisco would ask the time and when we told him he always looked up towards the sun as if for confirmation and then nodded with a smile. "*Si*," he'd say in his quizzical way. Unlike the other *amigos*' huts along the shore of the sound, there was no sign of a calendar on Isla Rucas. We knew Francisco was supposed to be returning to Las Colas in about ten days to meet the cutter, he always pronounced it 'Cooter', which came to the sawmill in mid-November and on which he served as a local pilot. The cutter was then sailed up to Isla Rucas to collect the cypress fence posts which were supposed to be cut and trimmed, ready and waiting for collection. The problem was that work had fallen rather behind owing to the extra delay caused by our long trip from Skyring to Isla Rucas; although the breakdown of Francisco's engine was a major cause of this delay, the enormous extra cargo he was carrying for us didn't help.

"What about going up and giving them a hand, Kris?" suggested Richard, one evening early on in our protracted stay on the island.

"Okay, let's go up with him in the morning," the tall Swede agreed.

Late next afternoon when they both returned with the grinning Francisco they were nursing very sore shoulders. The day had been spent carrying the seven-foot fence posts from the upper woodland where they had been cut, down to the chute which ran down to the water's edge. There were several difficulties: the posts, although beautifully dressed by the axes, varied in diameter from eight to twelve inches, there was no path to the shore and this meant stumbling down through the dense slippery undergrowth with a heavy load on sore shoulders. Francisco often carried two posts and never varied his stride up or down hill and seemed quite tireless.

"*Mucho trabacca*," grinned Francisco. Next day was a fiesta throughout Chile, and Krister and Richard were vastly relieved there was no work. The north-westerly gales raged on and on, Francisco said if there was bad weather on the fiesta then it would remain bad for a week, but we were no longer surprised.

It was at night that the weather seemed to be worse. Marie Christine and I would lie close together in our sleeping-bags as the squalls slithered through the channel and up the ridge to blast the hut. The roof was leaking so badly that we rigged the Australian Army lightweight groundsheet I'd been issued with in the Army and which has done me so well in the jungles of Malaysia and Amazonas. This time, instead of making an inverted V-shaped roof as in the jungle, we tied it at all four corners to make the sort of canopy one imagines used to hang above the four-poster beds of Tudor times. By this means, we managed to cover not only our own bed space but also the strips of floor on which Krister and Richard stretched their karrimats and sleeping-bags. Krister lay at the end of the bed by the table and Richard along the side in front of the fire. The majority of the leaks were caused because the corrugated sheeting had been used at least twice before Francisco bought it at Isla Rucas. The holes through which the bright sunlight shafted so attractively during the day, making pencils of blue light through the woodsmoke, made a huge puddle in the groundsheet by night. The rain came through worst of all of course where there were old nail holes in the troughs of the corrugation.

On the nights when it was not raining or blowing too hard, there were other sounds to be heard. The busy little mice rustled away everywhere in the room it seemed. At one time or another they found their way into biscuits, oats, mince, and even sank their teeth into Kendal Mint Cake. Marie Christine let out a great scream one night, and when I assured her there was nothing to fear she said she'd dreamt that one of the mice had jumped down on her face from the shelf box above. As I had heard more noise from the mice that night than at any previous time I wondered if the loud rustling might have triggered off the dream. Against that theory were the gnawed packets of biscuits we had found on the previous morning in that very box, directly above Marie Christine's head. The other visitors were unusually large spiders which secreted themselves in the vertical cracks between the interior frame of the hut and the horizontal planking which made up the outside skin of the building. Perhaps it was the heat of the fire which forced them to start moving around the hut after we had been in residence for a few days; once or twice we found them on our bed, but they were harmless.

Our several days at Isla Rucas were each passed in a similar general pattern, and since I found this little interlude so enjoyable perhaps it is worth describing. As a background it should be remembered that we four were really in an autumnal state of mind. That is to say we left Scotland at the end of a long hard-working summer, just when the first snows had touched the peaks and the green bracken was burned red by the early frosts. The days spent in the big-city atmosphere of London and Buenos Aires were not influenced by weather as such. Punta Arenas in mid-October came as a harsh shock; even though we expected cold, the rawness of winter in such a windy place is impossible to acclimatise to in advance. Only now, with time on our hands in Francisco's snug little home, did we really appreciate that spring was coming. In spite of the shaking walls, leaky roof and the clatter of loose corrugated iron, we could measure the slow retreat of the snowline up the mountains across the water from our window. Down on the beach when the sun was shining, where we were always sheltered from the wind, we could absorb the new life and hope that comes when winter is done. The many little shrubs which burst into fresh green leaf even though the branches on their windward sides were still bleached silver by the cruel wind. It was not only the brilliant mating plumage of the birds, like the little chestnut-backed tyrant, all jet-black save for its back, or the ordinary blackbird, but the perky way they held their heads as they hopped along the fallen tree pier to greet us. On the outlying islets flocks of steamer ducks were already making their nests of softest down in little hollows among the bushes and clumps of moss. They preferred the islets to the mainland, because they were there safe from the foxes and pumas: so safe they thought, that they nested up to twenty yards from the water even though they can't fly and waddle only with difficulty through the thick undergrowth.

Francisco was inevitably the first to rise in the mornings, he always seemed to come out of his room and light the fire so quietly that we only awoke when he called softly "*Pocito café?*" With the windy nights and the rain we never felt inclined to get up early and so prolong a day of waiting. Once up, however, Marie Christine would quickly make porridge for breakfast, usually with help from Krister, while Richard would busy himself with the first self-rolled cigarette of the day. I'd try to steal some hot water for a wash and shave before breakfast, and Francisco usually sat in a corner sucking on the long metal pipe leading from the *maté* bowl he held in his left hand.

After breakfast, and before he left to join Silva in the forest, Francisco always insisted on seeing we had sufficient wood on hand to keep the fire going, until he returned for supper at around six o'clock in the evening. He made quick work of this task, splitting logs with his razor-edged axe as if he were cutting kindling. When I suggested we might need an axe ourselves on the expedition he grinned and disappeared. We felt rather ashamed when he came back with an old axe head carefully sharpened with a file; I had insisted we didn't want his axe so he used an old head and transferred the fine long handle from his axe. The kind of wood he needed for a handle didn't grow on this island so he set off to work with a makeshift handle which not only didn't fit properly but was also the wrong length and split as well. This gesture was typical of Francisco, obviously he had practically no money and few material possessions, and yet he would always instantly give anything he had. As someone who has always suffered a dreadful compulsion to take the largest slice of cake from any plate offered, I perhaps admired Francisco more than most.

On one morning there was a lot of hammering outside after breakfast and eventually our friend came in with a stove and pipe to replace the smoky fire we had got used to in one corner of our room. Based on a square of gravel, on top of strips of tin on the floor, the fire had sent its smoke out through a hole in the roof directly above, via a couple of circuits round the room to set our eyes running. Now, with the top half of a rusty forty-gallon oil drum, and sections of tin curved into shape to form a chimney pipe leading up through the hole in the roof we were in luxury. It was as if someone had presented us with a new Aga cooker; with the smoke problem solved and a large flat surface to heat things on, Marie Christine found cooking much more attractive.

The ration packs so carefully assembled and heat sealed by Willy Isherwood back at Ardmore in May made up food for seventy days. The snag was that at the time of packing there were to be only three people on the expedition: Marie Christine, Richard and myself. It wasn't until August that Krister came

over to Ardmore for a few weeks from Sweden to join the team
of instructors for the remainder of the season. When he accepted
my invitation to join the expedition it was already mid-
September and our crate of stores and equipment was on the
high seas bound for Buenos Aires. Krister had to carry all his
clothing and much of the equipment he would be using, with
him on the plane. The weight limit of forty-four pounds left
no scope for extra food so we each agreed to carry a few packets
of light dehydrated meat to supplement the three main packs.
We had now been on rations for nearly a fortnight and even
with generous helpings of the biscuits and raw oats we bought
in Punta Arenas, it was clear that the three main packs couldn't
adequately be stretched to feed four hungry people.

The fishing tackle I had brought from home, added to the
stuff I bought in Punta Arenas when it seemed mine was lost
at Buenos Aires airport on the way down, was quite sufficient
for me to catch plenty of fish. Unfortunately Francisco said the
fishing for trout and '*salmo*', presumably a type of sea trout,
didn't come on until December. However, he assured us that
there were plenty of '*robalos*' in certain shallow bays, including
some around Chandler Island, which was the area in Canal
Gajardo where we hoped to establish Base 2. Base 1, of course,
was back at Estancia Skyring. *Robalos* could apparently be
caught quite easily on a spinner, although I wasn't really sure
how Francisco could be certain of this as he only ever fished
with a net back at Estancia Las Colas. This information was
coupled with that of the captain of the American ice-breaker
research ship *Hero* which had failed to get through the Gajardo
Narrows only a few weeks previously owing to the icebergs, he
had said that divers had seen no fish at all in Gajardo. All in all
the fishing prospects seemed rather too thin to pin much faith
on any realistic supplement to our diet; this particularly as we
might not have too much time to spare for fishing if we continued to fall behind our schedule owing to bad weather.

The other possible means of getting extra food was shooting
with the ·22 rifle Arturo had lent me back at Estancia Skyring.
I had done quite a lot of shooting with the Parachute Regiment
and Richard had also done some with the Special Air Service
Volunteer Reserve. Krister and Marie Christine had done none
at all. None of us was keen to shoot living creatures for sport,

Heading for the Andes

Fresia sipping *maté*

Alexandro and Calisto

Francisco takes a break from baking
at Isla Rucas

preferring to see wildlife at Ardmore rather than to eat it and then not to see it. I had enjoyed the stalking of the ashy-headed goose near Sergeo's home, and the clean kill seemed justifiable because we were hungry and ate it immediately after it was shot. I was less happy about missing several geese and ducks.

When I changed from the older ammunition to some new long-range high-velocity hollow-point ammunition at Las Rucas I began to account for one bird for each round fired. Again the snag here was time: at Las Rucas we had time on our hands and could well afford to spend several hours making a painstaking approach to within twenty-five yards of the surprisingly wary birds. But once on our own, it seemed unlikely that we would have much time for shooting, and even that time would be lessened because at the back of our minds we would rather not be doing it.

There remained three other possible sources of food: duck eggs which were easily found at Isla Rucas but which would be unobtainable at many places along the coast and in any case would mostly be hatched by the end of November. The *calafete* berries were abundant everywhere we had been and we had no shortage of sugar to cook them, but they did not ripen until December. Finally we were thrown back on the mussels: both Francisco and the captain of the *Hero* had assured us there were plenty of mussels, and all four of us liked them; this meant that whatever happened along the coast we were unlikely to starve.

The daylight hours at Isla Rucas were spent in an easily variable pattern that experience in the Amazon has taught me can only be achieved when the four people know each other well and are at ease with one another. The chores of washing up and looking after the wood for the fire got done without the need for any routine, and Marie Christine's skill at the cooking somehow always managed to surprise us with some new variation from a few basic incredients. Subtle use of garlic and a variety of herbs made eating a real pleasure rather than the duty it often becomes when men are cooking rough for themselves.

Krister wrote copiously in a tiny red diary from Sweden and he was always able to ratify erudite claims by anyone, such as the population of Indonesia or the ninetieth birthday of the

king of Sweden. Richard concentrated most of his energy into
maximising the effect and minimising the content of each 'last'
roll-up, while eventually and reluctantly confiding that he did
have a couple of packs of curious Chilian herbal tobacco for
when the English finally ran out. Marie Christine read all three
books '*A Horseman Riding By*' by R. F. Delderfield who I
remember meeting at the Hodder and Stoughton offices near
St. Paul's, shortly before his death. He described his writing
routine for me and I have tried to follow it myself: three hours
in the morning, a good break for physical exercise in the
afternoon to drum up fresh ideas and ease the frustrations of the
writing itself and three hours more in the latter part of the day.
In the same time, if I remember correctly, he would produce
roughly double the words I can manage. Having read the 1,500
pages myself at odd times when bad weather pinned us down
at places like Isla Rucas, I came to feel I knew the kindly fellow
rather well.

My own day was spent reading and writing and feeling the
general anxiety of civilised life slowly slough off like an old
unwanted skin. Between periods of writing when the small room
felt oppressive, I would do my 'rounds', feeling for all the world
like Smut Potter, the poacher in Delderfield's book. From the
back of the hut I'd move stealthily but quickly across the
saddle and down on to the windward shore. There I never once
saw any of my quarry: the wary steamer ducks, grey with a
reddish-yellow bill and bigger by far than the ashy-headed
geese which often landed on the sheltered beach in the lee of
the saddle. From the shelter of a boulder on an exposed point
I'd scan the shoreline of the next bay with the miniature Zeiss
monoscope given me by Dietrich Scharschmidt when he left
one of the businessmen's courses at Ardmore. Often I'd see the
ducks sheltering on the narrow beach far away. More often than
not, they'd see me and, by the time I'd doubled back on my
tracks and then moved up and round the back of the hill before
threading my way down through the trees and undergrowth
to the water's edge, they'd be gone. Once I outwitted them, and
we ate well next day on the rich dark meat of an old twelve-
pounder that should have known better. My stalking was at
first clumsy, but after a few days I began to get the feel of the
old days again: when I used to stalk the fat chub with my fly

rod, as they lay basking in the summer sun under the bushes in sheltered reaches of the Thames below Windsor.

On some afternoons, Marie Christine and I took one of the Avon Redseal inflatable dinghies and motored across to the island where the steamers nested. If we looked for long enough we usually managed to flush one of the ungainly birds from her nest leaving us up to ten huge cream-coloured eggs each about four inches by three inches in size. Old Donald Corbett at Ardmore had told us that in the old days if you took black-backed gull's eggs in the second tide in May they would be fresh. If uncertain about the freshness of the eggs he would take five of seven and return next day to the same nest to find a full seven again. The fresh five would sink in a pail of seawater and the bad two float. On Isla Rucas we tried to leave two eggs in the steamer's nest so she would lay a full ten and so in due course rear her complete quota of chicks and feed us at the same time.

In the evenings when Francisco returned from the forest we would all have supper on the rough table by the stove, some-times he brought *tortas* from Silva's hut, once he baked *tortilla* for us. Supper was always the main meal of the day for us, but Francisco and Silva seemed to prefer a big meal at noon and not so much at night, the main delight being the evening bowl of *maté*, the herbal tea. No matter what his regular eating habits were, Francisco never questioned the evening 'parties' we held in his hut, he always fell to on the duck, goose, scrambled egg, curry or whatever Marie Christine had prepared.

As the light began to fade, and before we got ready for bed, we usually tried to hold a conversation with Francisco in our disjointed Spanish. It was never long before he would turn to the subject of Chilean freedom from foreign domination. All his life peasants like himself had known nothing but hard work for next to no pay, while his European employers lived in a grand style in lavish houses not a stone's throw from his humble dwelling on the Estancia. He was a staunch communist and I could well sympathise with his view that Amerigo Fontana and President Allende were both '*bueno persona*', for they had, at one stroke, given him the dignity he desired. The long struggle as a small-time settler on this little island symbolised for him the struggle for freedom that Chile had won for itself. During his visit to Chile in 1972 Fidel Castro had stayed at the Estancia Rio Verde at the eastern end of Seno Skyring and Francisco had gone along to hear him speak and been much impressed. There appeared to be no doubt that for Francisco communism was the answer for Chile, he appeared never to have thought that it might result in a different and even worse tyranny for the Chilean peasant. My memories of the dead British Club in Punta Arenas only served to confirm my own feelings that some drastic change had had to come and to wish Francisco well the way it had turned out.

At ten o'clock on the morning of our tenth day on the island, we were still tidying up the hut after breakfast.

"What's that funny noise?" asked Marie Christine, and we all stood still to hear a sound rather like a lot of porpoises blowing in the sheltered bay.

"It's a change in the wind – it's from the north-east and the sound is ripples breaking on the beach," I almost shouted. We all rushed to the door and out into the sunlight: there it was, little waves sparkling as they splashed on the pebbles before the breeze. Overhead half a dozen black-and-white Chilean swallows played tag against the blue-and-white bowl of the morning sky.

"Tenth day – that was my forecast," grinned Richard. "We'll soon be off."

4

Base 2

IT WAS IN FACT in the late afternoon of the eleventh day, Tuesday, 7th November, when Krister and Richard ran the little grey Avon inflatable up on the pebble beach, at the end of their successful trip to Silva's hut to collect Francisco.

"He's with us, we've to get packed and move straight-away," laughed Krister as he jumped the steps clean through the open door in best Swedish ski-instructor style.

Within the hour we had collapsed the dinghy, transferred a motor to the stern of Francisco's boat, packed and loaded all our kit. Then we were on our way up through the channel to pick up Silva who was coming with us to help Francisco sail his boat back to Isla Rucas from our base in Canal Gajardo. In the event the dog Pellin came as well as the slim narrow-faced Riviera boy; so it was a big load of seven souls and a dog plus all our stores and equipment that set off across Seno Skyring at six o'clock that evening.

There was still quite a chop and a few white caps lingered on from the north-westerly gales of the previous ten days. On Francisco's advice, I headed well to windward of the seven-mile straight-line course from Isla Rucas to Punta Del Norte, the point guarding the entrance to the twenty-five-mile-long narrow Canal Gajardo which links Seno Skyring to the Pacific Ocean. Instead of keeping the waves more or less over the stern, Francisco's course meant something of a beam sea – every so often a rogue wave would lollop over the side, dousing our kit with liquid ice. Silva and I sat in the stern by the motor and the others sat up in the bow, on the other side of our mountain of cargo.

In spite of a steady drizzle the trip went smoothly enough. The Seagull engine worked well at its unfair task, making the clumsy boat amble across the waves with little of the harsh scream we remembered from pushing into a head sea round Punta Laura, or up from Sergeo's place to Vasquez's home, both of which now seemed a thousand years before. As we slipped past Isla Larga on our left, and slowly closed with the main Andean massif on the south-western shores of Seno Skyring it seemed to me as if we were moving towards another continent. After nearly a month of frustration on the wrong side of the sound it was exciting to realise that at last we were nearing our destination.

On our way across the grey rolling waters we passed a few black cormorants flapping heavily up-wind and sticking so close to the sea that their slow wing beats made occasional scratches of white on the grey. Up above, we saw our first terns, flying in their own inimitable style that is at once jerky and delicately graceful. Once or twice a tiny black-and-white bird, something a little smaller than the black guillemots of home, surfaced, looked hesitantly towards us and then dived in a splashy panic to resurface briefly at a safer distance before heading on its way.

At eight o'clock, with a couple of hours of daylight still in hand we rounded Punta del Norte and had our first sight down Canal Gajardo in a flat calm. It was narrow with its steep sides running up into the lowering cloud. Our attention was riveted by a huge glacier where it lay, a poised white tumble of snow blocks up in the sky, some ten miles down on the southern shore of the channel. A forewarning of things to come.

We ran on down towards Isla Chandler, keeping close under the western side which was heavily scarred by countless avalanches. Some were recent, probably the result of melting snows of the winter just past which had triggered off rock slides which carved a broad swathe straight down into the sea, obliterating everything in their path. Others were from earlier times, the white scars partly healed by a tissue of thin green undergrowth, the edges of the wounds still puckered by lines of dead grey cypress trunks tossed haphazardly aside by the falling rock of yesteryear. Immediately to our left the eastern shore was dominated by the sheer walls of Cerro Atalaya which rose clear from the water to its sharp peak at six thousand feet somewhere in the clouds directly above.

The evening drew into night. We moved farther and farther

down the long narrow channel, now made sinister by the flat calm, which lured us ever deeper into the heart of the mountains. Krister took over the motor and I moved up to the bow to be with Marie Christine who like all of us was now feeling cold and hungry. The distant glory of the Diadem Mountains finally disappeared from view. The stark tracks of the landslides became more numerous. Above the comforting purr of the Seagull we heard more often threatening rumbles from the ever-moving glaciers above and all round us. Dark cypress trees grew thickly from the water's edge up the nearly vertical slopes, hanging on at impossible angles.

"We'll have a hell of a job finding a camp site if we go on much longer, those trees are nearly growing out of the water," shouted Richard from the stern.

"It'll be okay," and I waved my arm to keep going. We'd spent too long waiting for calm; now it had come we'd make every inch we could, it was well worth an uncomfortable night.

"We'll just build a fire and sit round it till daylight," said Marie Christine brightly, and Krister grinned his assent.

Darkness covered the sky at last, leaving patches of bright white snow up on the sides of the blackness, the skeins of roaring waterfalls, and occasional luminous flares left by steamer ducks in their panic-stricken scramble across the phosphorescent waters ahead of us. Pellin, the cream and white mongrel collie, padded carefully up into the bow and we were grateful for his coming to keep us warm. Francisco and the Riviera boy were both half-asleep wrapped in the tattered grey sail, just forward of our pile of cargo. Marie Christine doled out equal shares of biscuits for all concerned, and Krister in the bow with us taught us all the words of 'Leavin' on a jet plane', which we sang softly to ourselves while drumming our feet to keep them warm.

At around eleven o'clock, the only traces of light came from the broad snows above, for there was no moon. Silva shouted rapid Spanish to Francisco from the stern. The bulk of Chandler Island appeared in the middle of the channel where it bent sharply to our right, somewhere above us lay the summit of Monte Inaccessible. We were now at last at that point on the brightly coloured map of southern South America which hung on the kitchen wall at Ardmore at which we had stared a thousand times in the past year.

"*Mucho monte*," proclaimed Francisco, pointing in the direction of the fiord to the north of Chandler Island, beside which I had hoped to establish Base 2. Instead we kept straight on, into the angle where the channel turned right. We left Chandler Island to our right and headed for the blackness of the forest in the corner of the bend, moving slowly now, Richard's engine at quarter throttle, intently watching Silva's impulsive gestures of guidance in the night. In the bow I kneeled ready with the torch. Suddenly there was a frenzy of activity in the water ahead, thin streaks of white fire zooming in all directions across the surface. "*Sardinas*," said Francisco phlegmatically, all the while keeping his eyes on the blackness ahead.

"*Bella*," cried Silva, and I hit the night ahead with the narrow beam of the torch. We were desperately anxious to save the batteries, having only one set for each of the two torches to last us for two months. After several brief flashes I finally managed to fasten on to the pale grey line of the beach under the tall trees. Then we were aground and Richard quickly cut the engine.

Immediately we were engulfed in the eerie silence of the flat calm. The slight drizzle which had persisted all evening blacked out the stars in the moonless sky. Above us on both the mountainsides projecting out from our corner of the channel, bright fields of snow provided our only light. Francisco and Silva jumped into the water, splashing white phosphorescent waves as they ran through the shallows and then disappeared into the night.

"Well, we'd better unload some of the stuff, then we can drag the boat up to the beach," suggested Krister quietly.

"Better go carefully on the torch," I added, anxious for the precious batteries.

We made our way to the shore, Krister carrying first Marie Christine, then me, for we were wearing our walking boots instead of the wellingtons we all had for boatwork.

Farther up the beach a single match flared, and then a small fire crackled into flame, illuminating the mouth of the small river which ran into the channel from the forest in our corner. Soon it was a great roaring fire, flames spurting up from the branches of fresh green birch leaves which our two *amigos* kept ramming in between the driftwood logs to get the blaze going.

We got all the rucksacks ashore with the help of the slim Riviera boy, who suddenly seemed to be having the time of his life. By the time the boat was made fast by a long rope to a fallen tree on the beach, the *amigos* had the strong black coffee already on the boil in their battered kettle. Squatting on our haunches watching the leaping flames, and stirring heaped spoonfuls of sugar into our steaming mugs, life seemed pretty good. We had almost finished the chunks of delicious *tortilla* when there was a grinding crash somewhere farther in the forest.

"*Grande ventisquero*," roared Silva waving his arms wildly. The four intrepid expeditionaries looked at each other in alarm.

"He means there is a big glacier just behind the trees here," I said. "That must be where the river comes from."

"They wouldn't bring us here if it weren't safe," said Marie Christine.

"No, it'll be safe enough, these trees wouldn't be here otherwise," Richard agreed.

It was one o'clock in the morning when Marie Christine and I unrolled our sleeping-bags on a bed of green branches laid on the pebble beach beneath the widespread branches of a big tree. We got into the bags and pulled the Australian ground-sheet over us, preferring its condensation to the accumulated drizzle of the five hours to dawn. Krister elected to sit up by the fire and keep all his kit dry, Richard tried a variation on that theme and simply lay down in the shelter of a tree trunk on a bed of leaves and covered himself with a couple of large polythene bags we had brought with us. At intervals we awoke to hear the growling roar of an avalanche or to try and arrange the groundsheet so as to stop heavy raindrops from falling on our faces from the branches above. This latter was made more difficult because the condensation had made the groundsheet stick wet to the sleeping-bags.

At five next morning the first rays of day stole down the channel on to the little camp. The *amigos* and the Riviera boy awoke, stretched themselves in the comfort of their bulky canvas bedrolls, then calmly got the coffee pot back on the embers and fanned the fire quickly back to life. For them it was just the start of another working day. For the four *gringos* it was the start of a period of discomfort which was to last until they dropped some of their silly city ways and became accustomed to the rigours of camp life.

It was still calm, a pair of condors wheeled in effortless circles above Chandler Island always waiting for something to die. The waters of the channel were a pale shade of milky green, and the woodsmoke from our fire made a curling wreath groping across the still waters as if uncertain whether to rise or fall. The *amigos* were in a hurry today, sensing they could row and sail clear of the treacherous channel before the wind made them prisoners with us. Breakfast was a quick affair of coffee, porridge and a chunk of Silva's *tortilla*; then shortly after six o'clock we were away.

The trip to our base camp under Monte Inaccessible was only three miles in a dogleg course round the western end of Chandler Island and up into the fiord to its north. Half-way across we had our first view down the next section of the channel: towards the dreaded narrows, and the icebergs in which had turned back the American icebreaker *Hero* a few weeks earlier. Directly above the area of the narrows lay the southern flank of the unexplored Gran Campo Nevado Ice-Cap still shrouded in cloud. As always it was the glaciers that demanded all our attention, visually as well as audibly. They were there just as the American skipper had said, clinging to the mountainside. Silva got very excited beside me in the stern and by means of elaborate gestures with his arms explained that when the glaciers calved ice falls, they hurtled straight down into the narrows. The resulting waves were much higher than the trees where we had been camping. I laughed it off and he kept looking at me, waiting for me to say something, but I couldn't think of anything.

What surprised me most about the glaciers was not so much their majesty, though I felt it should have been. Instead, from the angle we were looking, the light was such that in places the ice was exactly the same royal blue ink stain among the white that matched the light green ink-like stains I had seen in split tree branches at Isla Rucas. It was as if I had discovered a matching set of inks, one in ice, one in wood.

On the way up the fiord towards our camp the green water became increasingly milky until it was simply a pale grey and not nearly as attractive to the eye. We were making straight for a low grassy point on the west bank. As we approached a party of about twenty steamer ducks waddled into the shallow water and flapped their way to safety towards the far side, where the steep slopes of Monte Inaccessible fell into the sea. Five or six ashy-headed geese remained uncertainly on the pebbles of the point until we ran aground some way from the shore, then they took off and flew low over the water in the direction of the river which ran into the head of the fiord, a mile farther north. After a bit of indecision we settled on this place for the base and began the business of unloading the mountain of gear which had for so long made poor Francisco's boat look as if it were about to sink.

We were on a low flattish piece of ground which ran for a mile and a half along the western bank of the fiord, and about three-quarters of a mile inland. Heavily forested, the ground appeared to be made up of terminal moraine from a couple of ancient-looking glaciers behind the trees. The milky water came from the nearest of these and it ran into the fiord at our point, which turned out to be little more than a gravel delta.

The sun came out and soon we were all sweating with the exertion of stockpiling the many boxes of food and green metal jerrycans full of petrol. Francisco showed us a good sheltered place on the edge of some trees just a hundred yards south of the point, where we would escape the blasting north-westerly winds.

Suddenly the long grey boat was empty and the *amigos* jumped aboard with the Riviera boy and the dog. Then they were away, both men standing to row with one long sweep each while Riviera and Pellin sat crouched in the stern. They kept waving for the ten minutes or so that it took them to pass down the fiord along the northern side of Chandler Island and disappear north-east up Canal Gajardo, back towards Seno Skyring.

"Quick, light three fires," joked Krister, just before they were out of sight. Just before leaving, Francisco had gone to great pains to ensure we knew what to do if we got into trouble. If we made our way to the southern shores of Seno Skyring opposite Isla Rucas and lit two fires it would mean 'come with the boat'. Three fires mean 'come immediately, its life or death'.

"They shook hands very solemnly," Marie Christine mused.

"That fire lark won't help much once we go the other way, on down the channel," I added. Richard was already rolling another cigarette. We all missed the *amigos*.

We turned to the work of building the camp with a will: to get over the sadness of goodbye as much as anything. But the sun was hot and soon we felt tired from the cold trip of the previous evening and the miserable night in the drizzle. When the three tents were up, one large one for Marie Christine and me together, plus a small mountain tent each for Richard and Krister, we had a brew of milkless tea and sugar. Everyone decided the best thing would be to have a little doze before putting up the Australian groundsheet as a canopy over a cooking and eating area.

Although I lay down for a few minutes, I found the cup of tea combined with the view of the western side of Monte Inaccessible from the open end of our tent was enough to make me get up and get on with something. The sight of all the ducks and geese on the point on our arrival had seemed to me a promise of a steady supply of fresh meat if only I could stalk close enough to get in a shot at not more than thirty yards over the open sights of the ·22 rifle. The place favoured by the birds was nothing more than a strip of pebble beach and a similar islet rising perhaps to a foot above the surface of the water. The forest ran to the landward end of the point, providing a good cover of dense undergrowth and smallish trees: the shot I paced out at a maximum of thirty-five yards. Full of enthusiasm I set to work cutting a path from the back of our tents through the tangled thorn and birch bushes to the nearest place possible to the point. The task took two hours, and although I started well with Richard's S.A.S. jungle machete my hands were blistered by the end as well as having several thorns painfully embedded in my skin. Towards the end Krister appeared on the point itself and confirmed that it was an effective hide to his eyes, but that he wasn't sure if the birds might not have sharper eyes than his. I tottered back to the tent and collapsed; for a little doze before the birds appeared.

"Grub's up." Richard's gruff voice woke me from a dreamless sleep.

'Oh dear, he's feeling the tobacco shortage,' was my first thought as I crawled out of the tent to find the other three sitting on ration boxes under a temporary shelter shovelling hot mince into their faces. A mug of the milkless tea and sugar and my mince soon restored my spirits.

"What do you reckon about having a go at the mountain tomorrow," Krister suggested, nodding at the hulking grey and white mass which dominated the eastern shore of the fiord, only half a mile across the water from us.

"It's a pity we can't see the top," Richard chipped in, "the map is so vague – a few faint contour lines with Monte Inaccessible written across."

"I'd gamble the summit is this near one, straight up from the shore," I said. "That would make it the ring contour under the letter M of Monte on the map."

"Well, I think it could well be farther back from that. We'd get there in a day all right, but we might then find we had a lot farther to go."

So the discussion went on, and was bound to go on until we had climbed the blooming thing, then that would be that.

"Anyway we ought to climb it as soon as possible, from those slopes we should get a good view of possible ways up on to the ice cap," I said to close the Monte Inaccessible topic for a bit. Access to the Gran Campo Nevado Ice-Cap, henceforth always called by all of us simply 'The Ice-Cap', was the main reason for siting the camp in its present position. Beyond the half-mile belt of coastal forest at our backs lay the beginnings of two great spurs of rock, one on either side of the glacier valley directly behind us. Richard and I hoped that it would be one of these spurs that would lead us up through the clouds, keeping us always above the constant avalanches of the many glaciers. Unfortunately, as with Monte Inaccessible opposite, the snowline seemed to run up and away into cloud and we could never really see how far we had to go. Distances and altitudes are always difficult to judge in mountainous country, even with a good map showing clearly identifiable features. Our maps were simply 'fablonised' photo-copies of the only map available; one which had been made from air-photos taken by the U.S. Air Force in the 1950s – on cloudy days by the look of them too. No one had ever actually been to the places marked on the map, it was simply a projection from a photograph taken from a high-flying aircraft.

Anyway, as it turned out there was no solution to be found on the next day. After a night of ominous rumbles from avalanches, the dawn broke at around five in the morning. All was grey and misty, soft rain fell softly on a glassy sea. I went back to sleep.

"Marie Christine – here's some tea for you and John." The zip hummed up the front of the flysheet, stopped half-way to the apex of the A-frame, and Richard's hand thrust an aluminium pint mug of steaming tea through the gap.

"Oh, thanks a lot, Richard," murmured my wife, sitting up, leaning forward, and rubbing her eyes all in one startled movement. It was seven-thirty.

"Looks pretty grim out here, I doubt if we'll get up today – no visibility," said Richard, pulling the zip back down and then moving a few paces to repeat the performance at Krister's tent. It took a little longer with the Swede, who would never claim early rising to be his strongest quality.

When I joined Richard, under the little shelter, just beyond the tents, some twenty minutes later, we couldn't see far. "Do you reckon they could be icebergs down there?" he said nodding towards Chandler Island. I thought they were only whitish parts of the cliff and was just going to say so when I saw a small rise not more than six feet from the beach just in front of us. Richard noticed it too and said there had been several but he didn't think they could be very big as the water was barely six inches deep.

I wasn't so sure. Francisco had told me that the shallow bay on which we were camped, would probably be good for *robalos*. Back at Rucas he was often saying that they ran up to quite a size in these waters, indicating a couple of feet with his hands. I had made a point of asking him if we needed to use the Avon inflatables to get out after them, but he insisted the fish preferred shallow water. Our bay was certainly shallow, a curving pebbly place about three hundred yards from point to point and only fifty yards in from the two headlands at the centre of the curve. Thirty yards from the shore there was still a couple of inches to spare in our wellington boots.

I prefer fly fishing to any other method, but for quick results when I'm hungry I always go for my spinning gear. Whenever I leave Scotland I try to take my Hardy 'Traveller's' rod with me in case I manage a day's fishing somewhere along the way, for I prefer fishing to any other pastime. The Traveller's rod I had with me on this occasion was new but shop-soiled; I had been on the waiting list at Hardy's Pall Mall shop for ten years before this one had suddenly become available. They stopped making them about fifteen years ago, just after I bought my first one which still gives me good service at home. The rod comes in a short green cloth case about twenty-two inches in length and is made up of five sections of the famous Palakona split cane, including two top sections, one for fly and one for spinning. With the reversible handle the various sections can be assembled to make four separate types of rod to suit prevailing conditions.

Within ten minutes the tackle was set up: a six-foot trout spinning rod with a stiffish action was matched with the Japanese fixed spool reel and one hundred and fifty metres of nine pounds breaking strain monofilament nylon. The reel was also new but shop-soiled in a sense, for I had bought it in Lima, Peru, two years previously for use on the big trout of the headwaters of the Amazon, high up in the Andes. Sadly the glass-fibre rod I bought at the same time (I wouldn't risk my Traveller's in tropical jungle), had been rapidly converted from two to four pieces when 'Noddy' our tiresome white horse, had spitefully walked under a tree and smashed the rod, packed in its case on his back, against an overhanging branch.

My line for the *robalos* had to be light, yet I must be able to flick it thirty yards to the edge of the shelf with the springy cane rod. I chose a small silver Spinfix spinner barred with black. My first cast drew a blank – so did the first twenty! Sometimes the treble hooks came in garlanded with weed. The remedy for this weed was to snap on the bale arm while the spinner was still in the air; this brought it down with a bit of a 'plop' but it meant instant retrieval without giving the spinner a chance to sink and snag the weed. By holding the rod point high I was able to keep the spinner near the surface all the way in, and yet still wind slowly enough to attract the fish.

"Stop," I shouted at Richard who pulled up sharp half-way towards me along the water's edge. "Can't you see you're frightening the fish?" Richard is no fisherman and my twenty blank casts had told him all he needed to know – the twerp was wasting his time like all fishermen.

"Why aren't they scared of you, if they're scared of me," he asked with a rather hurt voice, for he had noticed the V's along the surface making for deeper water.

"I'll tell you why, it's because you're walking like a cart-horse. You have to move like the herons in the shallows at Ardmore – they creep along with tremendous care."

"Well, I only came to tell you breakfast is ready," and he stalked away looking more like an aged vicar than a heron.

After a few more casts I noticed a tell-tale lump on the surface of the water following the spinning line. I slowed my winding and the lump closed the gap on the spinner. Suddenly the line swung away at an angle and the rod tip arched. The automatic brake on the reel allowed the spool to pay out line, at a pressure well below the nine pounds breaking strain, in spite of my winding in with the handle. I quickly twisted on the drag star at the front of the spool and the flash of a silver flank shone through a welter of foam where the fish surfaced some twenty yards out owing to the increased tension on the line. After a brief plucky struggle I beached my first *robalos*, a clean silver fish and just on three-quarters of a pound. Breakfast was ready!

Later in the morning we rigged a proper shelter for cooking and eating, using the groundsheet as a canopy, strung taut between four trees at about seven feet above the ground. We sloped it down a little towards the back and attached the centre of the rear edge by a string to a bucket on the ground. This soon provided us with a pail of drinking water rather more appetising than the milky stuff from the river. We fiddled around making a fire of the wet wood in the drizzle and it was clear we had a lot to learn before we could conjure up a blaze as quickly as the *amigos* had done for us. Krister outflanked the *amigos* somewhat by coming up with the idea of using one of the Avon dinghy

One for the pot

John chopping wood at Isla Rucas

Preparing for the hunt

Our kitchen at 2nd Base Camp

foot-pumps as a pair of bellows and with this extra help we soon got the fires to go quite well enough to fry up the *robalos* I caught. Both Krister and Richard became keen and I lent them the German spinning set I bought in Punta Arenas. The fish came fast and thick, and the way Marie Christine fried them in butter, adding a few herbs and a touch of Aji chilli paste to the firm white flaky flesh, made sure we weren't going to starve.

Richard felt it would be a good idea to have one of the dinghies permanently inflated in case of emergencies, so while he was doing this Krister and I carried the remaining stores from the point to our concealed stockpile among the undergrowth. I still hoped the ducks would return to the point, but for the second day there was no chance of a shot. Although there were plenty of birds swimming around on the fiord, they all took good care to keep clear of the garish-looking orange tents.

The rain kept on and we had a stormy night but the site Francisco had selected for our camp was a real winner. No matter how hard the wind blew from the north-west it could not get through the belt of forest at our back. Although it was still drizzling next morning we were able to get up and cook our fried fish breakfast under the shelter without discomfort. The little bay just ten paces from our camp was calm and we were able to watch, with much satisfaction, as the wind whipped the water to foam, just beyond the point.

"That howling sounds as if the wind is furious because it can't reach us," said Marie Christine.

The fishing went well and Krister caught eight and Richard three. They were taking a break from their efforts, and we were all enjoying a brew of tea in the shelter when I got up to walk the twenty yards to our tent, which happened to be the farthest away. I took the usual glance up towards the point doubting if there would be anything there, but I was wrong. Two plump grey steamer ducks sat preening themselves right on the far edge of the little island.

I whispered to the others, grabbed the ·22 rifle from my tent together with a few rounds, and crept along the hidden path I had cut a couple of days before. Soon I was peering out through the cutaway tree at the target, just twenty-five yards to my front. I might have been a tiger for the concentration I was giving it. Desperately slowly I raised the rifle to my shoulder; my mother-in-law's green woollen golfing hat masking the upper half of my head, earflaps down, chin tied. I thought hard, 'Aim left and low, that's it, base of neck leading edge of breast. Check sight picture – tip of firesight blade just showing in bottom of backsight V. Relax, look away at something green to rest the eyes. Pause. Aim again. Breathe two, three, out. Steady. Take up trigger slack. Squeeze and FIRE! Check sight picture.'

The heavy duck was hurled a foot into the air by the impact of the high-velocity hollow-point round and splashed on to the edge of the water. It gave a couple of flaps with its wings and then lay still and dead on the surface. The eager wind seized at the bundle of pale grey feathers, sending them riffling the wrong way up the back of the carcass, and in doing so sent our supper on its way towards the middle of the fiord. There was no way through the bushes on to the beach, so I quickly ejected the empty case from the chamber of the rifle, applied the safety catch and ran back down my hidden path.

Krister had already seen what had happened and, with the help of Richard and Marie Christine, was launching the inflated dinghy. He then set off alone without a motor, paddling the short oars as fast as he could.

Then we saw them.

"Look out, Krister!" screamed Marie Christine. "Condors."

The Andean condor is the largest flying bird in the world. The wingspan of each one of the sinister black birds circling a hundred feet above Krister was broader than the entire length of his ten-foot dinghy. We saw him look up and then hesitate, uncertain whether or not to leave the dead duck to the huge birds. Then he obviously decided to give it a go. The paddles whipped up the foam and still the birds circled above. If they decided to come down and challenge for the duck we were powerless. The seconds ticked by, "Oh, I hope they go away," whispered Marie Christine – and they did. Contemptuously they went into a side-slipping glide and landed on a ledge on the cliff just the other side of the fiord. Perhaps it was their nest. Krister redoubled his efforts, picked up the bird and paddled back to us as fast as he was able. Grinning all over his bearded face he said, "I didn't really go for the duck until I saw them make for the cliff, you know."

Following Francisco's instructions, the duck was plucked straightaway. It proved to be rather smaller than those Silva always seemed to have in his larder on Isla Rucas, and everyone who had a go at the plucking found themselves covered in feathers. Later that afternoon I shot another ashy-headed goose and we caught several more *robalos*. The best weighed just over two pounds and was nineteen inches long. Over a fine kedgeree supper we discussed plans for an attempt on Monte Inaccessible for the following day: we had enough food now to cut right down on our use of ration packs.

5

First Ascent of Monte Inaccessible

THE DAY DAWNED GREY and misty again, but quite calm. After good helpings of porridge, fried fish and tea, the mountain seemed rather less of a problem, even though we couldn't be sure if we had ever really seen the summit through the cloud. The plan was a quick ascent and back again in time for supper. Marie Christine decided not to come with us and this strengthened the supper prospect for our return. Richard, Krister and I packed our kit quickly, hoping to make the most of the remaining fourteen hours of daylight. A hundred feet of No. 4 climbing rope, plenty of warm clothing and the Helly Hansen suits. A sleeping-bag each and a tent, together with rations for two days. For the snow we took glacier cream and goggles. We each had maps and compasses both to help us on the mountain and to check out possible routes up onto the ice-cap, which lay across the fiord from the mountain. By nine-thirty the weather was improving and we made the decision to leave at ten.

The boat trip across the fiord took only fifteen minutes. On the way we saw and heard porpoises gambolling in the still water. Away to our left close under the condors' nest we caught a glimpse of a stately pair of swans, snow-white save for their black necks.

We carried the dinghy across ten feet of pebble beach and laid it upside down on top of the short bushes at the fringe of the forest. In case of high winds, in our absence on the mountain, we made certain that the boat was tied securely both bow and stern. The little beach had been made in the course of time by a powerful torrent, whose roaring could be heard night and day even right across the fiord at our camp. Somewhere, high above in the mist, was the source of this stream, and higher still the summit of the mountain we had come halfway round the world to climb.

The first part of the climb was up through dense trees and bushes which clutched at our every move; underfoot the going was sometimes rock, sometimes swamp. Every so often we emerged on to the bald face of a rock band, to mop the perspiration from our eyes, and then shed another layer of clothing.

"I reckon this is still only the third band," grunted Richard, "we left base about four hours too late."

In my mind's eye, I tried to visualise how far up we were, against the mental picture of the mountain I had tried to memorise at the camp. The third layer of rock up didn't look too hopeful to me. Trees and brush clung to every inch of soil, and behind each rock band they choked the little valleys. However, Krister steadied us with a quote from Lord Slim, "It could be worse, it could be raining!" So for the next quarter of an hour it did rain.

At twelve-thirty we stopped for lunch on a rocky ledge, it was bare except for a few large boulders which provided shelter from a cold breeze. Underfoot there was some moss and several pools of water. The climb to this point had been particularly trying; up a steep gully full of slippery wet moss, and tangled with bushes which were so insecurely anchored to the rock as to offer little use as hand-holds. Our rucksacks, mounted on their high pack frames, weren't much of a help because they bumped the backs of our heads whenever we tried to look up.

"All in all, I'd rather be in Philadelphia," quoted Richard as we struggled into our duvet jackets and waterproof suits. Although the rain just managed to hold off, it was pretty chilly. We weren't too optimistic, so no one said much, and the little petrol burner roared away under the tall billy which was carefully placed in the shelter of a boulder and the artificial walls made by our rucksacks.

The cloud base had risen a bit during the morning and we could see well up into the tumbled icefields where they clung to the walls of the ice-cap on the far side of the fiord, although the top was still obscured. At our feet lay the fiord, a long narrow strip of milky green water, running from Canal Gajardo and Chandler Island on our left, to a short river which joined a couple of pale grey lakes and a huge glacier on our right. The orange specks of our three tents marked the base of a thin spiral of grey woodsmoke rising from our camp at the edge of the dark green trees directly opposite us on the far side of the fiord. What interested us was the ground between the orange tents and the blue white wall of the ice-cap; for somewhere here, if anywhere, lay our route through the towers and ramparts formed by the rumbling ice-falls. The southern ridge appeared to have the easier approach, because the trees quickly fell away where it rose sharply from the edge of the fiord; also there were broad tongues of yellowed winter grass which led through the worst of the woodland. But try as we would, we still could not get a proper view of either ridge, owing to the layers of grey-white cloud clinging to the side of the valley.

We knew by heart that there were eight thin slices in a pack of Kraft cheese, and twenty-two thin wine biscuits in one of Mackay's Vino packs from Santiago. Krister's chilled fingers made three neat little piles on the bare grey rock. Richard had an advantage with the scalding sweet tea, his plastic thermo-mug enabled him to drink comfortably while Krister and I made hasty sips against the hot edges of the empty butter tins. I thought of the old army trick of insulating the edge with silver paper, but Richard's packets of English cigarettes had run out long since, and with them our only source of foil.

It was too cold to sit for long over lunch. I led the next stage which rose sharply into the snowfields and cloud. Sadly the trees didn't end where the snow began, but rather changed into a low flat-topped type of bush which twisted hither and thither across the surface of the snow as if afraid to climb far from the mountainside. Progress became a matter of kicking footholds in the none-too-crisp snow, and wending a way in and out of the wind-blown bushes. To pass too close to one of these serpentine clumps of silver branches usually meant sinking through the icy crust until one leg was thigh deep in wet snow. This stage of the climb was rather like a tiring game of snakes and ladders, it didn't take long to exhaust both our interest and our new-found energy. We took it in turns to lead through this wilderness which was interrupted occasionally by rushing streams whose snow-covered banks caved in all too easily.

After an hour or so we were well up in the cloud and the whole project assumed a more stark atmosphere. Apart from one solitary snipe we had seen no living thing. It was cold and our world had shrunk to black rock and white snow. We stopped to eat a bar of Kendal Mint Cake, hoping it would give us the energy and enthusiasm to face the last assault, up through the cloud. We found a use for the scrub bushes; they made excellent springy seats which stopped us from sinking in the snow. A chill breeze from the north was blowing now through a saddle connecting Monte Inaccessible with another unnamed mountain to the north-west; we sat for only a few minutes in a fairly sheltered place, but the cold soon got us going again.

Ahead the going became much steeper, the bushes stopped and we were faced with sharp rocky spurs interspersed with gullies full of loose shale or gneiss. Snow lay in drifts here and there, and it blanketed every piece of sheltered flat ground; luckily the crust was hard and we were able to chip footholds in it without difficulty. Finished was the floundering about in wet snow up to our thighs. The best approach to the summit of Inaccessible appeared to be by way of the spur running up from the saddle, which joined the two mountains. Richard led us up in a general direction which would link with it. Once on the spur we would turn sharply to the right and follow it, hopefully to emerge on the summit soon after.

"If you wait here out of the wind I'll nip up and take a look," called Richard, when we were about thirty feet below the edge of the spur. Krister and I huddled together between a couple of big rocks and cracked jokes to take our minds off the cold. Soon Richard came into sight and clambered down to join us.

"You'd better go up and take a look, John. It's grim. I reckon we'll need a lot more time and a helluva lot more kit," he said, and Krister and I looked at each other. I could tell we were both thinking the same thing – 'Oh no, not all the way down, to come up and go through all this again.'

I left them there and crawled up on my own to see the way ahead, fearing the worst. As soon as I reached the crest of the spur the cold wind hit me, probing at every join in my clothing as if anxious to find a way in and freeze me. Across on the other side of the saddle there was a great area of snow-covered peaks, not at all like the friendly fiord and green trees below on the side from which we had come. The sky was above and all round me, like a huge grey blanket. Glancing urgently on up towards the summit of Monte Inaccessible, I could see a stern sight. The ridge of the spur disappeared from sight only thirty yards farther on, over what I guessed would be a false crest. Looking across up the other side of the spur I could see a great bowl of sheer black rock against which fields of snow clung, just ripe for avalanche. Across all this the grey clouds drifted in a most mysterious, melancholy fashion.

Laziness drove me on. I had no plans to go through this again on another day. We had come up here to climb the mountain and climb it we would. I scrambled down to Richard and Krister. They were both looking rather serious.

"Well, we've seen Foinavon look like that," I said. "If the cloud clears for a few minutes it will look very different. I'm for going on. I'm sure the spur will lead to the top." Krister looked relieved, Richard cautious and unconvinced, but they both nodded assent and we set off.

Once firmly on the spine of the spur, we found the going tricky in the cold wind. It was so steep that we could only move very slowly.

"See the condor, John," called Krister. I looked up and the great bird seemed close enough to touch. While we struggled for every foot of ground he sailed along with unconcerned ease, bending his ugly bald neck to peer intently at those whom he hoped 'are about to die'. From below he looked all black save for the bright white collar, but when he banked to turn for another run close over our heads we could see that the tops of his wings had a lot of white on them. Twice he lowered his legs as if about to land but changed his mind, content to circle above us until one or all of us finally lay still.

The loose rock on the spur was nervously and physically exhausting, and it was with some relief that I saw a substantial patch of snow ahead. But when we reached the point where it began I wished that we could simply carry on across rock instead of the time-consuming rope work that would be necessary to cross the insecure area of the snow cornice.

"This is the top of the big snowfield, John. Do you remember we saw it from the camp – the day we thought we saw the top of the mountain?" shouted Krister against the wind.

"Yes, I remember; this bit on the right will be where the avalanches were coming from," I shouted back, thinking the left windward side of the cornice looked pretty unstable as well.

While Richard belayed himself to the rock at the edge of the thirty-yard horseshoe snow walk, he explained how the formation had occurred. Basically this was a point on the spur where there was a sharp dip, rather like a bite taken out of a slice of melon. The winter snows had filled in the bite and drifting powder snow had found an overhang on the right-hand or sheltered leeward side of the spur. Now that summer was coming (believe it or not) the overhang would collapse and avalanche down the main snowfield which we had seen from the camp. On the left or windward side, the snow fell so steeply with the angle of the spur's side that it too might come unstuck and slide away down the face of the bowl.

Krister went first, with Richard carefully paying out the rope so that there was never too much slack. Watching him plod methodically across the glaring white, prodding the snow with the handle of his ice axe before each step to test the depth, reminded me to slide my sun visor down off my woolly hat to shield my eyes. The sun doesn't necessarily have to be out to cause snow blindness. He reached the rock on the far side of the cornice with only just enough rope to spare and Richard shouted to me that he wished we had brought the three hundred-foot length of 9-mm. Kernmantel instead of the hundred feet of No. 4 nylon rope.

By the time we were all three safely on the far side, almost fifteen minutes had elapsed, and we were numb with cold from the biting wind. We struck out for the top at a brisk rate, hoping that we might warm up a bit by the time we reached the summit. As always it took longer than we thought, and another half hour had passed before we all three strode onto the peak together, feeling for all the world like Hillary and Tenzing.

As if to acknowledge our effort the cloud lifted above us and the sun shone through on parts of the surrounding country. For a while the keen wind seemed to drop, or it might have been just the euphoria of achieving our objective. Every way we looked there were snow-capped mountains of all shapes and sizes, from gracefully rounded mounds to the thrusting pin-nacles of the cerros which looked like fairy towers encrusted with icing sugar. Ribbons of bright water wove in and out around the feet of the mountains. Nowhere in all this wilderness was there even the slightest trace of man's having ever existed.

Close above, the sinister shape of the black condor wheeled about us, the great splayed feathers at his wing-tips playing the wind like fingers on a piano.

Each one of us remarked on our feelings during the few minutes we spent on the summit. Together with the sense of achievement usually felt on reaching the top of something, there was this extra ingredient at standing where no human foot had ever trod. Richard took the tiny Union Jack from his rucksack and pinned it to the top with a couple of rocks. Krister buried a small Sundsvall badge from his home town in Sweden, and we each took a small chip of rock to remind us of the day we made the first ascent of Monte Inaccessible.

Far below we could still just make out the camp and behind that we could now see all but the top of the ice-cap. The approach spurs flanking the nearest glacier didn't look too difficult in themselves; but where they joined the north-east wall of the cap itself they seemed to rise nearly vertically: so much so that Richard began to mutter gloomily of 'super-alpinism' and 'major assault force'. To the left of the ice-cap we could see down the three-mile stretch of Canal Gajardo beyond Chandler Island to the pale green water where opaque icebergs jostled one another. There were plenty of problems in store.

It was already four o'clock in the afternoon and it seemed late although there were still six hours of daylight. Perhaps it was the thought of the curried duck awaiting us that sped us on our way, or simply the need to warm ourselves with physical activity. Anyway we set off at a fair old pace, choosing round-about routes where we could keep moving rather than the harder direct line of our approach. It is usually on the return from a successful patrol that soldiers blunder into ambushes, and it was with this kind of sobering thought that Richard and I kept urging half-heartedly for a slower pace. Once down on the smaller and less steep snowfields, Krister the ski-instructor came into his own; tobogganing down on his backside with the bottom of his orange waterproof jacket stretched tight across the back of his thighs to stop the snow from cascading up his back. Once, after shedding his pack, he showed us how to do a forward roll with skis and still come up to continue ski-ing on down the slope. Although he laughed as he told us it was a bit easier without the skis, I well believed the long hours he must have spent learning how to do it.

As we descended so it grew warmer and the trees came back into the landscape. First there were clumps of scrubby bushes and then almost suddenly they were small trees. Going down we seemed to have more time to take it all in, in spite of the fact that we were covering the ground much faster. We noticed that the trees, a sort of wiry birch, were burned white by the cold on the windward sides so that they looked like clusters of skeletons sprawled about the mountainside. Richard was ahead most of the time, having only contempt for Krister's frolics which had so impressed me; the mechanics of safety befitting the chief instructor of an adventure school occupied his thoughts far more than the *joie de vivre* expressed by the athletic young Swede.

We finally caught up with Richard where we had stopped for lunch, and we finished our bar of mint cake while Richard told us how a pair of tiny pipper-like birds had fluttered round him, as though afraid he might tread on their nest. While he was talking the cloud began to clear off the ice-cap, drifting past at first and then disappearing to reveal a hot sun and deep blue sky above the dazzling white line of the cap itself. Close to the eastern wall, nearest to us, a black dagger of rock thrust through the smooth white surface to reach for the sky. It looked so stark that I half expected it to move and so shake clear the mantle of snow which obscured its head from the golden sun.

We had before us, over the side of the ledge on which we sat, a broad sweep of sun-bright snow, rock, glacier, lake, iceberg, grass and forest. This splendid panorama was spoiled by only one small feature: the ugly black Face work involved in any ascent from the approach ridges on to the ice-cap.

"I don't think the old lady would like that," I said half aloud, thinking of what Marie Christine would think of 'super-alpinism'.

"I'm telling you now, we can't get up that," Richard said rather aggressively.

If we couldn't get up on this eastern side, where the wall rose five thousand feet from the sea in half a mile, there was only one alternative: a trip of nearly a hundred miles in the tiny rubber dinghies. The biggest glacier from the ice-cap ran

six miles from its north face and spilt its bergs into the cold
waters at the head of Bahia Beaufort. To get there meant having
to pass through the Gajardo Narrows with its icebergs clinking
in the treacherous current like so many cubes in a giant whisky
glass; on down the channel into Golfo Xaultegua, the mention
of which had had Francisco rolling his eyes and muttering
"*Mucho golfo*" and refusing to take us there. Beyond that there
was the sea reach of the Magellan Straits, which the Admiralty
Pilot warned no ship to enter except in daylight and which felt
the Pacific swell from Australia on even the calmest days.
Beyond that . . . well, what was the point of worrying about
the dangers beyond that? Best cross our bridges as we came to
them.

We had come prepared to make this trip in two ten-foot
rubber boats, but the dire warnings from the captain of the
American ice-breaker in Punta Arenas had made me think
twice about it. The aggressive note in Richard's voice was as
much due to my stubborn determination to climb the sheer
black eastern wall and so cross and recross the ice-cap from
this side in order to cut out the need for the perilous sea voyage,
as it was caused by the first sight of the wall itself.

"Well, anyway, let's get down for the duck curry," said
Krister lightly, and we dropped the subject for the time being
to concentrate all our effort on negotiating a way down round
the rock bands and through the grasping undergrowth which
had caused us so much trouble on the way up. All the same I
kept on hearing Marie Christine's mother's voice, as we said
goodbye in Brighton months before, "Make sure you look after
her!"

Eventually we emerged on the little beach and mopped the
sweat from our faces. The trip across the fiord took only ten
minutes in the sun and then it was supper time. Not duck curry
because Marie Christine had decided the duck should hang
for a couple of days, but instead a splendid feast of fish cakes,
mince and *aji*, followed by a chocolate biscuit cake. The whole
lot was washed down with several brews of hot sweet tea while
we basked in front of the wood fire, and glowed with the warm
feeling of content always associated with physical achievement.

The ice-cap was finally ruled out from the eastern side, and
Krister chimed in to say that anyway the main reason he had

come on the trip was to navigate 'Estrecho Magellanes' in a rubber dinghy. We concentrated our discussion not on the hazards but on the merits of one dash round, with only what stores and fuel we could carry in the two dinghies, compared with the possible benefits of ferrying more equipment to and fro on short sections of the voyage. We came down heavily on the side of one dash for two reasons. Firstly, to ferry anything meant going to a point, emptying the boat, returning for another load and setting off again for the point: three journeys for two loads. Secondly, ferrying meant more time, and I felt strongly that the voyage was simply an opportunist venture: when the right weather came we must dash as far as we could, then hole up until conditions improved again. In a place where ocean-going ships were warned not to enter by dark I felt we shouldn't linger in our ten-foot rubber dinghies.

We all went to bed in a thoughtful mood.

The next couple of days were spent in preparing for the move, nobody raised the possibility of climbing on to the ice-cap. The weather was reasonable, with not too much rain: in fact it always seemed thus when we sat round the fire in the camp which Francisco had so cunningly chosen for us. The wind never bothered us there.

Richard and Krister took a dinghy and spent one whole day on a careful reconnaissance of the Gajardo Narrows. Their report was a cautious confirmation that we should be able to get through: a lot of icebergs ten to twelve feet high, impossible to motor against a full tide but feasible in a slack; vertical williwaw squalls, glaciers clinging to the vertical walls of the gorge.

Marie Christine and I worked at calculating the greatest load we could pack into the Avon Redseal dinghies. Chafe is a great problem on boats where everything is constantly on the move in tune with the motion of the boat itself; a motor-boat is extra flexible in a choppy sea, so my loading trials were carried out with this uppermost in my mind. Marie Christine had managed to pack sixty days' food for four people into seven plywood arctic sledging boxes two foot by one foot by one foot, four green plastic four-and-a-half gallon jerrycans, and most of the space afforded by the two green canvas bags supplied by Avon for the carriage of their two deflated dinghies. I planned to load fourteen of the green metal four-and-a-half gallon petrol jerrycans and twenty-eight of the one-litre cans of two-stroke oil. Richard had an old Peruvian salt bag full of climbing ropes, ice axes, crampons and other small articles of climbing hardware. There was an army kitbag of tools and an assortment of pots and pans to be squeezed in. Finally six rucksacks and three tents were lashed on top of the heavy gear.

One of the first things I had noticed about the dinghies, when I inflated them at Las Colas sawmill weeks before, was that some cautious soul in the Avon factory in Wales had gone to the trouble with a ruler and red biro to box in the stern warning that eight hundred and fifty pounds was the maximum load. Now on this remote little beach I smiled at the peremptory rubber label and felt rather pleased that I was just about going to manage it for the unknown 'Welsh warner'.

While Richard and Krister were away at the Narrows I was able to catch twenty-five *robalos*, the best of which was twenty-two inches long and weighed two and three-quarter pounds. Also I managed to shoot another goose. By this means we were able to eat well, and at the same time avoid using the ration packs which would be vital once we left our comfortable base.

Porpoises and seals came to our beach – we could hear the former from inside our tents at night – and in the early hours of one morning Richard felt sure that he heard something blowing much harder than any porpoise as it made its way along the outer edge of the shallow bank formed by our bay.

"I reckon they could have been killer whales," he told us over breakfast. "I read in Scott's diaries that once they got the taste for his ponies and dogs, they would come from below and smash the ice to tumble the animals into the water."

I had read how they caught seals by tipping over icebergs with their snouts, and Krister and I both remembered seeing their spiky dorsal fins and white patches breaking the surface near my yacht off Handa Island during the summer. Perhaps the most vicious creatures in the sea, we could certainly do without their mistaking our small dinghies for seals.

We were surprised to find jellyfish on our beach. Surrounded by lofty mountains and snow, the ugly heaps of brown jelly seemed the more incongruous, as if they had got lost and been swept the wrong way.

Visitors to the little pebble island at the mouth of the milky glacier river were not confined to species which I shot to restock our larder; we saw plenty of rock cormorants, black-backed gulls, great oystercatchers and the occasional hawk, land there. Smaller birds like the delightful little chestnut-backed tyrant, hopped about on the beach at our feet, quite unconcerned at our activities.

On the afternoon before our attempt on the Narrows, Krister, Marie Christine and I took one of the dinghies to explore the main river at the head of the fiord and the lake half a mile beyond. There were many pairs of ashy-headed geese and plenty evidence of *robalos* in the shallows. The river was as milky as the one near the camp, and this didn't help our fishing. We tried hard with the spinner where the lake emptied into the river, usually a good place for fish, but we were not in luck. Marie Christine gathered a handful of clay from the mud bank and said she felt sure it was pale grey china clay of the kind she had used to make pots as a child at school. When we entered the lake we were at once shadowed by a pair of condors as we motored round the entire circumference trolling a Toby lure and a large minnow, again without any success. A blank day like this always manages to get me down a bit and we returned to camp feeling rather sorry for ourselves, in spite of the sun and magnificent scenery, but this temporary lowering of spirits was quickly allayed by the long-awaited curried steamer duck for supper.

We were all ready to move on.

6

Killer Whales at the Narrows

AT FIVE O'CLOCK IN the morning I awoke to the sound of porpoises blowing as they cruised along the edge of the bank in our bay. Or were they killer whales? But as soon as I opened my eyes and saw the sun was shining gold into our tent, the walls of which were quite still, indicating calm, I dismissed the idea of horse-gobbling killer whales in our bay as a load of rubbish. Our tendency was always to bask in the cosiness of dry sleeping-bags and sheltered warmth; not so this morning – we were off.

"Krister," I called, without reply, for the Swede was a notorious late-nighter, reading by candlelight until two in the morning. He was an equally notorious late-riser.

At the third call came a sleepy response, then a half-hearted call to Richard. We were started.

Breakfast and packing took much longer than we hoped it ever would again, for it was important to leave nothing essential behind and at the same time to pack the dinghies perfectly with the heaviest load they would ever carry.

At eight-thirty on the morning of the finest day we had yet seen in Patagonia we listened happily as the Seagull motors stuttered into life. The plan was to try one engine at first, for I had hoped to tow the second boat and so save fuel; after five minutes I changed my mind. If there was to be any economy, then fine days were more important than fuel.

With the two boats moving as separate units down the channel on the three-mile journey to the narrows we made a brave sight, pale grey dinghies with yellow trim and scarlet spray sheets and us in our orange suits. The green water was glassy calm except where steamer ducks traced lines of foam in their panicky escape. A hot sun shone from a cloudless blue sky. Ahead lay the dazzling blue and white wall of the ice-cap, towering five thousand feet above the channel, which was only twenty-two yards wide where it made a sharp turn to the south-east. Behind us our retreat was barred by rows of silent white peaks. On either side rock walls, clad here and there with dark green trees, rose sheer to the snows above. Sometimes we passed tree-strewn avalanches and roaring waterfalls, but the day was still young and the calm created an atmosphere of expectancy rather than action.

To some extent we were all tensed for an emergency at the narrows, but none of us was prepared for the form in which that emergency showed itself. Things were going nicely I thought; we had got away in good time in good weather, the cooling system we had rigged up for the broken engine at Isla Rucas was working faultlessly. I could hear the roar of avalanches from somewhere above us, where the glaciers hung seemingly motionless on the rocks walls, only rarely could I see the final traces of a recent fall, then my eye caught sight of what looked like a ribbon of salt spilt from some giant dispenser. The sound always arrived long after the event. I couldn't believe we should be so unlucky as to arrive under the main wall when a major collapse sent hundreds of thousands of tons of rock and ice plunging into the water to displace a tidal wave: if it happened I still felt the dinghies would ride the wave.

The sides of the channel drew in considerably as we approached the narrows. 'No,' I thought, 'we'll just pull in on the right there before we reach that pack of bergs – it's a beautiful day, we'll be quite all right, as long as we're careful.'

It was in this mood of cautious optimism that I led the way down the middle of the channel. I was no more than mildly surprised to see the three black submarine creatures rise up a couple of hundred yards or so to our front. Marie Christine said nothing and I smiled across at Richard and Krister to our left. I was much more surprised to see that they had changed station and were heading across our stern, straight for the shore a hundred and fifty yards away to our right.

Richard was at the helm, I thought he looked worried.

"Killer whales," he mouthed. I still didn't believe it and looked again at the place where the three had surfaced. They didn't keep me waiting long this time, instead of rolling gently up they came up all three facing in our direction. Massively larger than porpoises, wicked spiky fins high on top of their black backs and white patches along the sides of their bodies. By this time I was heading for the shore.

"We'll be okay if they don't chase us – we'll get into the shallows where they can't reach us," I said to Marie Christine, trying to smile calmly, but remembering the speed with which the creatures could swim and that there might be no shallows by the rocky shore.

They came up again nearer this time but they didn't look as if they were after us. Richard was well inshore of us by this time. With no sight of the whales, Marie Christine and I just held on to the sides of the dinghy while we made for the shore at full speed, expecting at every second to be tossed in the air when a whale surfaced under us. It was a rather unpleasant wait.

We made it to the shore and coasted round until we reached a low rocky promontory which marked the inward end of the narrows. Here we got out and looked back up the channel to ascertain the position of the three whales. To our relief they surfaced at speed, line abreast, half a mile away and heading for Isla Chandler.

The first thing we noticed about the narrows was that the tide was coming in towards us, bearing stately icebergs like stagecoaches through the whirling green water until they joined a pack of bergs in an eddy on our side of the narrows. Here the ice creaked, groaned and clinked its way round in a tight mass, rotating clockwise. Pieces of different size and hue jostled for position, some appearing from beneath to make a space for themselves, others turning on to their sides or rolling completely upside down. The water behind the jumble of ice was at a lower level than that which rushed down through the narrows; this gave evidence of the pressure and depth of the bergs many of which must have been grounded. I could understand how the American ice-breaker had turned back for the wider waters of the Magellan Straits, for the rocks seemed everywhere in the channel itself, not on the surface but somewhere beneath, sending up great welts of surging water.

"Let's just sit here a while and enjoy the sun, while we work out what to do next," I said, sitting myself comfortably on a springy bush.

"I hope those whales don't come back," muttered Richard.

While we admired the colony of white-chested rock cormorants and the busy pairs of orange-billed grey steamer ducks, we tried to make various calculations: the speed of the current, the time of high tide, the distance through the channel, how long the good weather might last, and the many other factors which had a bearing on our next move. Second to the absence of the killer whales the most important thing was whether or not the Seagull motors had the power to push the dinghies through the channel against the rushing tide. I felt sure we must make the most of the good weather, and that meant pushing on against the tide. However, the only entrance to the channel at our end was an oblique entry to the current just above the iceberg eddy. If the motors failed or if they couldn't make headway, then we should be pushed back among the pack of milling icebergs with all sorts of possibly nasty results.

"Well, if the price was right, and we were at home, I'd have a go at taking one of these inflatables through the ice – I reckon they'd ride it out," I said, "but here the engines and boats are vital to us. All the same, I'll bet the motor will push us through. We'll go first, you wait until you're sure we are right through before you start. If anything happens to us let us drift clear of the ice, upside down or otherwise, before you come out to pick us up." As I said all this I noticed a few hands fiddling with lifejacket strings.

"Okay, I'll come down with you and fill up the fuel cans," said Krister, as Marie Christine and I got up to walk the few yards back to where the little grey rubber boats bobbed silently to their painters.

Marie Christine paddled out into deep water, leaning against the big mound of gear in our boat as she took a few strokes on one side and then a few on the other side to keep us going straight. I checked the fuel through to the carburettor, and after a couple of pulls on the starter cord the motor burst into life. "Choke out, fuel on," I said to myself, and checked the air-screw on top of the fuel tank one last time. We both made ourselves comfortable on the yellow fibreglass seat in the stern and I did a trial circle with the boat in the back water, just to make sure the motor was well into its stride.

"Here we go!" I headed for the line of little green whirlpools which marked the edge of the racing current. We hit it with the throttle at three-quarters open and the boat moving smoothly. Immediately we were swung violently to the left, exposing all our right side to the full weight of the tide and bearing us down to the ice-laden eddy only a few yards downstream of us. I pushed the steering arm away from me and the bow, only some eight feet in front of me, swung decisively up into the current. The engine roared solidly and the wake boiled white.

"We're not making any headway!" Marie Christine looked worried, there was an urgent edge to her voice. On the little headland perhaps ten yards to our right, Richard and Krister stood helpless and looking worried too.

But we were making ground, only inch by inch but we were going forward and we had fuel enough in the tank for at least an hour. The total distance through the channel I estimated at not more than three hundred yards. We were on the outside of the curve and so I gradually edged across to the inside, right across the front of the ice. If the engine failed nothing could save us from hurtling down among the bergs, all that was needed was a speck of dirt or water in the fuel line . . .

"You stand up and watch for rocks and ice," I shouted above the roar of the engine, and Marie Christine gingerly pulled herself up and leant forward on the cargo shooting her arms to left or right when we seemed too close to any obstruction.

We reached a point two-thirds of the way through, where the channel was at its narrowest, and where we had to bend sharply left and so out of sight of the two orange figures on the far shore. Here we just stopped, unable to move any farther forward owing to the force of the current flooding between two submerged rocks. The ice-pack still looked dangerously close astern and we looked at each other seeking some inspiration. Carefully I slid the boat over the top of the inshore slab of rock clearly in sight below us. The trick was not to go too shallow, where the propeller needed only to strike the rock once at three-quarter throttle to break the shear pin and so leave us at the mercy of the current to spin out of control among the ice downstream. All the same, if we could just clear the main force of the stream passing between the rocks, then we could inch forward and work our way into less constricted and less forceful water. We managed it, more by luck than judgment, and eventually emerged, after the sharp left turn, into a much wider part of the channel.

We had now to wait for the other boat to make its run. Above us were millions of tons of ice frozen to the rock wall, perhaps four thousand feet above the sea. To our right the channel ran back into the mountains in a cul-de-sac, for about three-quarters of a mile. A big glacier ran down to the sea, at the end of this cul-de-sac, and all along its face icebergs were calving into the sea. Rather than hang about under the hanging glaciers high above, or be swept back into the narrows by the fierce current on the opposite side of the channel from the ice-covered walls, I decided it would be best to take a look at the glacier in the cul-de-sac, where at least there would be no current to waste our fuel.

With the throttle set so low that the cooling system was just sending its thin stream of warm water down the outside of the silence, we cruised gently through the flat, calm green water. There was no great hurry, for it would take the other boat at least half an hour to work up through the narrows; if they didn't appear then, we would go ashore and climb up on to some high ground to see where they were. We passed well clear of the larger bergs which were grounded along the shore, fearful they might turn over on top of us. Soon we were among small stationary pieces of ice which seemed harmless: perhaps no more than a stalk one inch thick and a foot high supporting a six-inch horizontal sliver of ice melting steadily in the hot sun. On getting close to such a piece we might find it was simply a pennant on top of a large submerged block several feet in size. There were two snags here: one, the block might hit the propeller and break the shear pin; two, the block might be unstable and suddenly a ripple from a previous turn of our dinghy might cause it to roll and reveal a large bulk above the surface, upsetting our boat at the same time. Slowly we moved into an ever-thickening field of ice, but warning bumps on the side and taps on the engine forced us to turn back and watch from farther away than I had hoped. All along the front of the glacier chunks of ice of all shapes and sizes lay in profusion. We never actually saw a berg calve from the face because we weren't able to stay for long. High above and to the left I saw the wispy aftermath of an avalanche but I missed the main fall, although our ears rang with the rumble of avalanches from all points of the compass.

The incredible weather held, it was as if we had suddenly arrived in paradise. The danger of this particular heaven was sunburn, the ultra-violet rays reflecting strongly off both the snow and the mirror-like surface of the sea. We had liberally smeared our faces with glacier cream before we set out and now we needed our sun visors as well. All the time we were looking at the glacier where it emptied into the sea, we were both thinking of the others in the narrows and long before the half hour was up we were pulling into the shore and climbing a headland to see how they were getting on. Even here, large chunks of ice, half the size of a house, were aground and in much deeper water than we would ever have imagined necessary to support such a relatively small size above the surface.

From the shoulder of a spur running down to the sharp bend of the narrows I was able to see the complete course we had followed. It was with a sinking feeling that I saw no sign of the other boat.

"You bloody fool." I cursed myself for not coming ashore immediately we got through ourselves. I was sure they were back under the ice somewhere. Marie Christine was making her way up the spur to join me, and I was quickly trying to think of some way to break the awful news to her, while at the same time deciding whether we should unload the boat before going back to look for any sign of them.

Just then their little grey and red boat came out round the same headland from where we had started.

"Bloody fools," I shouted, "why the hell do you have to take so long?"

"Here they come," I called to Marie Christine.

"Okay, I'll go on down to the boat," she replied as I watched the other dinghy make a much more rapid passage than ours and realised that the tide must be nearly full and falling slack. Krister was standing up and signalling the direction as Richard weaved in and out of ice and rock. Quite soon they were below me and out of the current, with Richard making hand signals to enquire whether or not we were stopping for a brew of tea. Scrambling down through the moss I waved that we must push on to make the most of the good weather.

Marie Christine and I carefully edged our way down the side of our grey dinghy, leaning over the pile of three rucksacks lashed on top of the cans of fuel, boxes of food and bags of climbing gear. We definitely did not want to slip into the icy water with many hours of travel before us. It was around noon as we pushed off from the narrows and headed on our way down the twelve miles of channel to the dreaded Golfo Xaulte-gua, which had caused Francisco to shake his head so vigorously when I suggested he might take us there in his boat. I was determined that we should cover as many miles as we possibly could; because if we ran into any sort of a headwind, then we might be stranded on some desperate piece of shore, even below a cliff, for weeks until the weather came good again.

"Let's have lunch now," said Marie Christine, pulling two packets of biscuits and two half packets of Kraft cheese slices from the square yellow and blue Milady toffee tin in which she carried all the culinary knick-knacks which made our meals so much better than those of any trip I'd ever been on before.

I only needed to hold the blue packet of twenty-two wine biscuits in the air and Krister had already turned their boat in towards ours.

"I know it's very cramped, but I feel sure we must keep going," I said as I handed them their lunch.

"Oh yes," agreed Krister, smiling as always. "Why don't we refuel now and we can tell you why we were so long coming through the narrows?"

It transpired that there was more to it than simply waiting for the tide to slack and while we fiddled with filler caps and struggled not to waste a drop of precious fuel, they told us what had happened to them when we had disappeared from their view.

"That big iceberg that came through just as you left turned over and caused a bit of a commotion in the eddy with the others. We saw how you only just made it so we waited a bit when the wind sprang up," said Richard.

"Yes, and while we waited the three killers came back," interrupted the Swede.

"Yeah, fins like bloody guillotines – we weren't going while they were around," Richard went on. "Well, then the tide began to slacken off so we had a go at it. I reckon you must have all but hit the big rock we saw in the middle."

"Yes, you could say that," mused Marie Christine, as Krister put the petrol can under his seat and wound the starter cord on to his engine.

We made our way down the channel, away from the main bulk of the ice-cap; slowly at first, but with gathering speed as the tide turned in our favour and started to run away towards the Pacific. The first stretch was a five-and-a-half-mile straight heading south-east, there wasn't so much as a breath of wind and the whole dazzling massif above us was utterly still. The awesome silence was broken only occasionally by the ice-falls and the steady purr of our motors. To our right a high spur from the ice-cap ran parallel with us for the whole length of the straight, and on the left we gazed up at a jumble of peaks and jagged 'cerros' which we could hardly place on the map as it was mostly unmarked and unnamed.

The pair of gaily coloured little boats looked like a couple of two-man bobsleighs; short and stubby with their red spray sheets rising steeply from the bows like windshields streamlined for speed. In the back of their boat, sitting crouched behind a pile of carefully lashed equipment, the bulky orange-clad figures of Krister and Richard with faces half-obscured by sun visors, looked for all the world like a pair of racers. Our own boat at closer inspection didn't look so speedy after all. True, the spare red rucksack set off the British Racing Green of our two main rucksacks in most racy fashion, but the fair-haired girl with her white Arran hat was plucking a goose as she went along. The man at the motor had his knees tucked up almost to his chin because of the crush of black cooking pots and pans, and along his side lay a hooked stick securing half a dozen fine silver fish.

Overhead a few inquisitive seabirds, up from the ocean for the day, paused to inspect the two dinghies which may have looked like a couple of crippled seals roaring out their death agony, to a hungry black-backed gull. We no longer saw any condors, but as we drew nearer to the ocean, birds like the Great Skua appeared to be more numerous; often harrying the gulls and cormorants until the unfortunate victims dropped their hard-won fish and fled.

The sunny afternoon wore on and a gentle breeze dappled the waters of the fiord. It was a long time since reveille at five in the morning. There had been no brew of tea, nor any real pause. Richard suggested we might start looking for a good place to camp, mentioning that most accidents occur in the latter part of a hard day, when people get careless through fatigue. The boats were cramped with their maximum load but I felt certain that we must capitalise on the fine weather and drive ourselves as far as possible until conditions worsened.

All round us lay the great grey and white mountains, imposing an atmosphere of stillness. Apart from the occasional bird, there was absolutely no sign of life, and even the birds appeared to be flying in slow motion.

Eventually, in the late afternoon, we entered the Gulf of Xaultegua and the mountains drew back on one side exposing us to a great area of sea, it was as if we were coming into a new world. Cutting across a bay we might have been as much as a mile from the nearest shore and three from the other. Ahead the gulf grew wider and we all dreaded the point where sooner or later we must round a headland and feel the impact of the ocean swell which would have built up on its way right round the world without the hindrance of any land in its path.

By five o'clock the breeze from the south-west had strengthened, and we were taking quite a bit of water over the bows. Marie Christine was busy most of the time scooping the unwanted water with a tin mug from between the clutter of pots and pans around our feet. It was time for a brew up, so we made for a pretty little pebble beach, neatly sheltered beneath the heavily wooded sides of a rearing black peak with slabs of white quartz near its summit.

7

Tide-Race

"THERE'S A NASTY tide-race about here." At the back of my mind I remembered the evening we spent on the American ice-breaker, and Captain Lenie's finger stubbing on to the chart by Isla Entrada. "We experienced heavy overfalls here, where the waters of the Skyring complex meet the Pacific tides," he had said.

The steep little beach where we were boiling our billy-can of tea was just north-east of Punta Quidora. Half a mile offshore I could see Isla Entrada – for us it meant Entrada into the Pacific in a heavily laden ten-foot rubber dinghy. The reason I had agreed to Richard's plans, gestured from his dinghy, to make for the beach and brew up, was rather more than just a shared need to stretch our legs. I had seen what I had been dreading ever since the idea of rubber dinghies near Cape Horn had entered my mind.

There was white water breaking on the southern end of Entrada.

We had twenty-five miles of open coastline ahead of us. If the sea was breaking heavily on such a calm day as this, what realistic chance did we have of getting round?

The hot tea was a help but it didn't seem to do enough. We should really have been putting up our tents for the night after a long day.

"Look at these enormous mussels, Johnny," said Marie Christine, holding up a couple of giants, each fully four inches long, "let's just boil up a few of these and eat them now." So we had a couple of dozen between us, each one was as big inside as their Scottish cousins are outside.

"There's a bit of white on the end of the island, but it's such a fine evening that I'd like to get this part over – remember the captain of the *Hero* said there was a tide-race around here." I said this quietly and the others all nodded their heads in agreement.

"So what's the plan then, John?" Richard reaffirmed. "Push on now and hope to make it to Portaluppi for eight-thirty this evening. Is that it?" He gave one of his quizzical looks from under furrowed brows.

"Yes, I reckon that's it; camp at Portaluppi for the night, that's ten miles on from here; get a place near the mouth. Then first thing tomorrow morning make a dash to get on up the fifteen miles of coast and on through Canal Cripples before nightfall."

It was already six o'clock; to make it up the coast to Portaluppi for eight-thirty we needed to do four miles an hour. In the evening calm this was not impossible.

We threw the empty mussel shells back into the sea, then slid the boats gently off the tide-line and out into the water, hopping aboard before the water could slop over the tops of our wellington boots. Both motors started straightaway and we headed for Punta Quidora with full tanks. It was a perfect evening, the sun was well on its way into the west mellowing the harshness of our surroundings with its soft light. The breeze which had earlier slurped the sea over our bows had died away. High up and far away above the horizon the clouds had a placid flat-topped look to them. We were going well, riding out into the gulf on the last of the Skyring ebb-tide. It took scarcely twenty minutes to cover the couple of miles down to the innocently rounded headland that is Punta Quidora; the swell was long and low and the two little dinghies rode it easily. I looked across at the other boat and felt greatly relieved that Richard and Krister seemed to be completely unworried. Beside me in the back of our dinghy Marie Christine, too, appeared calm. It had been a long day, thirteen hours since reveille; some of those hours had been pretty hectic, the others had been spent perched on the back of the boats while the fresh sea air and dazzling sun leached the energy from us. Now the reward for our perseverance was near: Neptune was dozing, unaccustomed to the warmth of a still and sunny evening. We were going to slip cheekily through his fingers before he had time to awake and tighten his fists.

Pleasantly relaxed with fatigue we arrived at the point and

then suddenly conditions changed. The long gentle swell we had encountered in the lee of the point became a short steep sea with white-crested waves over-falling themselves into deep troughs. Immediately we were in trouble; the boats heaved up and down over the seas and the angle of rise and fall became too great. Both engines were swamped almost at the same time leaving the boats helpless hardly fifty yards from where the waves broke heavily on the rocky shore. In between lay the banks of kelp weed, showing brown in the troughs against the white and grey of the sea. At each successive wave more water spilled over the stern of the boat swamping the boxes of provisions.

"Get up on the boxes and paddle!" I shouted. While I struggled to bring the engine in board, Marie Christine crawled along the top of our cargo on her stomach and bravely tried to prevent us from drifting back into the weed which would surely choke the propeller if I managed to restart the motor. The same feverish activity was going on in the other boat. Richard swiftly changed sparking plugs and his motor roared back to life. I waved to them to motor away out of the rough water. They went. We were not so lucky. I changed the plug and at the first pull of the starting cord the engine coughed hopefully, just failing to start. Ten further attempts failed damply. About one wave in five was still flooding over the back and we were in danger of swamping to a point where the water levels inside and outside the boat would be equal. We wouldn't sink, but instead we would go to pieces – literally. The cargo of stores, fuel and equipment would float away in the general direction of the shore where it would quickly break up in the surf. As for us, ten minutes in the icy water would finish us . . . no doubt the other boat would come back for us but they might fare no better.

Marie Christine was paddling hard first to one side then the other and we were just about keeping our position. Sprawled on her stomach she was beginning to tire.

The water was now up to the yellow fibreglass seat on which I was sitting. I had to stop fiddling with the engine and get bailing with a saucepan, so I left the engine tilted on its bracket and let the spanner fall into the water inboard on the end of its string. So much stuff was jammed in the little space by my feet that I couldn't get the saucepan under the surface.

"To hell with these fish," I shouted and threw a stick of a dozen *robalos* over the side. Several minor cooking utensils followed them, until a dismayed cry from the paddler put a stop to further deck clearance. I discarded the saucepan in favour of a frying pan and soon had us reasonably free of water, then I turned my attention to the motor once more. The spanner string came up without the spanner and frantic groping under the remaining water swilling in the bilges yielded nothing more than a cold hand. Another fifty pulls on the starting cord achieved only wet noises from the engine and a squandering of the time we had left before Marie Christine became too exhausted to keep paddling.

"We'll have to call up the other boat and get a tow," shouted Marie Christine, now pale with fatigue.

"Okay, but let's just borrow their spanner first, towing us would probably swamp their engine again." I waved my arms, and Krister turned the other boat towards us from a calm spot a quarter of a mile away.

A few more pulls on the cord and then more bailing. Richard threw us the spanner on the first pass and Krister headed for the calm again. Another fifteen minutes of plug changing, drying with damp handkerchiefs, pulling on the starting cord, bailing and Marie Christine paddling all the while got us nowhere.

"I can't go on much longer – call for a tow," she called.

"Okay, let's turn round and both paddle to try and clear the point, it'll give them a better chance when they reach us." I grabbed the other paddle, and after waving it to attract the others I got stuck into the tricky business of running with the floating tide, while at the same time cutting across it to clear the weed banks and the point, in readiness for a tow.

It worked out all right and soon we were flailing away with the starting cord again in the sheltered calm of the lee-side of the point, under the curious gaze of a cruel-looking osprey which perched motionless on the bough of a tree not twenty yards away. Another half hour passed quickly and all we achieved was the immobilisation of both motors. I tried the dry plug from the other boat in our motor but it too became sodden to the point where it failed to spark even in the original engine. There was nothing left but to get paddling.

It was a disconsolate foursome which beached three hours later back at the spot where we had cooked the mussels so confidently at five o'clock that afternoon. It was almost dark, the tide was rising fast and what had been a gently shelving pebble beach fifty yards or more in depth, was now only a thin ribbon of gravel between the cold sea and the impenetrable forest. Marie Christine set to work in the half light with the faithful Optimus petrol cookers to prepare a quick hot meal of curry, while Richard, Krister and I put up the three tents at the very top of the beach, where we fondly hoped the tide wouldn't get us that night.

"Semolina's ruined, Johnny," Marie Christine's voice reached me as I was clearing a mound of rotting seaweed from under the big tree where I planned to site our tent.

"Oats have had it too," called Krister, who had been checking the contents of each dripping ration box after Richard and I stacked them in the undergrowth.

"It's just like the bloody rowing again," I muttered to myself, remembering the thirty-three per cent ration loss we had suffered on the North Atlantic after Hurricane Alma.

Supper was a pretty dismal affair in the dark, illuminated only by the white patches of ruined semolina and oats on the dark grey pebble beach. But we cheered up as the double portions of curry seeped into our stomachs, washed down with steaming cocoa.

"Could be worse, could be raining," the big Swede chuckled, again quoting the late Field-Marshal Slim.

"Probably will be in the morning," I replied, "then we'll be stuck here for ten days – it won't be like Isla Rucas here."

"Oh, don't be so gloomy, John, it'll be quite all right in the morning and we'll get up to Portaluppi," came Marie Christine's weary voice from the entrance to our tent.

We all packed up and went to bed filled with the dogged optimism borne of exhaustion, which argued that we had done enough and that the tide would not be allowed to come up into our tents.

In spite of the steep angle of the tents we all slept well. Too well. We didn't wake up until seven o'clock. A couple of vital hours of calm, wasted through idleness. We baked the four sparking plugs over the flames of the cookers while swallowing

hot porridge purposely burnt to disguise the salt water con-
tamination of the oats.

Richard was none too cheerful, having lost a part of his
awful Chilean tobacco supply in the bilges during the excitement of the previous night. He was now convinced that we must
avoid further progress up the sea reach of the Magellan Straits
at all costs. He argued that we should make for the far end of
the fiord Portaluppi and carry everything across the mountains
to the sheltered waters of Fiordo Northbrook; but Krister was
not convinced that we could get down through the forest on
the far side of the mountains.

In the space of a few mouthfuls of burnt porridge I agreed
to give the mountain portage a try. Perhaps it was my right
hand, sore from pulling the starting cord on damp plugs which
decided me.

By ten-thirty the boats were all loaded once more. It was
sunny and flat calm, really we might have been in Shangri-la
. . . blue skies, warm sun, green forest below snowy mountains:
just miles and miles of utter peace. Behind us we left twenty
cartons of oats and all five packs of semolina, also two of the
arctic sledging ration boxes as well as a five-gallon jerrycan.

We took care to load the boats so they were a little nose
heavy, to achieve the maximum clearance above the water for
the air intake of the carburettor on the back of each craft. For
half an hour I pulled and pulled at my engine while Marie
Christine paddled us round in circles and Richard and Krister
returned to the beach to wait. I began to fear permanent salt
damage in the engine, but at last after pulls without a plug,
pulls after drying the plug each time, and pulls with the plug
dipped in fuel, the motor finally stuttered into life and we were
away. Our start coincided with the first ripples of breeze on the
glassy surface of the sea. I cursed myself for wasting the hours
of early morning calm and looked fearfully at the horizon now
ringed with cloud. 'At least,' I thought, 'we have missed the
turbulence of a rising tide in the Race, it should be calm in the
slack water of the next hour or so.'

We rounded Punta Quidora once more and the wind began
to rise, gently at first, from the west. We slipped through the
Race while it was calm and headed across the mouth of an
unnamed fiord for Anderson Island. Soon we were a mile and a

half from the shore and our engines stuttered once or twice as spray hit the carburettors from the rising sea. Around us albatrosses wheeled, inquisitive at the pair of stubby grey boats coughing their way towards the island some three miles distant. Distinctive among the other seabirds, the albatross has long thin wings and a comparatively small body. In the distance the slight droop of the wing span, which is said occasionally to reach fourteen feet, makes the bird look rather like a self-propelled boomerang as it scribes figures of eight and tight S's above the waves. Down in these latitudes where the winds blow continuously between the southern tips of the continents and the antarctic ice, the albatrosses are most at home. At only 40° south latitude the distance round the world is about nineteen thousand miles. Riding a wind of twenty knots will carry a bird five hundred miles in a day. So it would not strain an albatross to circle the world in eighty days with much less effort than Jules Verne's hero. In 1887 an albatross was found on the beach at Freemantle, Australia, with a tin round its neck on which some French sailors had scratched a message, telling that they had been shipwrecked on the Crozet islands over 3,500 miles away. There is something haunting about the way they fly, symbolic of great lonely places where men lived hard and raw on salt beef and hardtack aboard creaking wooden ships.

Quite close to Anderson Island we passed a flock of Magellan penguins, black-and-white as they sat low on the water, diving only at the last minute to avoid the oncoming boats, and surfacing astern a moment later to stare in wonder at our ungainly grey shapes. We ran along in the lee of the island as the wind got up and up, until we had to make for a little bay to refuel. We passed through a barrier of yellow brown kelp, which grew from a great depth, and beached the boats on a steeply shelving pebble shore. Richard scrambled up on to the high ground through the dense wind-flattened bush which covered the low island, soon he came back to report that if we started immediately then we ought to make it to the shelter of the Arturo group of islands which guard the eastern entrance to Fiordo Portaluppi. I had been exploring the beach and I was intrigued to find numerous upturned empty barnacle shells above the ebbing tide wherein lived individual tiny shrimps in private artificial rockpools.

We pushed off again with full fuel tanks and we could see down thirty feet or so into the clear waters among the beds of mussels with their sinister enemies the starfish creeping among them. Once out of the bay Krister pointed to what looked like a small white-washed pillar at the edge of the kelp beds, a short distance up along the island shore. We kept close in by the weed to see if it might be some trace of man, for we were filled with a strange sort of longing to round a headland and find people with whom we might share the sense of wonder we felt at our surroundings. Soon we realised that it was no stone we were approaching, but a solitary bird standing amid the weed at the water's edge. Startlingly white, it showed some consternation as we drew near, but in spite of nervously pacing up and down it stood its ground until we could clearly discern the black bill and eyes, and the yellow legs of the rare kelp goose. Bob Risebrough, the friendly American marine biologist who had shown us around the ice-breaker research ship in Punta Arenas, had singled out the kelp goose as a species for which he felt special concern because he thought they were dying out. Standing there white on the contrasting brown of the shore, the poor thing seemed quite defenceless and easy prey for even a short-sighted predator.

As we cleared the end of the island we had to face the full force of a swiftly rising wind and sea. The albatrosses now seemed much more at home in this kind of weather as they glided effortlessly over the sea in search of their favourite food, the cuttle fish, and any other edible titbits near the surface.

Conditions became so bad that we only just made it to the Arturo group of islands. The sea was now streaked white with ribbons of spindrift but the careful loading of the boats paid dividends. Although nose-heavy and shipping a lot of water around the edges of the red spray sheets in the bows, the stern-up attitude stopped spray from flooding the carburettors and all that was needed was continuous bailing by the person not actually controlling the motor.

The Arturo group was similar to Anderson Island, low and covered only by a dense mat of windswept brush. The islands formed a sheltered lagoon about the headland of Punta Este, and once we got into this we were in a haven for the many kinds of bird that frequent the seashore. Not only do the islands offer shelter from the almost unceasing winds that sweep in from the Pacific, but they provide a breeding ground free from the foxes and rats which would plague them if they were to nest on the mainland shore. Our entry into the lagoon surprised a pair of steamer ducks who were making their way from one side to another with a convoy of eight chicks behind them. At our appearance the two adults set off in opposite directions making long white wakes of froth as their wildly flapping wings built up a speed of about twelve knots. We were sorry to see that the parents were not content with simply making a decoy to draw us the enemy after them, but that they continued their flight for a quarter-mile or more until they were out of sight at the far end of the lagoon. The poor little chicks, not much more than tiny balls of floating grey feathers, were left to scatter hither and thither in our path. Marie Christine was horrified at this and it took the stormy conditions outside the other end of the lagoon to drive away her concern for their safety.

At one o'clock in the afternoon we rounded Punta Este and headed up Fiordo Portaluppi, presenting our port side to the westerly gale. We kept edging out to windward, rolling danger-ously across the big flank sea, trying to make some sea room between ourselves and the surf crashing on to the rocks all along the western side of Punta Este.

"You call this my summer holiday? You must be joking," screamed Marie Christine against the wind.

After half a mile we opened the full length of Portaluppi and ran straight into a driving headwind. The sea became very confused – so did I – for I couldn't recall having ever en-countered a gale blowing from the north and the west at the same time. Blinding sheets of spray, driving over the bows, forced us to keep our heads down with the hoods of our trusty orange suits pulled right forward to form a kind of spray visor.

"No wonder nobody lives here," I shouted. "Why don't you stop bailing for a moment and save your energy?" I shouted at my wife.

"I must keep busy, I feel so frightened – it's just like an ostrich, if I keep doing this flat out I can't see what the sea looks like!" she shrieked back, her face streaming with spray and long strands of blonde hair.

We really needed good luck now, if the engines failed no

amount of paddling could save the boats from skittering across the raging seas and on to the rocks a couple of hundred yards downwind of us. I could sense that Krister, like me, felt a part of his bobbing little craft and as such shared my confidence that twist and leap though they might, they would not fail us. Richard and Marie Christine felt much less confidence in the future. After this Richard would need a great deal of persuasion to chance going farther up the unprotected coast if we failed to find a way over the mountains.

An hour and a half later we pulled into a sheltered bay at the mouth of a cascading stream on the southern side of Punta Araya. Richard and Krister had been driving forward through the gale wearing their snow-goggles, and now with these pushed up on their orange hoods they looked like a pair of Cresta-run bobsleigh racers as they nosed into the shallows with their compact grey and yellow craft with its dashing red spray cover. The beach was carpeted with even bigger mussels than those we had seen before, and as we waded ashore on to the beach they made an unpleasant crunching sound as they broke under our feet. Once on the gravel beach at the forest's edge we set about making a quick brew of tea in the blessed windbreak. Even the pink footsteps through the dense, black mussel-bed couldn't prevent our spirits from rising when the sun broke through racing clouds above. We had made it through the worst; now we could surely portage everything across the mountains to Fiordo Northbrook.

We didn't stay long because Richard had suffered badly when a wave splashed up the inside of his orange jacket while we were rounding Punta Este. The freezing water had run down inside his trousers and even though he hurriedly changed his trousers when we landed, our hot tea still failed to stop his shivering.

Creeping up the eastern shore of Portaluppi, I was impressed once more by the grandeur of our surroundings, the sun was more often out than in now and the afternoon promised to improve into a warm sunny evening. It was as if we were in the Rocky Mountains of British Columbia: patches of blue sky were mirrored in the waters of the fiord, as was the strong dark green of the forest, and towering above us were the stark white snows of Cerro Finger to our left and the dazzling ice-cap itself way ahead of us. Savage williwaws raced down from the mountain, driving black-and-white across the blue waters, every few minutes, but they lacked the steady high wind base to keep the fiord in turmoil. Although our heavily laden dinghies rocked before their onslaught they never looked like capsizing in the gusts, which soon passed and allowed the sea to drop calm again.

It was already well on in the day when we reached the islets guarding the mouth of the narrow branch fiord leading west from Portaluppi, and we were further delayed when our engines both fouled the kelp beds. We had to paddle through into the deeper water beyond, before restarting the motors for the mile's run to our Base Camp. The steep sides of the fiord were lined with dense forest, some of the Nothofagus trees surprisingly tall compared to those we had seen before. Above the tree-line white ribbons of water cascaded down from the snow through a belt of moss-covered rock before disappearing into the forest. The surface of the sheltered fiord was calm, disturbed here and there only by the occasional catspaw of wind tracing its erratic path across the mirror stillness.

Suddenly the calm was shattered close to our left. I looked for the other boat which had been following us to avoid the weed. It was already well on the way to the shore on our right. Krister had heard quite enough of killer whales to make him race for the shallows the moment any living creature appeared from the depths. I could see him laughing as he realised these were only dolphins six or eight feet long, and he headed back towards us. For the next five minutes we enjoyed a spectacular show as the ten friendly creatures weaved and jumped about us, passing within touching distance at tremendous speed. We were now only a few hundred yards from the end of the fiord, but our pleasure turned to alarm when the dolphins extended their play to something rather more serious.

"That one hit the bottom of the boat," Marie Christine looked just a little worried. The next one hit us hard, just to the right of centre, and our boat lurched up and sideways.

"I'm sure they're only playing," I shouted over the noise of the motor. But I wasn't too sure and I looked anxiously for the beach growing ever nearer: if they really decided that hitting the boat was fun they could have us over. In the other boat, hands were already tightening lifejacket strings. This glorious show continued full swing all about us right up to the edge of the beach where the water grew too shallow for the dolphins to follow.

Once we were out of their reach, they disappeared completely, quite suddenly there was no trace of their ever having been there at all. Somehow this served to heighten the loneliness of the place. It was as if we were in a valley belonging to a different geological age; now the dolphins were gone the present seemed to have gone with them. The water was still again, the day mellowing into a warm evening lent an atmosphere like the end of a long hot summer – if a dinosaur had come waddling down the stream we would have been shocked but not really surprised.

Once again we found ourselves hard pressed to find somewhere to put up the three tents. It had been a hard day and we were tired: I reckoned that the two-man tent for Marie Christine and I would fit on the beach. If I balanced the floorboards from the dinghies on rocks astride a small stream we could sleep on them with the tent over us and the stream beneath. Krister and Richard sited their tents end to end, on a narrow grassy spit of land projecting down into the mouth of the main stream which flowed down from the valley into the end of the fiord. Again we were gambling with the tide, again we were too tired to care. I lay on my back on the floorboards to test if they were properly balanced by the rocks, the blue sky was already clouding over from the north-west with fluffy white clouds like ice-floes jamming together to blot out the blue. My life seemed to be the blue – already half gone.

"Hey, look at this – you've got a puncture!" Krister was unloading the last of the stuff from the boats. Tight in the bows of our dinghy the big black cooking pot seemed to be stuck, the handle of fencing wire was sharp at either end where it was twisted through the handles of the pot. Flexing of the boat had caused one jagged end of the wire to pierce the side – it was a good thing we hadn't known while rounding Punta Este that we had a puncture. The wire was stuck a full half inch through the skin into the forward air chamber.

It says much for the Avon dinghies that the forward buoyancy compartment was still hard; even after removing the wire the escape of air was still almost imperceptible. We all felt even more confidence in the little craft which had carried us safely thus far in such a dangerous place.

I cursed myself for being so foolish as to put the pot in such a stupid place. The consequences of a collapse in the front half of the boat while we were rounding Punta Este didn't bear thinking about.

In the late evening, seating round the fire eating our supper of fried mussels, mince and potato, and hot cocoa, it was the first chance we had had to relax and chat. It had been a wonderful couple of days, full of excitement and progress. We had come forty miles, and taken over-all we had made the most of the unusually fine weather. Now we had some hard physical work ahead of us, but on the land at low altitude we would be less dependent on the weather than on the sea.

8

The Portaluppi Portage Catastrophe

"WHAT ABOUT THAT half bar of Kendal Mint Cake we saved yesterday?" I said to Marie Christine from the depths of my sleeping-bag, inside the orange world of our tent next morning.

"Okay, it's in my jacket," she replied, sitting up and making the slatted floorboards rock precariously over the steady rushing noise of the stream directly beneath us, which was now swollen by the heavy rain of the past eight hours.

"John! We're awash!"

"Where?" I jerked into a sitting position.

"Don't panic – you'll upset the floorboards."

Very carefully she raised one flap of the flysheet. The tide was rising. The forward right corner of our tent, by her feet, was under water. The lifejackets at the front were afloat. Outside the rain drummed on the flysheet and the wind howled down the valley.

"It won't come any higher," I said, adopting a sort of defensive Canute-like attitude. Acute discomfort symptoms jumped up and down my nervous system in anticipation of the worst.

We waited patiently, willing the water to retreat, at the same time gradually withdrawing our effects farther back into the higher top left-hand corner of the tent. Minutes ticked slowly away and at last the advance stopped; the freezing water halted by one of our marker sticks, a quarter of the way across the tent floor, and then ever so slowly it began to ebb.

Marie Christine waded away along the shore to see 'how the others have fared'. When she reached the mouth of the stream at what we had already christened 'Windy Gap', the place was transformed. What had been a gently meandering stream the night before was now a racing torrent. The two tents were perched pathetically in the estuary on what is best described in Spanish as a '*Chicitita Islota*'.

"How are you?" she called across the froth-streaked waters.

"See you at supper time," came Krister's reply, muffled but still cheerful. From Richard's tent there was no sound, doubtless he was busy trying to extract some little pleasure from his 'cigarettes', made up from a few carefully counted strands of cheapest Chilean tobacco rolled in the outside wrapping from a Kendal Mint Cake bar. He had to puff hard to get much pleasure from the finished product.

Before returning to our tent, Marie Christine decided to check that nothing else had been washed away from the corner of the beach we had decided to use as a kitchen.

"Both the geese have been stolen from up in the tree during the night," she said angrily, when she had crawled back into the tent. Not only had she spent hours plucking them on the journey round, but a special dinner was planned that night to celebrate our arrival at the Base Camp.

"We are not as alone as we think here," I said, imagining a puma watching our approach from its cave on the mountain-side during the previous afternoon. "Probably a fox," I added as an afterthought.

While we silently devoured the ritual breakfast of raw porridge oats, swilled down with milkless tea from our oily tin mug which had been used as a bailer on the boat, I tried to make a rough plan for the portage. Rain and wind whipped the fiord into a turmoil, the fine weather of the past two days seemed to have lasted a whole month. Our complete list of equipment, rations, boats, engines and fuel could be broken down into thirty by one man-loads. We had to carry a horizontal distance of three-quarters of a mile rising about eight hundred feet to a narrow freshwater lake running two miles east to west. Once there we would inflate the dinghies and motor to the north-western corner of the lake and then stockpile everything while the four of us made a preliminary reconnaissance of a two-and-a-half-mile route up a thousand feet over a saddle and down the other side to join a sheltered subsidiary fiord off the main Fiordo Northbrook. By this means we would never have to cope with the open Pacific coast where we had heard on a radio programme just before leaving the United Kingdom that the sound of the waves breaking on the cliffs could be heard fifteen miles inland. Richard and particularly Krister had recommended a reconnaissance of the whole route before we moved any loads up Stage 1 to the freshwater lake. The sound of those waves breaking left me in no doubt but that we would get over the mountains all right. The idea of the reconnaissance was dropped.

Krister interrupted my thoughts, and Marie Christine's reading of Akuaku, when he kindly offered to help me flatten a new site for our tent. Another night of tide watching was out, so we began the tricky operation of moving house in the drenching storm.

First we rolled our karrimats and some of our personal kit into a thin red polythene bag such as we use for rubbish at Ardmore. Then the inside of the tent was taken down and rolled in the groundsheet. After this the dinghy floorboards were carefully taken from their precarious situation over the stream. They were then laid level on the site Krister and I had prepared some three feet higher than his own site which had survived the previous night. Then the flysheet and poles were taken down and erected on the new site. When the inner tent was carefully put up inside the flysheet Marie Christine and I were so delighted that everything was still dry that we decided to celebrate by making a reconnaissance of the route up to the freshwater lake.

We crossed the stream by a narrow point, hopping from one submerged boulder to another and then we trod a path through thick bushes on to the hillside which was wonderfully clear of the forest for some reason. It was rather farther up to the saddle than we had calculated from the map since we crossed no contour line. I took this as a blessing in disguise because on the map there was only one contour line to cross on the two-and-a-half mile stretch from the far end of the freshwater lake over to Northbrook, and from this I reckoned that if we had had to rise so high to the freshwater lake, then the saddle between it and Northbrook would not be so very much higher.

The weather was appalling but as we were carrying nothing the going was easy enough across yellow grass, sodden brown moss and past several plants bearing flowers like reddish honeysuckle. When at length we reached the ridge and looked over the lake we half expected to find Conan Doyle's 'Forgotten World'. Perhaps ours were the first human eyes to see the lake – perhaps they weren't: anyway we could have been overlooking any one of the many freshwater lakes at Ardmore with Foinavon in the background during a winter gale. The heavy rollers breaking on the rock-bound shores made even launching our boats impossible, much less motoring up the middle. All along the north side of the lake, the steep sides of the mountain range we were to cross disappeared into the cloud. There was no sign of a saddle. Directly across the lake, above the tree-line, a steep glacier lay beneath a portion of mountain which had recently been subject to heavy avalanches.

"Have we really got to go up there, Johnny?" Marie Christine was trying to sound unworried – I could tell.

"Well, when the weather clears it won't look nearly as bad," I said reassuringly, "there's bound to be a saddle up there at the far end – the map says so."

It was cold up there, where the wind shrieked over the pass blowing the waterfalls back up in the air in clouds of spray. We had to lean right forward at an acute angle to the ground to get back on to the steep slope, down to our camp, now just a splash of orange among the drab greys and browns far below us.

The storm continued. We dried our tent with the petrol cooker, for there was petrol to spare now we were going to make the portage instead of the coastal trip in the boats. In fact we planned to leave five full cans of fuel behind.

Next day the weather was, if anything, even worse. Conditions on Golfo Xaultegua would be as bad as anything I had ever read about Cape Horn. Our three tents in 'windy gap' had taken quite a battering. Their poles were bending badly and the nine-inch valance of material which we had sewn round the bottom of the flysheets to carry rocks which would help pin the tents to the ground, were now tearing in places. All the same, both tents had escaped the tide and it looked as if they would be all right if they could keep upright until the storm abated.

At ten o'clock we held a conference in our tent. In spite of the rising wind we all agreed the best thing was to get on with the business in hand. That of carrying thirty loads up the mountainside to the freshwater lake, and there establishing a stockpile to make for an easy start to the boating phase just as soon as the weather permitted boatwork.

Outside in the weather, conditions took some believing. The first thing we had to do was to bring everything round from the beach at the end of the fiord, up to a point on the bank of the stream by the tents from which we could operate without hindrance by the tide. Although only a distance of approximately a hundred yards, this entailed wading through the flooded mouth of the stream. The winds, shrieking down the stream bed from the devil's cauldron above, were so severe that when a squall came the water over the large black mussel-bed in the mouth of the stream was sucked dry. Great sheets of foam would suddenly whirl into the air, and then, as the tornado moved on down the fiord, so the water would rush back to cover the mussel-beds in a sort of minor tidal wave.

Our first loads were a five-gallon metal jerrycan of petrol for Richard, Krister and myself, and the green plastic jerrycan of sugar for Marie Christine. I think we were all surprised how well she carried a load of forty to fifty pounds. We made our way in single file, up through the undergrowth and out on to the grass, moss and naked rock of the mountainside. Clad from head to toe in our orange waterproof suits, with hoods up and drawstrings tightened to minimise the sleet intake through the face opening, we didn't feel cold. Wellington boots, although slippery, did keep our feet warm and dry. We walked in places that, if given months of sunshine, might turn into beds of bluebells. At that time, however, they only seemed to entrap our sinking feet.

When we gained the 'devil's cauldron' itself, a mountain bowl at the head of the valley, the effect of the wind on the sleet was beautifully illustrated like a demonstration of a magnetic field at school. The visible sleet served as the iron filings, the darker background on the mountainside served as the paper, and the invisible wind performed the part of the magnet moving beneath the sheet of paper. The result was remarkable; different areas of sleet moved up, down and across, spinning clockwise and anti-clockwise. Uplifted spume from the waterfalls danced in tune.

Above everything else there was the noise. The wind and

the water: sometimes deafening, sometimes gentle. Sounds which could easily frighten four lonely people bowed low under their pathetic little burdens.

The moving pattern of sleet was not only beautiful to watch, but also it served as a useful guide map. We found places where we could get the benefit of the up-currents of wind in stream beds on the way up to the saddle. For the route down there was a more exposed place where the wind whirled along the side of the valley, building up pressure to burst down and out along the fiord.

On the saddle itself it was like the tundra. The winds of centuries had eroded everything, made everything lie flat and along the lines of its floor. Plants, grass, peat, even gravel banks conformed to the wind. We too either scurried like crabs before it or bowed low into it. Every time we crossed, one or other of us would fall.

Across the saddle lay the narrow lake, alternately a sheet of white mist and a sea of white rollers laced on a black background. Behind the lake, on the mountain, a great blue glacier overhung the jumbled snowfields of its own avalanches.

Unpacking the rucksacks on a roaring shore of flattened rocks we stood a moment with our backs to the wind.

"The saddle over to Northbrook must be round the corner at the far end somewhere," I said to Richard, who was also trying to solve the riddle of some route through the snow.

"Yes, it surely can't be anywhere that we can see now," he replied.

"Well, when the weather clears it won't look nearly as bad," I said hopefully.

The day wore on. Marie Christine battled bravely with two loads and minded the tents, while the rest of us made a total of five trips each. The wind was so strong that someone needed to be with the tents all the time now, constantly adjusting the rock walls which held the flysheet valances to the sodden ground. Lunch was biscuits, cheese and boiled mussels followed by a small piece of Kendal Mint Cake. Conditions up at the lake were now so grim that we doubted if it would be possible to camp there at all. In mid-afternoon, down at the fiord, one of Richard's tent poles broke under the strain. At six in the evening we agreed to call a halt, we had a quick dip in the melted snow of the stream, and this made the air seem suddenly warmer.

Everything we had, was by this time, either wringing wet or very damp. Over a delicious supper of hot mince and cocoa Marie Christine came through with a long-expected policy statement:

"I'm never again coming on one of these trips with you!"

The weather got worse in the evening, after dark. Our tent suffered a semi-collapse when the rock wall failed to hold. We repaired it. The candles became unreliable for reading, because the tent walls under the flysheet jumped in and out with a bellows action. Just before midnight I decided to take a last look outside before trying to sleep. Kneeling on my wellington boots I cautiously unzipped the flysheet a little: it flapped in my hand like the reins of a runaway horse. At first I could see nothing but grey, the roaring torrent alongside our tent seemed too close for comfort. Gradually I could just make out the shape of the other two tents twenty yards away on the grassy spit.

"Krister!!" I roared, and Marie Christine sat up like as if she had been stung.

"What is it?" she cried in alarm.

"They're going to be flooded – the tide is right at their fly-sheets now."

"Krister!!"

I was shouting myself hoarse. At last a sleepy voice replied as if it thought it was we who were in trouble.

"Tell Richard you're both going to be flooded," I shouted.

Minutes later Richard appeared. Soaking wet. Tent abandoned.

"My tent's a bit lower than Krister's – he's staying," Richard muttered and eased himself into our tent. Within seconds he was fast asleep, his head down at the entrance end of the tent.

Twenty minutes later Krister arrived for the night. "I stayed until I realised that every time I put my hand on the groundsheet it left a phosphorescent mark in the sea water."

It was a bad night. Marie Christine and I found ourselves lying in a puddle in the middle of our tent formed by the condensation running down on to the groundsheet from where Krister and Richard rubbed against the tent walls. Dawn came at five-thirty in the morning and our two guests went home;

the tide had ebbed, leaving their sewn-in groundsheets like miniature swimming pools. They dismantled the tents, no mean task in the gale, and then moved to a new site cut a little higher up than our tent. We mopped out our tent with my towel, and then curled up in our wet sleeping-bags to try and dry them out with our body heat. It was far from Granny's electric blankets back in Brighton.

In mid-morning Richard decided to move his tent again, right up on the mountainside. His second site had failed and his tent collapsed. On top of all his discomfort, he was going through a private hell of his own, because his supply of tobacco had finally run out. There were all the symptoms of cold turkey. Never again would I agree to someone choosing an expedition as an opportunity to give up smoking.

Marie Christine had been reading the biography of Gino Watkins and she became determined that whatever else befell us, we must not run out of food. When not working the diet must be mussels.

"We've got to get the right perspective," she declared. "Gino was always running out of food – we aren't going to end up on biscuits and boot polish like him."

In the afternoon things improved a bit, there was a hint of sun and the wind dropped a little. Richard returned and set up his tent by Krister. But as soon as we hung out some of our sodden clothing on the bushes it came on to sleet again. We decided to make more trips up to the lake, this provided an opportunity to dry some wet clothing by wearing it, although it wasn't very pleasant putting it all on, cold and wet. Richard was temporarily disabled by a splinter in his foot, suffered during the tent evacuation of the previous night, but we managed to lift both the Avon dinghies up to the lake which we found had risen eighteen inches, and Marie Christine made two trips with rations.

"It's not my day at all," poor Richard said, when we came down to find he had burned the curry supper.

There followed a night of heavy rain. Inside the tents battle continued; wet clothing versus human slow radiators. Marie Christine and I talked long into the night; if nothing else this kind of shared experience provides plenty of communication between man and wife. We had been married for the best part of a decade and together we had seen plenty of married couples sit at restaurant tables with scarcely a word passing between them during the course of a whole meal. What really is the point of going on such a trip? Lying there side by side in that wet gale-racked tent it seemed there were two main reasons. First it brings me back to reality, out from under the plastic dome of present-day life with all its pace and shallowness. Away, from the false sense of security offered by double-glazing, central heating, hot baths, regular meals and electric blankets, which can twist a man to believe in his own immortality. Out here the obviousness of mortality, quickly dispersed that sad fog of cynicism that clings so persistently to the affluent society, and in its place there blew a fresh breeze bearing before it all my blessings for my eyes to count. Secondly this temporary removal from the race of existence provides an opportunity to take stock of the position, to stand back and look at the way life is going, then plan any alterations that appear necessary.

Perhaps a good way to describe the experience gained from an expedition is to look at life like a map, with contour lines marking the ups and downs. Many people prefer to live on the plains, moving steadily with the minimum of disturbance. I prefer the mountains, life is so short and I want it to be full, not empty. There is so little time. An expedition provides a high concentration of contour lines in a short space of time, a whole life can be lived in just a few days. Perhaps you get to know yourself.

The following day it was far too windy for any movement on the lake, Richard's Rolex watch told us it was Sunday, 19th November, so we decided to spend the morning on 'make and mend' and see what the afternoon might bring. We did a pretty good job of drying out our tent with the little petrol cooker, and when Richard and Krister came in for a light lunch I was all set to make a speech designed to rally our efforts for the future.

The gist of my thinking was as follows:

The skylarking was over, we were now on an expedition. There were no army trucks to come and pick us up, neither was there any senior authority responsible if something went wrong. We had no communication with the outside world, if we fell sick or had an accident it might be three or four months before one of us on foot could bring help to our position by way of the sea.

We should look at the situation through the three principles we used at Ardmore –

1. Self-reliance. Each one of us had a duty to the expedition. What we had with us was all there was. There was no way of getting more. If a tent blew away, or a dinghy, it was gone for good. There must be no more cooking-pot handles puncturing dinghies as I had done. We must keep our own personal equipment in impeccable condition at all times.

2. Positive thinking. We were going to complete the expedition. We had learnt a good deal about ourselves and each other, now we should put the knowledge to good use. To succeed we should have to keep moving on the land and take the rare chances offered by the weather to move long distances on the sea. We each owed it to the expedition to think ahead and provide ideas. Discomfort exists only in the mind.

3. Leaving people and things better than you found them. Each individual had a duty to stop thinking about himself and to transfer the thought to trying to cheer up the others. There must be no question of isolating one of us from the others. It was not fair to increase the burden on the others by walking around looking like a long drink of water.

At five-twenty next morning we had a cup of tea and a couple of biscuits, then we got on with the job. By lunch time everything was up at the lake, our tents were pitched in a small dell and a nearby wood. The sun even came out, and we dried some kit and got the dinghies pumped up in readiness for an early move next day.

In the event it was noon next day before the wind dropped enough to allow us to launch the boats. We managed to get the motors going and we were more than sorry to find that half-way up the lake it turned into a river too rapid and shallow for the boats to pass through under power. At this point there was a brief family row during which my wife threatened to kill me, and I imagine I paled a little under my tan.

Eventually we reached the far end of the lake, stockpiled everything, deflated the dinghies, tied everything securely to the trees and had a cup of tea. The next phase looked far from easy.

Fishing for *robalos*

Richard explains his plan to navigate the Narrows to John

THE NARROWS

Dodging the icebergs afterwards

"I think we should all go over the top and see what it's like down to Northbrook," Krister said over his mug of tea.

"Leave everything here and just take tents and a couple of days' food," Richard chipped in.

"And the ice axes and a rope," added Marie Christine. "I don't like the look of it at all."

"Okay then, let's get on – it's two and a half miles and there's not much of the day left," I said, getting to my feet and looking for the ice axes while changing into my walking boots.

It took us a little more than an hour to reach the top, up through thick trees at first, and then out on to slippery moss-covered rock. Below us the lake was stained pale brown by the water from the end of the main Cerro Finger glacier. Not much moved up where we were, but we did see our first pair of flighted steamer duck winging low across the face of the lake. Away to the right, where the vivid green weed marked the delta of the glacier river, we fancied we could see a flamingo, but it was far below the snow cornice on which we stood. Marie Christine had a real crisis of confidence half-way up the steep snow-face, but all the same she made it up to the top by looking only at the snow itself, never down. She made a zigzag track upwards, turning exactly as we called the moves to her.

We reached the top at the lowest possible point on the ridge. Here a stream plunged through a narrow defile of rime-covered rock, down a hundred feet or so into a black pool which was covered by ice and snow at its downstream end. Above the defile the stream was running under the snow and we looked for a narrow point at which to cross.

Much careful probing with Richard's ice axe got us across without incident, and we then followed the course of the stream to a small lake marked on the map. Here we began to run into difficulties. It was cold and windy and starting to sleet again, visibility was poor and it looked a rotten place to have to spend the night. The map was wrong. We came to a point where a rushing stream ran down out of the cloud to the east; when it reached the lowest point of the saddle this stream divided, one branch flowing south into the defile, the other running north into the lake which was for the most part frozen over.

It was apparent therefore that the water from the lake must flow north-west and so down to Fiordo Northbrook. If the map could be wrong in this manner, could it not also be wrong over the question of altitude and contours? We all wondered gloomily what we might find when we left the three-quarter-mile plateau on top of the ridge and started the descent to Northbrook.

We set off again with sleet driving into our faces from the north-west. Marie Christine did well, keeping her head down and following the blue footprints in the snow made by Richard and me, but I noticed that when we stopped her legs were shaking a bit. Krister, quiet and dependable, was bringing up the rear. As soon as we began to descend Richard ran into a hard time as pathfinder; the snow covering was not reliable and the great clump of moss and brush beneath concealed some nasty pitfalls. After ten minutes he fell heavily, hurting his left leg and tearing his orange waterproof trousers.

It was a dreadfully lonely place and Marie Christine quickly nicknamed it the 'haunt'. A bitter cold wet wind, lowering grey cloud, rushing streams thundering eerily down into the misty forest below.

We kept on going for another hour, the primeval forest crowded us into a gorge, and the streams continued to make one unfordable torrent of roaring water. It was now seven o'clock, visibility was poor and we were all tired, wet through with sweat under our suits, and very hungry. We paused where yet another stream raced into the river from the west, the age-less trees were festooned with great beards of dripping grey green moss. It didn't look very hospitable.

"Well, I suppose we must sleep here," said I, sounding pretty half-hearted.

"If Krister and M.C. look for tent sites, you and I can go on down on a recce," replied Richard wriggling out of his pack.

The pair of us went down the gorge for a couple of hundred yards or so and then found we were forced to hop from one island to another as the river split into several arms on its head-long descent. To our left the mountain rose sheer wet rock into the cloud, it was overhanging in places and the ground was covered with the débris of recent rock-falls.

"Let's get past this," said Richard enthusiastically.

The going became more difficult and we had to make a

tricky traverse along a vertical rock-face some twenty yards long and thirty feet above the river.

After this I said, "Look, Richard, I could only just manage that without a pack – I don't think that the four of us could make a combined total of sixty passes across that face, half with kit, without an accident. What do you think?"

"Well, it would take a long time. There's no sign of the sea. It's getting harder as we go down. I don't think it's on with all that kit."

"Let's go back to the others and put up the tents," I said.

Richard went back across the traverse first, moving with the expert speed and balance born of countless hours of teaching this sort of thing at Ardmore. It looked easy. The roar of the river made communication impossible. He reached the end of the rock-face and walked on up into the mist just as I was starting. Quite suddenly I felt afraid and completely alone. If I slipped now . . . I'd go straight down into the river. My knees began to tremble. The rock seemed much more slippery now, the ledge much narrower for my toes below. If only Richard had waited for me.

Crossing that face seemed to take an age. When I was across I felt sick and cold. This was a dreadful place. What were we going to do now? Plodding back up the way we had come only a few minutes previously, the old familiar sense of hopelessness began to swill over me, the whole scheme was now looking impossible. Why on earth had I come in the first place, with so little knowledge of the area? Now here we were, completely cut off and unable to move forwards, backwards or even sideways. As to crossing the ice-cap, well, we could hardly stand the conditions where we were now, we certainly wouldn't last long in the snow with the kind of conditions that seemed to prevail in this dreadful place. 'Well, you've done it this time, it was bound to happen. Serve you right. It's all your fault – and you're responsible for the others too, you know.' The doubts were crowding in like a swarm of bees round a honeypot.

"There's space here for one single tent," a voice called and I looked up from the streaming ground to see Richard, arms outstretched, showing the site for a tent on a small low island in the river.

"What if the water rises during the night?" I shouted, full of self-pity.

"Well, it's just a possible place to bear in mind if they've found nothing farther up," he replied.

"Anyway, you left me behind down there – I thought I was going to end up like Harsh Bahuguma." We had both just read *Doctor on Everest* which gives a graphic account of the Indian climber's death on the mountain.

"Oh, I'm sorry, John – you got down it so easily, I never thought you'd have trouble getting back up. Look, don't you think we'd better get the tents up for the night, we're all tired and this is just when accidents do happen."

He was quite right. This was the kind of situation when people have a row for having a row's sake. A good hot meal and a night's sleep would produce better conditions for deciding what we should do next.

When we rejoined Krister and Marie Christine, they were still scratching about in the rain looking for sites. The ground was one great tracery of streams weaving about low islands on their way down to the gorge below. Swirling mist cut visibility to little more than a hundred yards, and the moss-hung trees presented such an air of desolation that we felt no living creature had ever been here.

"It looks impossible for load-carrying any farther. We'll just get the tents up, have a meal and get our heads down – it'll all be better in the morning. You were right, Krister, and I was wrong, we should have come and looked at it first, before carrying all that gear up to the lake."

With my small speech over we all fell to, and in no time we were tucked up warm in our sleeping-bags. We had got pretty good at putting our tents up quickly, and the rapid preparation of hot meals. Our small world revolved about these two simple tasks. If we failed in either the level of discomfort rose so rapidly that it goaded us into expertise.

Conditions were precisely the same when I called Richard and Krister at seven next morning. Crawling into the cold wet clothing hardly cheered the thought of having to retrace our steps all the way back to the fiord. Nobody said much. The rain meant we had the breakfast of tea and hot porridge in our own tents.

There was one advantage when we started: the wind was at our backs. By pushing steadily forward we managed to reach the stockpile by the lake before noon. Launching the dinghies was made easier by the lake having risen a further foot during the night, and after half a pack of cheese each and a brew of tea we loaded up and pushed off back the way we had come. Each of us was thinking of the load we had to carry and trying to come up with some better route, where we might avoid having to climb up to the pass before descending to the fiord.

When we arrived at the rapids, the extra foot of water helped us to float right on down the middle, steering with our paddles. Both motors were cut and stowed upon their brackets, to avoid any chance of the propellers getting damaged on the rocks as we shot through.

Once in the bottom half of the lake, Richard signalled that we should take a look at where the river ran out at the north-eastern end on its way down to another fiord, to the north of the one which had been our previous base. Any new route seemed less depressing than the old one, and we could always motor back up the original fiord later to collect the five cans of fuel and oil we had left there. The main thing was to complete the task quickly and safely.

The river left the lake by way of a mighty waterfall, and as we edged into the shore we had to be careful not to shut off the engines too soon for fear of getting caught in the powerful flow at the edge of the waterfall. I was especially careful about this because I had been the leader of an Army canoeing party going down the Thames one dark winter night ten years before. On that occasion I had led the single file of five canoes into the bank by the weir at Cookham, the second, third and fourth canoes dove-tailed in behind each other. The fifth pair failed to get in and overshot the landing place. Too late they saw the iron girders looming up in the dark. We shouted a warning but it was drowned by the booming waters of the weir. They back-paddled frantically and it seemed, as they turned broadside to the current, that they might claw themselves clear. Then the suck at the edge of the weir caught them in its grip – suddenly they were gone. The white fibre glass canoe shattered on the lattice work of platform and posts and both men disappeared into the maelstrom below.

We had been lucky on that occasion, with the help of a hospital both men survived. I wanted no repetition here, there would be no second chance for anyone going over this waterfall.

Krister helped Marie Christine secure the boat and get a brew going while Richard and I set off to see whether or not we could be quicker following the course of the river to the sea. We walked a couple of hundred yards and sat on a boulder to discuss the matter. The sun was trying its best to shine through rising white clouds and we were sheltered from the main force of the wind by the huge boulders scattered on the mountainside. The first thing was that there was no climb up on this route, the way fell straight down along the river from the edge of the lake. It had the advantage of novelty but it did seem a bit longer and the lower part was mainly flat through scrub. The way we felt, we could have sat there all day discussing the pros and cons and generally doing nothing at all. The happy situation came to an end when we saw the big athletic shape of Krister leaping from boulder to boulder on his way down to us. We got wearily to our feet.

"What do you reckon, Kris?" asked Richard.

"Oh well, it's obvious, isn't it? The other way is best."

"Oh no," Richard and I groaned aloud.

"I suppose you're right, we'd better get on with it," I said, and we slowly followed the skipping Swede back to where my wife prepared a brew of hot coffee in the shelter of three rucksacks laid on their sides. Four equally small portions of cheese and biscuits were soon eaten and we loaded the boats again to make for the other side of the lake, and our old route back to the fiord. A great sense of weariness overwhelmed everything.

"Race you down the rapids," grinned Krister as he pushed off from the bank.

"Okay, I'll give you a start!" I joked half-heartedly, and we set off for an afternoon's heavy work undoing all the labours of the past eight days, which seemed to stretch back into a lifetime.

Nobody said much as we went up and down with the heavy loads in deteriorating weather, and by six o'clock we had all had enough for the day. We put the tents up in the old sodden places, rebuilt the rock walls on the valances, crawled inside and got on with the cooking as the weather grew worse and worse.

After supper Marie Christine and I each had a good wash, using one of the small saucepans. Water was no problem, but petrol was, now we were faced with having to motor up round the Pacific coast if we hoped to reach the foot of the seven-mile-long glacier. We couldn't afford to use the cooker to dry out the tent and it had got pretty well wet through during the carriage to and from the 'haunt'. Now the flysheet was sticking to the inner tent in places and thin veins of water trickled down the sides to form pools on the floor of the sewn-in groundsheet. We used our towels to dam the worst and snuggled into our damp sleeping-bags, hoping to dry our wet underclothes with body heat during the course of the night.

It was at four-thirty in the morning when it happened. Dark and raining heavily outside. The roar of the stream vying with the noise of the wind for ascendancy. We had slept well enough from exhaustion. Quite suddenly I was awake, something was wrong, for a moment or two my eyes gazed blankly into the black above, trying to work out what it was that had woken me.

"Bloody hell!" I shouted through clenched teeth, coming violently to a sitting position.

"What is it now?" came Marie Christine's sleepy voice in the dark.

"I'm lying in a puddle – that's what! The bloody tent must be leaking everywhere, draining down the sides and forming a puddle under me. *I'm sick of it!*"

Marie Christine sat up too. Her groping fingers splashed in a puddle at her side. Carefully she leaned forward and unzipped the flysheet to reveal the appalling truth.

"It's the tide," she said calmly. "We are sitting in the sea."

There was nothing for it but to get on and do something. Paddling on hands and knees out through the mouth of the tent, I had this vague hope that someone might intercede and let us off. Meanwhile the tide just kept on rising.

We bundled everything we could into the waterproof stuff bags and stacked them under the bushes out of reach of the tide. There was no point in waking the others until it was finally light. We were shivering with cold so we set about doing anything which would keep us warm, like removing the rock wall from the valance and looking for a new site for the tent.

Shortly after five it was light enough to walk about freely so we decided to make a trip up to the lake for a load before breakfast. The wind and rain were driving fiercely from the north-west and each gust threatened to batter us to our knees; on an empty stomach the manoeuvre was quite memorable. When we got to the camp again we felt weak and decided to look for a fresh site for our tent, erect it and get inside for some breakfast. We agreed to use some of the valuable petrol in the cooker to dry out the sopping wet tent and it was while we were doing this that a propeller-driven plane flew north over us at a fairly low speed.

"I wonder if Rebecca is all right," said Marie Christine, thinking of our small daughter and assuming that the plane was searching for us. It was, after all, the first plane we had seen for six weeks.

"More likely there's been a revolution and it's civil war," I said, trying to reassure her and thinking of the angry people we had seen queueing for loo paper in Punta Arenas.

We got on with the business of drying out and I thought how the Optimus cooker was a real life-giver, where would we be without it? The driftwood was soaking wet most of the time, and once above the snowline there was no wood at all.

At eleven-twenty-five the plane returned, flying south this time, low and slow. We all stood by the tents and waved, but got no response. If they were looking we felt sure they would see the bright orange tent cloth, but we didn't want to light a fire lest they weren't looking for us at all. It would be silly to mount a huge rescue operation just for us, when there was nothing wrong anyway.

In the afternoon we set off once again to try and get everything down from the lake by nightfall. While we were doing this, the plane flew over again, back south to north. In our enthusiasm to get the job done we carried heavier and heavier loads, like two five-gallon metal jerrycans of petrol together with five small one-litre cans of oil for the two-stroke mixture. Finally, at five-thirty that afternoon the job was done – we were back at square one. The four-party tent conference finally, and not without some discussion, decided that the only route now open to us was on up the Pacific coast, through Canal Cripples into Fiordo Northbrook. From there by way of a long narrow channel we could gain Bahia Beaufort, Glacier Sound and so on to the entrance of Lago Munoz Gamero where the main northern glacier spilled its icebergs into the sea. Marie Christine echoed all our thoughts when she said, "Surely after all this bad weather we're due a couple of days fine – that's all we need if we start early."

At six next morning we awoke to find heavy rain and a gale from the north-west as usual; all right for plodding up to the lake but no good for boat work on the open sea. By ten o'clock there was a touch of watery sun and the wind was dropping. Another brief conference and we agreed to move down to Punta Alfredo, the western side of the mouth of Portaluppi in the afternoon; in readiness for a quick dash up the coast when the weather gave us a chance. We packed up in the rain as usual.

9

Sea Reach of the Magellan

IT WAS RAINING steadily as we set off from our camp at two
o'clock in the afternoon. We hoped to cover seven or eight miles
down Portaluppi and over towards the sea reach of the Magellan
Straits. Our motor started easily enough but Richard had a lot
of trouble with his, the one which had suffered a broken union
in the water-cooling pipe, in the early part of the expedition.

"It won't be much good if we have to do the Pacific coast
with one boat towing the other," said Marie Christine looking
worried at the lifeless dinghy astern of us.

Luckily for us Richard managed to get it going, using a trick
he had learned from a Bermudan boy who had come on one of
our courses at Ardmore. This involved dipping the spark plug
in the petrol tank, replacing the plug in its correct position, and
then using the petrol on the plug to aid the spark produced by
hand starting. We grinned at each other, making faces to show
the relief we all felt at having both engines going again, just as
we approached what looked as if it might be the most dangerous
waterborne phase of the expedition.

"Look!" Marie Christine pulled excitedly at my right arm.
"Over there in the trees – a huge pile of mussel shells. It must be
Indians."

I glanced across in the direction she was pointing. We were
at the narrow mouth of the fiord about a mile and a half from
where we had just been camping. The channel into Portaluppi
was choked with beds of kelp and it needed all my attention to
keep the engine running. I wasn't keen to stop, but sure enough
just inside the tall trees on the edge of the fiord, there glittered a
pile of shells, maybe five feet high. Just behind I could make out
the shape of a crude dwelling-place.

"We're going in," I said, cutting the engine and waving to
the other boat, which had been tailing us through the channel

to avoid the weed. They cut their engine and suddenly everything was silent.

Page 41, South America Pilot, Vol. II: The Alacalufes do not merit the same confidence; they are refractory to the least civilisation, aggressive and treacherous. The larger number to appear, the more they should be feared; as a general rule, they will not attack a group of three or four persons; all danger vanishes if one carries a firearm or anything which appears as such.

Marie Christine had read this to me only a couple of nights before and I had laughed. Now I was feeling very sorry that the ·22 rifle was buried under all our kit in an effort to keep it free from the seawater.

"Now I know how Captain Cook felt, when he landed on Fiji." My whispered voice echoed like a shout in the silence. The others stopped paddling for a moment to look at me. We were alone and defenceless, spears and arrows from the protection of the forest would find an easy target.

"Kris and I'll go first," said Richard as we closed the shore. "You wait here – just in case."

I found myself winding the starting end back on the engine – just in case – as they got out of their boat and disappeared into the trees.

For a minute or two nothing happened. Marie Christine was looking at me with her serious expression.

"It's okay," came Krister's voice from somewhere in the forest. "It's deserted."

We paddled to the shore, hitched the painter to a bush and scrambled through the trees.

"They must have been very small Indians," said Krister, standing by the entrance to a skeleton of a hut, the roof of which came only to his chest. He is six foot three inches and we thought of Alexandro and Fresia back on Isla Unicornio, they could have got in and out of the shelter easily enough.

"It looks as if they haven't been here for some years," said Richard, as he examined the crude construction of a few poles and a shallow sloping roof.

"I bet this place is mentioned in your survival talks next

year," I laughed; Richard's survival camp in the Ardmore wood is always popular with the city fellows from the plate glass and steel shelters in London.

Lying all around were little reminders of a home long since abandoned. Hanging from one of the main supporting poles was a battered and bottomless tin coffee pot with a rusty wire handle. The atmosphere was dank and ghostly, the big trees enshrouded by dripping moss reminded us again of our night over at the 'haunt'. In a small cave in the grey cliff, only twenty feet from one side of the derelict shelter, we found the open fireplace where they probably smoked all those mussels the wife would have dived for in the freezing water. We had seen the long strings of these large smoked mussels for sale in the run-down shops of Punta Arenas. Also we had choked down a most unsavoury soup of the things to relieve the monotony of rotten mutton back at Estancia Skyring.

There was no sign of any activity other than the mussel gathering. It must have taken a long time to amass such a huge pile of shells, all of which were of the very largest size and which needed careful selection in the first place. The shelter seemed a fairly permanent place, and it certainly looked as if the Indians had lived entirely on the mussels they had gathered. It may have been that they had only come to the place on a seasonal basis, and perhaps brought sacks of provisions with them to last the duration of their stay. All the same there was no evidence of any alternative food supply.

We were not sorry to leave the dismal place, and head on down to Portaluppi; running at speed before a freshening wind. It was exhilarating to be on our way again after the gloom of the past two weeks; at least we were driving forward once more.

No matter how rough the passage might be we were ready to give it a good go. Things went well at first and we made good speed with the water getting rougher by the minute. We knew that once we reached the mouth of Portaluppi we could turn right and run along the shore in the lee of the Cerro Finger massif. The problem was the strengthening north-west wind which was going to meet head on with the incoming Pacific tide when it began to flow in after low water. The first refuelling operation was completed without a hitch under the shelter of the western shore, but the second time it would not be nearly as easy. There would be no shelter in the mouth of Portaluppi, only reefs and kelp beds. We gambled on just getting round the corner under the lee of Punta Alfredo before our tanks ran dry. Towards the mouth we began to experience heavy overfalls as the tide turned and began to run into the wind. Our engine stuttered a few times as spray was sucked into the air intake on the carburettor, but we were loaded well forward this time and the extra few inches of freeboard gained for the motor at the stern saw us through.

The other boat didn't fare so well and at the critical moment their engine swamped. Try as they might, neither Richard nor Krister could restart the motor: there was nothing for it but to try and tow them clear of the tide-race. We were now in a serious position, with the following wind much stronger than we could ever operate in if we had been driving into it. As with a sailing boat, the ease and speed with which we handled running before the wind was deceptive. The moment we tried to go against the wind to circle the other boat we were in grave danger of being swamped ourselves.

Something had to be done rapidly. If we delayed for just a few minutes longer the wind would sweep us clear out into the gulf. Then there was no hope of our fighting back against it on our own in the rough seas, much less chance of towing the other boat. Paddling in these conditions would be about as useful as trying to paddle the *Queen Mary*.

The only chance was to make an immediate tow across the wind, hoping to find a way through the seaweed-covered reefs to the shelter of Punta Alfredo, a quarter of a mile away, before we ran out of fuel.

Marie Christine caught the painter from Krister at the first pass we made by the other boat. She quickly took a couple of turns round the rubber rowlock on her side and held the end of the painter in her hand in case of emergency. Then she got down to the usual business of bailing which kept her mind busy and her eye on the floorboards while she waited for what might happen next.

I had to keep the engine at less than half throttle to avoid swamping the air intake. Krister and Richard helped speed our progress by paddling with an oar each. Gradually we crabbed our way towards the shelter. All the time the wind was pushing us farther out towards the open sea, where every wave seemed to have a breaking crest. I could see the spray leaping for the sky where the booming rollers broke out on the islands of Groupo Arturo farther out. No one said anything, we all sat and prayed we would get across Portaluppi before we were too far out to benefit from the shelter of Punta Alfredo. Once or twice I opened the throttle a bit, but it seemed to make little difference and the extra splash soon had the engine stuttering and everyone waving at me to lower the throttle again. Agonisingly slowly we bounced along, seeming to go more up and down than across. I bitterly regretted the short visit we had made to the ruined Indian shelter; those few minutes might have made it so much easier, before the tide started to flow in there would have been little or no turbulence. I started to work out a plan of survival if we were blown out to sea: fresh water would be our main shortage but we could trap it in groundsheets. Keeping warm and dry would be the main problems . . .

At last the water started to get calmer, we seemed to have made it all right. Smiles of relief were flashing between the boats when suddenly our motor stuttered and stopped. The grins were quickly replaced by looks of grim dismay.

"I reckon it's fuel not water in the air intake," I shouted. "Keep paddling hard while I refuel."

The other two fairly dug into the water with their paddles and Marie Christine crawled up along the cargo on her stomach to repeat her efforts of the previous tidal race. I set about filling the fuel tank as quickly as possible, hoping on hope that my diagnosis was correct and that the engine was not after all drowned. Certainly the tank looked dry but there is always a bit of fuel swilling about the bottom of the tank when there is some motion to the boat. It was a messy job even with the big filler, because the boat slopped up and down on each wave and I had to be careful not to drown the engine even though it was not running.

"Hooray!" I could hear the cheer from Marie Christine above the noise of the engine, as it started at first pull on the cord.

I towed the others into a really sheltered place right under the headland, and while they worked away at their motor we saw a big brown seal with a blunt nose playing about in the weeds.

After a while Richard managed to get his motor going again, and we crept along the shore looking for a place to camp for the night.

It was nearly five o'clock when we approached Punta Janequeo, once round that point we would come into the full weight of the Pacific swell backed by the strong north-west wind. Out to our left we could see the waves breaking heavily on the western end of Grupo Soto. I could feel the tension building up again among us as we began to experience the first lift and fall of the swell hundreds of feet from the crest of one low wall of water to the top of the next. Quite soon I had seen enough, the guide to conditions was the western tip of Grupo Soto, at the moment it was impossible for us to go any farther. We should look for a place to camp from where we could see the western end of the island, when it stopped breaking there it would be time to make our dash up along the eleven miles of bare coast to the protection of Canal Cripples. This was the big one for rubber dinghies; the one we had come half-way round the world to have a go at. Three hundred days at sea off the north-west coast of Scotland made me sure that if I hit the weather right, then we could do it. The same experience had taught me only too clearly, to realise that if the weather fooled me on the lonely coastline ahead, where the cliffs plunged steep into the ocean from the snow-capped mountains above, then nothing would save us.

We found a little pebble beach where a rumbling torrent flowed into the sea. There was a thirty-foot waterfall at the head of a deep pool twenty-five yards in from the shore and it was not easy for us to unload the boats, while Richard plunged off into the undergrowth to find some flattish place where we might pitch the tents for the night. He had an awful job and returned, with his waterproof trousers badly torn, to announce that there was a place for the big tent but there would be digging for the two small ones. Two hours later we were in our tents cooking up the mince for supper. In the interval the stream had risen a couple of feet and Marie Christine had fallen in it during the arduous business of carrying up the equipment from the shore. Now at last the wind and rain were beginning to relent. A glimmer of sunlight from the west made a great rain-bow span over the mountains and sea to the east; Krister kept shouting the wonder of it all from the top of a small hill near by, and I tried to make my mince last as long as possible.

By the light of a candle I studied our salt-stained Admiralty Pilot, trying to read more about Paso Del Mar (Sea Reach) into the terse sentences than really existed.

'But on opening Paso Del Mar (Sea Reach), a heavy swell will be felt coming from the Pacific. This swell prevails to a certain extent even on the calmest days.'

The following described the grim coastline ahead of us to Canal Cripples:

Peninsula Munoz Gamero [the mainland] consists of a succession of high and jagged peaks, with deep ravines and precipitous cliffs; the highest summit, capped with perpetual snow, rises to an elevation of 5,200 feet about twenty-one miles north-north-east of Punta Havannah [Habanah], near the head of Seno [Fiordo] Northbrook. Bahia Clift [Escarpo], five miles north-north-west of Punta Havannah [Habanah] is backed by mountains more than 3,000 feet high, covered with glaciers and snow. Bahia Thomas and Bahia Corkscrew [Caracol] are entered one mile and two miles, respectively north-west of Bahia Clift [Escarpo]. These three small inlets are too deep and narrow to be used as anchorage.

Isla Richardson lies from eight to nine and three quarter miles north-west of Punta Havannah [Habanah] and is separated from Peninsula Munoz Gamero [the mainland] by Canal Cripples.

It didn't really look a suitable cruise for ten-foot rubber dinghies up to Canal Cripples with my wife. If and when we got there, we should find:

Canal Cripples has a least width of one and a quarter cables; it is clear of dangers, and deep in the fairway. At its south-western end, there are several patches of kelp on either side of the fairway; these are all easily distinguished and can be avoided by keeping in mid-channel. Punta Cummins, on the northern side of the north-western entrance, is steep-to. The channel is useful to a low-powered vessel [at 3 h.p. that certainly described us], which cannot contend against

luppi – diurnal variation
of the tides

to the Straits of Magellan

Towards 1189

Marie Christine and Krist
putting the tent up in a bli

the wind and sea so often found in Paso Del Mar [Sea Reach].

Isla Richardson is mostly low, but has two hills; the southern hill 325 feet high appears conical from the eastward; the northern hill is 375 feet high, with a square summit. The island is covered with moss, with low tangled trees on its sheltered sides. Islets and rocky shoals extend up to the one mile south-eastward, southward and south-westward from Isla Richardson; but the shoals are all marked by kelp.

The depths in Canal Cripples are too great for convenient anchorage; but in 1883, H.M.S. *Sylvia* rode out a heavy gale, having a steady wind, when anchored in a depth of thirty-five fathoms, with the northern hill of Isla Richardson bearing 268°. The kelp patches south-eastward of Isla Richardson are the principal dangers to be avoided. [These were the ones we were to go through.]

Sitting there in our tent among the tangled undergrowth, I realised that the Pilot information alone was all I had to go on. The wind had died away and I wished I could see through the dark to the western tip of Grupo Soto and so discover if the swell had stopped breaking on the cruel cliffs between us and Canal Cripples.

Marie Christine seemed keen to push on, although obviously worried by the danger of the dash up the exposed coast. I could tell she thought I would be able to get us there. This increased my responsibility.

Krister was the most suited to the situation. Still young enough at twenty-three to assume the devil-may-care attitude which is the staunch ally of unattached young men, he also felt at home on the water. Before leaving London several of his friends had bet him that he had no chance at all in a rubber dinghy in the 'dreaded Magellanes' – now he felt a part of his little craft and he was keen to prove he could do it to his friends at home. In fact he had been disappointed when Richard's plan for the Portaluppi portage had won acceptance over the sea reach trip up to Canal Cripples some two weeks previously. Yes, Krister was looking forward to the stark challenge of the dash up the coast in the face of the worst sea conditions in the world.

Richard was the most worried among us. He was feeling the pressure of the isolation very hard. A shy reserved man with studied good manners, he found it increasingly hard to relieve the pressures mounting inside him with the sort of banter with which Krister, Marie Christine and I kept open the channels of communication with each other. The isolation is something to which I have become accustomed during my various projects, it is something which should not be taken too lightly and it cannot be imagined at home. Perhaps this is the main reason why it is so difficult to choose the members of an expedition; back in Britain, in the easy company of his fellows, a man may seem one thing but after a period of isolation he may seem quite another. The closest similar pressure I have found is that of responsibility, hidden but ever present. As well as the feeling of isolation Richard also felt ill-at-ease on the sea, he had suffered increasingly severe sickness on his last three days at sea on the yacht at Ardmore. This fuelled the fires of his anxiety which was based on a book he had read about how the Smeetons had had their large yacht rolled stern over bow on two occasions in these waters. Nothing could convince him that the captain of the *Hero* back in Punta Arenas could be wrong about the thirty-foot swells rolling interminably round the world and crashing on the cliffs. In spite of the aggravation of being without cigarettes on top of his other worries, Richard was always the first to take the lead on land and he worked tirelessly to find good camp sites and good routes wherever we went.

The other three of us sympathised strongly with Richard's troubles, we each knew and liked him well and we tried consciously to stop him splintering away from us in an attempt to keep his problems to himself as was his nature. We felt sure that the best cure was open communication with us, and we were determined to try to cheer him up. While I read the grim warnings in the Pilot, I knew that poor Richard would be finding sleep hard to win as he worried about the perils of the coming day in his lonely tent.

I read on:

> Mariners are warned that during heavy snowstorms, which are very prevalent in the western part of Estrecho de Magallanes, the visibility of the lights is frequently much reduced

owing to the glasses of the lanterns becoming coated with ice . . .

The heavy williwaws which so frequently descend the mountains, cause vessels to sheer about a great deal . . .

A good rule, and one largely used by regular trading vessels is never to pass Cabo Pilar except in daylight . . .

The approach to Estrecho de Magallanes from the Pacific ocean requires the greatest attention. Misty and stormy weather, which is very frequently found in this region, a continuously high-running sea, and the current which runs chiefly southward and towards the land, render navigation extremely difficult and call for the greatest attention . . .

I fell asleep with plenty on my mind.

At five-thirty a.m. I was out of the tent to get a look at the sea conditions at the western tip of Grupo Soto. It was ten days since we entered Portaluppi and our luck turned for the worse – now at last our fortunes would change. Wasn't this what life is all about? Hanging on through the bad times and jumping on to the inevitable upswing? Now the sea was glassy calm in the channel between us on the mainland of Peninsula Munoz Gamero and Grupo Soto. Out there in the Paso del Mar, the sea reach of the Magellan Straits, the surface of the sea was gently riffled by a gentle southerly breeze, which was an air-stream completely unknown to the four of us who were now nearly punch-drunk with the bludgeoning force of the north-westerly gales. At the tip of Grupo Soto, the ocean heaved gently, rising and falling as if asleep. I tiptoed round the tents and roused the others as if fearful the giant out there might awake and decide to squash us like so many ants on the huge cliffs at the edge of his domain.

We had a good breakfast and packed up to move in record time. By the time we actually got on the water the sky was dark and sinister. The rain which had started as a mist an hour previously was now falling with a persisting drumming rhythm on the surface of the water which was still flat calm.

"The heavier it rains, the less chance there is of wind," I muttered to no one in particular. "It's now or never."

Our motor started like a dream, but the other one was very difficult, as in my impatience to get on I decided to tow the other boat. From the look on poor Richard's face I could tell he felt he was being towed like a bull to the slaughter. But every minute counted now. The longer we delayed – the sooner old Neptune would awake and start blasting the cliffs again.

We moved slowly again, imperceptibly closing on the point of no return – Punta Janequeo. The sea was oily calm and we lifted and fell like feathers on a mighty long but low swell. Above us, the uniform grey of the cloud wove wreaths of mist about the cliff tops standing grim and silent to our right. Here and there we glimpsed patches of white glacier and snowfield farther inland, whenever there was a break in the cloud. There was an air of grim expectancy, as if everything was waiting silently for the next scene to unfold. The mounting tension was reflected in ourselves. No one dared talk for fear of saying something that could never be unsaid.

We rounded Punta Janequeo and looked clear down along the outside of Grupo Soto for the first time. The southerly breeze gained a little strength and the curtains of rain slanted a fraction from the vertical. There was no going back now.

"Why the hell can't they . . ." I started to say to Marie Christine, just as the other engine gave a prolonged cough and settled down to a steady note. We all raised our arms as if we had won the cup final at Wembley. I throttled back to let the other boat come up alongside. Marie Christine threw the painter to Krister who was grinning hugely and even Richard managed a smile of temporary relief.

On we went with fingers crossed. We passed close by a group of fifteen albatrosses sitting on the water, temporarily grounded by the calm. They looked at us in an odd 'you must be crazy' sort of way but didn't do much more than paddle out of our way as we approached. A few hundred yards to our left, a clumsy great skua all chocolate brown with bars of white on his heavy wings, was desperately harassing a group of delicate fork-tailed tern. It was like any grey spring day below the cliffs of Handa at home, except I wasn't in the yacht but more like in the life raft!

The rain held on and the mist with it, sometimes crowding in so close that we lost sight of the land and I had to grope in my pockets for my compass. When the mist cleared a bit we could see that the clouds above were still moving down from the north-west. The gentle breeze on the sea held good from the south, it only needed to keep blowing for three hours and we would be round Punta Cummings and heading up Fiordo Northbrook. Around us the natural world went about the routines of another day; it was as if we were in some kind of giant zoo. The grey-green water lapped gently at the foot of the still grey cliffs; the tropical green of the spring trees in tiny bays contrasted freshly with the ominous rock and the eternal white of the snow behind. Once or twice we could make out the familiar white blobs on the shore which we now recognised as the rare kelp geese. A group of about a dozen Magellan penguins let us come quite close before bobbing below the surface to streak away in their favourite element.

We passed Bahia Escarpo and the weather began to clear a little more. Although the cruel white peak of Cerro Finger was beginning to drop astern, and Grupo Soto had now nearly disappeared, we found the low mass of our objective, Isla Richardson, was growing nearer only with agonising slowness. The main clouds above were clearly still being moved by a north-westerly airstream, our time was running out and we were far from home yet.

Each hour we stopped the boats together and refuelled in the rain, and each time they both started at the first pull. We kept close together matching the engines so they would push the grey craft at exactly the same speed, in spite of the pair of wooden runners we had fitted on the bottom of each dinghy at Las Colas they were not easy to keep on a straight course. The helmsman had to make small alterations of course with the tiller arm all the time and he needed gloves to keep his hands warm. So responsive to the helm were the boats that when one engine ran out of fuel the other boat could make a complete circle almost literally within its own ten-foot length and so skid up alongside the other boat within seconds.

We forged along hardly able to believe our luck; past Bahia Thomas and Bahia Caracol, keeping close to the shore except where we had to cross the mouth of one of the cliff-lined bays. Even though the main wind was only a gentle breeze there was always the chance of a williwaw 'descending the mountains', as the Admiralty Pilot puts it, and sending us helter-skelter out to sea, perhaps too far out to get back when the main wind woke up again.

Ahead the many rocks surrounding Isla Richardson grew higher and higher out of the sea as we approached. At last we reached the first of several thick beds of kelp whose floating masses nearly blocked the entire entrance to the Canal Cripples just as the Pilot had described. These would be one great area of breakers in a storm, linking up with all the other shoals to make a deadly white necklace of foam around the seaward sides of the island.

The rain had now stopped and the cloud lifted as we wove carefully through the weed-covered rocks into the channel beyond; here we paused to refuel to the sound of roaring water-falls. And before restarting we sank one of our green metal jerrycans which was now empty of fuel. Marie Christine couldn't bear to watch as it slid slowly below the surface after gasping out its last breath of air. Down and down it went into the awful green gloom below.

"Well, it's come a long way from Czechoslovakia," I said, while trying to shake some warmth back into my frozen hand after holding the can below the surface. I felt as if I had just drowned my dog.

"We've been wonderfully lucky with the weather," said Richard cheerfully and we all smiled and nodded our heads, delighted at the weather and the way our friend was perking up at last. 'It's all in the mind' is a saying that is often heard among athletes who have just triumphed over physical pain. There is great truth in this, for things are seldom if ever as bad as they are imagined before the event. Once the blood is up and thoughts are transformed into action, the senses become almost immune to pain – almost.

Both engines started again and we motored up the mile or so of Canal Cripples. Flat calm except for the disturbance caused by fleeing steamer duck, and the splashy take-off of the pond-erous cormorants. The sky began to clear as if to celebrate our delivery from the trial. I almost expected to hear distant organ music heralding a new era in our lives, rather like the frivolous music which is played as the congregation leave a cathedral after the Sunday-morning service. To our left lay yellowy brown kelp beds along the shore of Isla Richardson, whose low, matted brush knitted by countless storms rose gently to the square summit of its highest hill only three hundred and seventy-five feet above the channel. On our right the whole majesty of the mountainous hinterland was slowly being revealed as the patches of blue sky advanced from the north-west to dispel the cloud.

I thought of H.M.S. *Sylvia* straining at her anchor here in 1883, as she rode out a heavy gale. How surprised the jolly jack tars would have been to see us in our two little rubber boats. I shuddered to think of the breakers that would have been pounding the white necklace around Isla Richardson on that day.

It was eleven-forty-five in the morning as we rounded the kelp beds off Punta Cummings, and headed north to pass between Isla Big and Isla Vince on our way up Fiordo North-brook. From the map it seemed likely that the mass of islands and bays had been named after members of the H.M.S. *Sylvia*'s crew back in 1883 – Pike, Brown, Hayes, Vince, Sullews, Cummings, Richardson, Ward. When they ran out of officers' names perhaps they turned to description: Big, Round, Maze, Roughwater and even Sylvia, after their own ship, which they must often have had cause to bless in these waters.

But what about Cripples? I do think they might have been a little more considerate of little rubber dinghy mariners in years to come. I had spotted this unfortunate name in the Royal Geographic Society with Eric Shipton in January 1972 and it had lurked malignantly at the back of my mind for eleven months. Now it was past, and I shared with Krister a wonderful private sense of achievement. We had done it. Looking over at the other boat across twenty-five yards of blue sunlit water I could see Richard's animated face as one huge grin. It was grand.

The fresh sunlight and the crystal-clear air, after all those days of rain, produced a wonderful scene for us. The sea in the foreground was an optimistic blue, to match the sky above. The islands were vivid green at sea level passing to bright yellow grass and brush at their tops. Far ahead of us, to the north-east, the Gran Campo Nevado presented a motionless, dazzling white, its glacier beards tinged with blue. Out to our left the stately Monte Muggeridge (what was Muggeridge doing here?) rose symmetrically to its own crown of white.

The euphoria continued. The snowy kelp goose with his

black-brown mate and fleet of fluffy young appeared more sprightly, the oystercatchers long beak a brighter vermilion. Suddenly the glossy surface was shattered by a school of racing porpoises, who must have been attracted by the noise of the motors or the vibrations from the propellers. They gave a wonderful performance for a couple of minutes but then one of the engines ran out of fuel, so we cut the other motor and rafted up to refuel both at the same time. Just as before, in Skyring and Portaluppi, when the engines were cut and the boats lay still, the porpoises lost interest immediately and disappeared below the surface, their games over.

We were heading eight miles north-east along Fiordo North-brook to enter the eastern end of the narrow Canal Almirante Martinez which would lead us eleven miles into Bahia Beaufort. At one o'clock in the afternoon we had just passed between Islas Vince and Big when the conditions changed quite dramatically. The tide turned and began to flow up Northbrook in the direction we were going. The sky rapidly clouded over and a willi-waw 'descended the mountain', rushing headlong against the incoming tide. Within minutes we were taking water badly over the bows as the surface of the sea erupted into a curious pattern of spiky vertical waves which I had seen on other seas before, but always from boats with a greater freeboard than the dinghies.

We turned hard left and made a dash due north, trying to cover the half mile of turbulent water between ourselves and the sheltered waters in the lee of Monte Muggeridge, before the conditions grew worse. We were lucky the squall passed as quickly as it had come, and the purple jellyfish drifting on the tide, were returned to a more sedate progress. We reached the shore and grinned with relief at one another. The sky didn't clear and the old familiar rain resumed its steady descent from leaden clouds above.

We began to conjure with the possibility of driving on and on until we reached the foot of the seven-mile glacier. Richard, who was always making calculations and planning ahead, announced a possible E.T.A. for midnight if we kept up present progress. We stopped briefly on a mussel-clad rock point half-way up Northbrook to attend to the pressing needs of nature, then pushed on declaiming that we should not land again before reaching the glacier. Even after seven hours cramped painfully in the back of the boats, we were all but ecstatic at the thought of completing the trip to the glacier in just one day.

The entrance to Canal Almirante Martinez is narrow and concealed. It would be easy in thick weather to go up the rather wider fiord which has to be crossed before reaching the channel itself. These were the problems which had worried Richard and me so much back at Ardmore. We were delighted to find that when it came to it, on a calm if rainy day, that we moved so slowly across the long stretches of water that we had no difficulty at all in finding our way.

A fast tidal stream drew us into the shallow mouth of the channel, only fifty yards wide at this point. There was a strange air of desolation about the place which led Marie Christine and I into a lengthy discussion about the cause of the eerie emptiness. She felt some of the reason was the absence of any sign of people having ever been there, while I thought it was the rounded grassy hills that showed a lot of sky. If there had been tall trees to relieve the bareness then I was sure the hostility would disappear. We were left with the feeling that a psychiatrist might read a lot into our differing views.

There was no shortage of bird life, and when a beautiful pair of ashy-headed geese flew off from a low island as we passed, I felt quite ashamed that I should have shot such beauty just for a meal a few weeks earlier. We moved slowly up the narrow channel, past the silent mountains on either side, at one point crossing a sort of bar where the flowing tide lifted us slightly above normal sea level and then deposited us safely on the inside of the gravel bank which caused the obstruction. We were surprised when only a mile and a half farther up the channel, where it narrowed to only twenty yards, we found the tide flowing against us. In other words it was flowing in from both ends.

In spite of the numerous pretty jellyfish, various gulls, cormorants, duck and geese the stretch up to Bahia Beaufort seemed to take an interminable length of time. We went through the inevitable 'favourite meal' discussion, which took all of half an hour with Marie Christine's final choice being a complicated dinner at the Melita restaurant in the King's Road, London. Parts of the remaining two and a half hours dragged terribly as we squirmed uncomfortably in the tiny sitting space in the stern of our boat. There was one small period of relief when Richard cut his engine to examine the floating body of a dead fish; some four feet long, it had wicked teeth and in some ways it resembled a hake. But in fact it was a *merluza de cola*, and very good eating it would have made if we had been a bit hungrier and it a bit fresher. The gulls had already taken most of the best cuts.

At six o'clock we were nearing the point on the northern shore of Canal Almirante Martinez, where we should turn right into Bahia Beaufort. As we drew nearer, we noticed what looked like a flag-pole with a red ball hanging from it. This produced a sort of frenzied hunger in us to meet people and talk with them. Eagerly we approached the pole, hoping on hope that someone would bob into sight from behind one of the grassy hillocks and start waving to us. Nothing occurred. We drew right up to the point and cut both motors, three of us intent on landing.

"Why waste time on this," said Krister. "We'd be much better getting on."

The other three of us looked rather shamefacedly at each other feeling guilty at having let sentimentality get the better of us.

"Yes, of course . . . you're right," I said, and we started up again. The bleached wooden spar with its dangling red buoy stared forlornly down on us. A relic of some shore party from a Chilian Navy ship a long time before, which had perhaps been overcome with the pioneering spirit, rather as boys carve their names on desks at school. (I remember getting beaten for it myself.) Or were there really the skeletons of a shipwrecked crew gathered round the base of their last desperate distress signal, erected when too weak to continue fueling their fire? We'll never know now.

Evening was drawing on, and far away on the south-west horizon we could see a magnificent seascape of saw-toothed islands outlined against the bright evening light in the west. The water we were now passing through was especially cold; a pale milky green, the product of the melting glaciers just round the corner at the foot of the Gran Campo Nevado. In order to cut this corner short and enter Seno (Sound) Glacier with a bit of the failing light still to spare, we passed through a narrow steep-sided channel between a small rocky island and the mainland.

At the far end of the three hundred-yard passage one of the engines ran out of fuel; we circled and rafted up immediately to refuel jointly. Another hour, one tank full of fuel, should see us across the Seno Glacier to Isla Xanadu where we would spend the night. Night navigation we ruled out, for fear of hitting icebergs in Glacier Sound.

"Hey, look at that," said Krister, pointing up at the trees on the island. We all looked up, and there among the upper branches of almost every single tree, were the big nests of the black neotropic cormorant. A few flew off, but the majority seemed unwilling to leave. After a minute or two we spotted the reason for their uncertainty – a pair of vicious-looking hawks which were stalking about the rock-face below, as if waiting for a chance to get into the nests, once the parents left. A pale gingery colour, with feathers well down their legs, I thought they might be some kind of harrier. We moved off and left the status quo.

Quickly it grew dark, and with night came the wind. We were tired after fourteen hours in the boats. Cold and hungry too. Now was the classical situation for a mistake. We began to take the icy water over the bows, both boats were bailing hard. I began measuring the distances and wind angles to the various pieces of land; it was either Xanadu or back with the wind to the mainland. Back to cliffs and a rough sea in the dark? No, it must be forward to Xanadu. Twenty minutes would do it. Keep bailing. Feel the stomach knotting with fear that the engines will swamp, knowing that I deserve it for being too casual late in the day. Hanging on in the dark, cold and frightened. Religion beginning to assume reality again, far from home, far from help.

For some reason we are allowed to escape again. We beach on south-west Xanadu. It has been a long day but still we must unload the boats and lash things down in case the wind grows stronger.

"It could be worse – it could be raining," Krister murmurs happily as he staggers up the beach with a jerrycan of fuel in each hand. Marie Christine has both burners going in a sheltered spot in the dark – it's going to be curry. Hurrah! Never learning, I gamble on the tide being nearly high and pitch our tent on the ground verge of the undergrowth. Richard disappears to find a bush for Krister and himself to sleep under, wrapped in groundsheets. Soon we were all asleep, buried under a great leaden wave of fatigue.

Dawn. It's sunny and calm, the tide is inside the flysheet but not the tent. We are on a pile of rotting seaweed which is swarming with minute black sandhoppers. We are all swallowing hot porridge. Then, gradually the hot tea brings back perspective and things slow down. The blurred images of exhaustion come back into focus. Everything could so easily have come to disaster on the previous evening. Now we should take stock and make a plan.

The morning passed while we motored gently up the narrow channel between Caldera and Xanadu in the sort of perfect weather that one associates only with the unreality of motion pictures.

By midday the wind was back again, but we had landed at the mouth of a river, seventy-five yards wide, which brought the cold clear, fresh water of Lago Munoz Gamero to the sea. It was running high and very fast, great boils surging up from below where the racing water encountered sunken rocks. Our beach was fine white sand. It seemed like paradise, until we looked at the icebergs floating down another river just round the corner from the glacier. The trip had hardly started.

10

Base Camp Blues

AFTER TWELVE MONTHS of preparation, we were poised to make our attempt at the first crossing of the Gran Campo Nevado (Big Snow Field). If we failed from this Base Camp, it was most unlikely that we should make the crossing at all. Far from feeling fresh, we sank back exhausted from the efforts of the past weeks. We used the continuously unpleasant weather as an excuse to lie low in our tents; we took a break from the Sunday of our arrival to Friday. Five days of rations we could ill afford at that stage.

I think we all felt we had done enough. We had got round the outside of the peninsula in two tiny rubber boats. We should now wake up and find ourselves at home in front of the peat fire talking about it. But ugly rumbles from the ice-falls, lying behind the precipitous mountains which guarded the shores of the bay, kept reminding us what we didn't want to know: the ice-cap was ready and waiting for us to make the first move.

Perhaps some of our inactivity at least sprang from the simple fact that we had chosen an uncomfortable camp site when we first arrived. We had discounted comfort in favour of the sheer grandeur of the scenery. We had arrived on a sunny Sunday morning with a wind fast rising from the familiar north-westerly quarter. It was really a preliminary camp that we were looking for; a place from which to reconnoitre the site for the first Base Camp of the ascent of the ice-cap.

"Be sure and make plenty of recce's," Shipton had told me in the Royal Geographical Society's Kensington headquarters. I had already paid for not following his advice at Portaluppi. This time it would be different.

Our broad sandy beach, running across the head of a rocky peninsula, flanked by the racing black waters of the Munoz Gamero river on the one side and the milky green waters from the foot of the glacier on the other, seemed a fine place to start from. Soft white sand, warmed by the touch of the sun, made a welcome change from scrambling over slippery rock or stumbling through wet shifting pebble beaches. Just back from the high-tide mark there was a piece of flat ground running to the foot of a sheer fifty-foot cliff. This ground was easy to clear, and it had plenty of small saplings to which we could tie the ground-sheet we used as a roof for our cookhouse. Fresh water ran past our new home at millions of gallons per hour. We looked no farther. The tents went up with the speed we considered a simple expression of our expertise in this kind of living – it was fun.

A packet of vegetable soup, with a few biscuits spread thinly with the precious canned butter, and a good draught of hot tea fuelled us for an exploration of the local area.

"Look at these footprints!" exclaimed Marie Christine pointing at the sand a few yards from our tent.

"Puma," said Richard. "Let's follow them both ways – first this way – oh, they seem to lead to your tent, John!" he laughed. Sure enough the prints led into the grass towards our tent. Marie Christine glanced anxiously about to see if the big cat was watching us.

"Here, look at these bones!" called Krister who had gone on ahead of us, "and he's left some fur behind," he continued, holding up a clump of sandy coloured hairs which looked very much like lion's fur to me. The place where the puma hid in the grass was littered with the bones of geese and duck which abounded in the low ground by the water's edge. It looked as if he made a pretty fat living, and when he grew tired of fowl, there was evidence of a few fish, and even the long shiny legs of the great king crab we had so enjoyed in Punta Arenas. We had been told how to catch them: by dipping a rag wrapped round a long pole into the sea just off shore – but we never tried.

Filled with interest, we followed the footprints along the sand, just below the high-tide mark, which meant they had been made on the previous night. They led a couple of hundred yards to a point where the cliff ran down into the sea by the edge of the glacier river, thus sealing off the sandy beach. At the foot of this cliff we found a small cave from which the puma could spring up some loose rocks and into the forest on the cliff top. There were several mounds of sand in the cave.

"I know that smell," laughed Marie Christine, "that's Pussy Ridgway when he was a kitten. This is the puma's loo!"

We walked back to the tents, keeping close to the water's edge, and I found the corpse of a large half-eaten *merluza de cola* swilling about in the tide.

"I bet the birds will come down for that if we keep an eye on it. We can watch from the tents with the little Zeiss monocular," I said.

"Yes, it's going to rain," said Krister unnecessarily, for at that moment a great clap of thunder rolled out from the black cloud which was coming fast over the top of the mountain on the other side of the Munoz Gamero river.

"A better place would be under the shelter," said Richard. The wind fell away and heavy drops of rain pattered down to join the rings of a rising fish I had marked by the mouth of the black river.

We huddled together under the shelter, two to each of the pneumatic rubber centre seats from the dinghies. But it was no good, the water leaked off the edge of the groundsheet and began to wet our polar sweaters. The very last thing we wanted was to get our precious dry clothes wet; we had learned that well at Portaluppi. We ran for our tents.

The thunderstorm lasted perhaps half an hour and I thumbed through the Admiralty Pilot once more to pass the time, idly looking for some explanation of the region we were now in. Apart from saying that some of it was unsurveyed and that there are no anchorages in the rest of it, I learned nothing. Instead I turned again to Chapter I of the thick navy blue cloth-bound volume; the chapter giving general information on the southern and western coasts of South America.

"Oh no! Listen to this," I gasped and Marie Christine looked up in surprise from her miniature anthology of English verse. "If only I'd read this earlier on, listen: 'On the Pacific ocean side of the continent, there is a certain amount of diurnal inequality in the tidal streams: that is, one of the two streams running in a particular direction, during any period of 24 hours, is stronger and of longer duration than the other . . . 8.'"

"That's what swamped us at Portaluppi that night," I said,

"Oh, I remember all right!" said Marie Christine, escaping from the memory back into her English verse.

The thunderstorm passed by and we scrambled out of the tents to continue improving our new home. Richard and Krister set about gathering some driftwood for a fire to dry bags full of their clothing still wet from Portaluppi, and Marie Christine put the big black pot on their fire to boil up some water to wash clothes in. I sneaked away in search of the fish I had seen rising. "For supper," I said importantly to disguise my idleness.

The black river was the sort of dream that preserves the sanity of so many office workers in hundreds of dirty cities, those who each weekend escape from the screech of the telephone and 'go fishing'. This was a different river from the mighty Amazon, yet in its way it possessed the same kind of power. The human body doesn't float as well in a river as it does in the sea; the power of even a mild current is too great for a man to fight. One mistake and he is whisked away . . . standing there on the bank I remembered seeing a blackened corpse bob on the surface of a pool in a jungle river in Malaysia; a soldier dead for making one mistake on a river not half as powerful as this one in Chile. We would need to be careful when we tried to get the dinghies up this one on our way home. Each boat would have to be hauled along the bank, the engines couldn't push against the flood that was for sure. The banks are heavily wooded, how would we . . . The fish rose again and I remembered why I had come in the first place. I flicked the spinner in the direction of the rise, it was just out of reach and there was no sign of a fish as I retrieved the lure, trying to give it some life by varying the pace of winding in the reel. I added a half-moon-shaped lead to the cast, which would serve the double purpose of giving extra range and stopping the revolving lure from kinking the line. My next cast was a good one and crossed the rise with six feet to spare. Still no reply from the fish. A dozen more casts and no sign; the wind was freshening again and the rising tide threatened to cut off my line of retreat to the beach. I left the scene muttering darkly. What was needed was the fly and a pair of waders. I didn't deserve anything anyway for 'dredging' with a spinner.

We were quietly eating our supper under the shelter when the eagle came. He had probably never seen a man before and he showed no sign of resenting our presence at first. Almost as big as a condor, but without the bald head, the bird was dark brown generally with black and white bars on the wings. He was flying fairly low, as if to surprise some small living creature along the tide-line, just as he had surprised us. He saw the dead fish slopping back and forth in the rising water; he hovered for a while and then dropped lower for a closer inspection. We could almost hear the broad wings thwacking the air to keep his heavy body from falling into the sea. After a few seconds he rolled smoothly on to his side, and swung away to glide perfectly into the onshore breeze, which quickly gave his outspread wings the lift to send him soaring up off the face of the sea, round and back over our heads to disappear beyond the cliff top. He didn't come back. The neat little Chilean swallows were then able to continue their insect hunts without interruption.

Next day we wished we had chosen a more sheltered site to camp and forgone the view. Purple rain squalls came rolling up the bay from the west, churning the mouth of the black river into a turmoil, where its racing waters plunged into the wind.

So it went on for a couple of days, foul weather at sea level and the imagination of what it would be like on the ice-cap keeping us pinned in our sleeping-bags, fiddling away at 'make and mend'. Not that there wasn't plenty of this to do: torn waterproof trousers, torn rucksacks, broken zips, buttons off shirts, stitching undone on sleeping bags, holes in socks, etc. The medical department was clear except for Richard, who was suffering from septic splinters in his hands. These came from a lot of good work, breaking the trail through thorn bushes particularly, whenever we had been moving on the land.

At around lunch time on the fourth day, the rain stopped and the sun came out for a little. The wind kept on fairly strongly and it wasn't worth putting up the shelter. Over the usual snack lunch of biscuits, cheese and tea, we decided to do something positive at last. Richard set off alone in one boat to cross the mouth of the black river, land on the far side and climb to the top of the two thousand-foot mountain there. His aim was to climb high enough to overlook the approaches to the ice-cap on the far side of the bay and then to return and report on the most favourable route. Krister, Marie Christine and I were to take five cans of fuel, the two plastic cans, one of sugar, one of oats, a box of rations and some oil up the black river to establish a stockpile and to assess the problems presented by the river as far as our access to Lago Munoz Gamero was concerned on the homeward leg of our journey.

Soon Richard was gone, leaving us his route and estimated time of return in case we had to search for him later. The other three of us loaded the remaining dinghy and set off into the bay and round in a wide curve to meet the middle of the river at its mouth. We had a full tank of fuel, enough to last one hour at three-quarter throttle. Timing was important, for the middle of the river with its stranded tree trunks and boulders was no place to run out of fuel. Things went well at first, the engine surprised me with its ability to push the heavy load against the current. After twenty minutes we had covered about two hundred yards or more up against the stream. But the river was getting narrower and the snags more numerous. No one was saying much. We reached a point where we were static in the current, even with Marie Christine and Krister both paddling hard with the oars. Behind us, some forty yards downstream, the water frothed white over a stranded tree trunk; there was also one to our left and the overgrown bank was to our right. Fear comes quickly in such a situation. I had used these motors a great deal in the past ten years: now I really needed to know what I was doing, for we had to go through a sort of slalom gate backwards.

I waved to the others to tighten the strings on their yellow lifejackets and then eased the throttle. Too much, and we swung round at angle to the stream losing twenty of the vital forty yards in three or four seconds. I raced the engine and we came head to stream again, inching forward. Next time I eased the throttle a little less and we began to lose way. Very gently I moved the handle of the motor towards me a fraction, this pushed the bow to the left a little and we began to move back and to the left under some semblance of control.

Soon we had passed between the trees and were in open water in midstream. Looking down I could see the current racing over big smooth stones about the size of bowls. Krister started to use his paddle to sound the depth. There was a bulge in the water, about two-thirds of the way across the river which indicated shallows – maybe too shallow for the propeller. One tap would break the shear spring and a great racing whine from the motor would herald the start of our uncontrolled spinning descent of the river. If we were lucky it would end in the sea, if not we might be upturned by one of the several stranded trees on the way downstream.

I decided not to risk the shallows but to make for the far bank a little farther downstream. We could start hauling the boat along the side of the river from there, at least the first part didn't look too difficult to walk along.

Once on the bank, it looked more overgrown than I had thought. We could also see rapids about half a mile farther upstream. Krister suggested we try to find a short cut to the lake by examining an empty watercourse to the left of the river. We stumbled about in the undergrowth for half an hour, maybe more, before agreeing on the depressing conclusion that the only way was up the side of the main river. While on our reconnaissance we had passed three or four shallow ponds; they were each about fifty yards long by twenty wide, six inches of clear water lay over a bed of bowl-sized pebbles similar to those in the main river. In the ponds we saw several shoals of fish fry about an inch in length, but no sign of the larger parent fish. The same situation prevailed in the river, for except at the mouth there seemed to be no full-grown fish at all. From this I reckoned that the fry were possibly the young of a migratory fish, such as the sea trout which were not due in the rivers of that part of South America for another month or two.

Our progress up the river was slow, we all felt strangely tired and even the least exertion only increased the lethargy. Marie Christine's job was to recce ahead up the bank, looking for possible ways round the various obstacles. Krister held the boat off the bank with a paddle, while I hauled it along the shallows by a long rope from the bow. This went well, until we reached a steep section of the bank scoured by deep racing water where the forest grew right to the top of the six-foot bank, toppling several dead trees over the edge. These half-in, half-out trunks posed a serious problem and Krister had to balance on the bow of the dinghy while I pulled on the rope to get him round the outside of the tree. The dangers here were several: either I might fall in if the bank crumbled, or the dinghy might capsize with its top-heavy load. Krister might fall off the boat or the rope might be dragged from my hands by the weight of the current. We were all relieved when at last we reached the rapids where at least the work was safe if tiresome, for everything had to be carried round the edge of the rough water, including the boat. On the upstream side we relaunched and reloaded again and then continued with the mixture as before.

When we arrived at the next rapids we tied the boat to a rock and went on upstream to check the distance to the lake. The afternoon was wearing on and we didn't want Richard to get back to the camp and start worrying because we weren't there; also there was the question of delaying supper and we all felt hungry most of the time. We were delighted to find the end of the lake, Munoz Gamero, only just a short distance up from the rapids. The three of us sat for a few minutes on a huge slab of grey rock which slanted down into the speeding river in a smooth curve, just as the retreating ice had left it some thousands of years before. The lake was as black as the river, even the sunlight and calm of late afternoon failed to relieve the sinister atmosphere of the place. On either side the mountains rose steeply and this only served to increase an air of foreboding gloom.

"A lot will happen before we pass here again," I murmured to myself as we got carefully to our feet and made our way back to the boat, disturbing a pair of steamer duck who clattered along the surface and then rose into the air as if to prove they were of the superior flighted variety. We left the dinghy below the rapids and carried all the stores and fuel to a stockpile in the forest, close to the entrance to the lake.

Our journey home was a fast one once we had portaged round the lower rapids. With an empty boat and two people to paddle if the engine should fail, I chanced powering straight down the middle of the river, swinging to left or right where necessary to avoid islands, trees and shallows. It was a brief and exhilarating trip and the engine never failed. Back at the camp we found Richard, who had already got the fire going in readiness for the evening meal. While Marie Christine and Krister got on with the cooking, Richard and I got down to assessing the best way up on to the ice-cap; we were aided by an

excellent sketch he had made while up at his observation point
on the mountain.

"The cap itself was under cloud all the time," he said, "but
I think I got a pretty good idea of the approaches. I reckon we
should steer clear of the glacier – it looks very broken for a long
way up from the foot. Ice plates thrown against one another,
with their ends forced into the air. Masses of crevasses."

"I'm sure the best bet is to go along this ridge," he added,
pointing across the bay to the mountain marking the seaward
end of the southern side of the glacier valley. "I know it's steep
to start with, but we can try and pick a route up by eye from
here; then cross over the bay by boat and set up a camp again
at the foot of the mountain itself."

"Why is it that Shipton always goes up the glaciers then?"
Marie Christine interrupted from the fire where she was busy
stirring the curry. "I've read the book two and a half times now
and he has always gone up a glacier."

"Well, we aren't experienced in glacier work, and the noises
and the look of it are far from encouraging," Richard replied,
and I nodded in agreement.

"At least if we keep to the ridge there shouldn't be any
crevasses," I added.

"What if it turns out like the ridge on the other side of the
valley? We've all seen how jagged that is," asked Krister.

"This side doesn't look as bad and I'm all for going up to
have a look at it anyway," Richard said in a determined
fashion.

"Okay, let's give it a spin, if it works out it will give us a much
easier access to the cap itself. Surely we can do it somehow,"
I said, and no one seemed to disagree.

"Let's get on with the grub and at the same time we can work
out what rations we have available for the rest of the trip.
Today should be Wednesday, 30th November," I said. "We've
got . . ."

"Sorry, I make it the 29th," Richard broke in holding up his
Rolex watch.

"Oh! Well, that must be right then. Krister's diary will
confirm the day," I said and Krister felt in the breast pocket of
his purple windcheater, like a village constable.

"Wednesday, 29th November," he read slowly. "Tomorrow

is my mother's forty-ninth birthday. I'll do the cooking to celebrate it," he said gravely.

"Thank goodness the watches are keeping good time, we could all go cuckoo otherwise," laughed Marie Christine. "Who's for some of these berries? They need plenty of sugar, I warn you."

We had taken to eating the purple or red berries because their rather tart taste was refreshing when we were walking with the heavy loads. This was the first time we had tried cooking them, because we had never seen them in such abundance as they were here. We were not sure if they were in fact *calafate* or *murtilla* but they did need plenty of sugar when stewed and then they tasted rather like unripe cherries. There were quite enough of the bushes around for us to survive off them for a while if all else failed. Combined with the mussels I dare say we might have done quite well.

The next day was disappointing, except for the splendid cake Krister made for his mother's birthday party, out of cocoa, crushed biscuits and sugar. The weather was hopeless, far too strong in the bay for us to launch the boats; and so we lay huddled in the tents, trying not to think what conditions would be like in the clouds five thousand feet above up on the ice-cap.

On the first day of December we got up at six in the morning, had a quick breakfast and motored across to the forest, below the only place on the three thousand-foot cliff which we thought we might be able to get up. We found a crystal-clear stream running into the bay. It came from the foot of a mighty water-fall about a mile or so back in the forest at an unscalable part of the cliff. The trees were tall by this stream, and promised complete protection from the wind. There were also the remains of another Indian dwelling but on this occasion there were no signs of any mussel shells; instead we found a frame about the size of a small soccer goal, with an angle post behind each upright to support it. There was no sign of cultivation, and we concluded the Indians must have brought their food with them, relying on that supply until they began to catch the fish which they dried on the frame. Once again there was nothing to indicate the place had been visited in recent years, although we found a good supply of split cypress logs for firewood. It is customary in such a situation to leave wood, so that on return a fire could be lit immediately without all the bother of having to cut unsuitable wood near by. There was no cypress growing anywhere near this camp, so we tried to burn local wood in case the Indians should ever return.

We brought the boats ashore and set up the tents, then Richard and Krister set off to find a route to the top of the cliff and to establish a stockpile there of eleven days rations for four people, and five gallons of petrol for the cookers. The weather was not too bad, reasonable winds and only occasional showers of rain and hail at sea level, although probably this would fall as snow on high ground.

In the camp Marie Christine and I set about preparations for the main ascent which was planned for the morrow. We cut forty whippy saplings, not much thicker than a cigarette and each three feet long; to the top of each one we tied a strip of red polythene in a tight clove hitch. These were to be the markers we would use when crossing the ice-cap; they would show us the route back when we retraced our steps – if the visibility was good enough to pick them out. If it wasn't, then we should be able to pick them up using a compass bearing and a measured number of paces. I carefully disconnected the fuel pipes on the outboard fuel tanks and then removed them from the engines. These oblong black tanks each held three litres of petrol, which was the equivalent of fifteen refills for one Optimus cooker; and the tanks were the most convenient receptacle we possessed for carrying bulk fuel in anything less than the fifty-pound weight of a five-gallon jerrycan. Tampering with the motors in such a remote place seemed to be asking for trouble, but it had to be done. The aluminium fuel bottles only contained one litre, and the big whisky bottle the same, although the latter was cunningly misshapen to look as if it held a lot more! Altogether this meant we could carry on us, two full cookers, fifteen refills in each of two fuel tanks, one litre in each of two aluminium bottles, and a litre in the whisky bottle. A total of forty-seven fills, each one of which lasted for one and a half hours. Enough to last the four of us perhaps three weeks on the snow.

We made up carefully waterproofed loads of food, checked all the tents, poles and distributed the spare pegs from the reserve tent. Then we deflated the rubber boats and stowed them away with the other equipment we would not be taking, storing it all in a safe place in the trees.

When everything was ready for the morrow, we set about improving our camp site. First the trusty Australian ground-sheet was rigged over half the ruined Indian hut, then we got the fire lit in the centre of the hut and placed the inflated dinghy seats round the blaze which had a sort of pole table rigged over the top of it for drying, or more correctly, smoking things. Our tents were sited well into the trees, back from the river bank in case of flooding. The trees were thirty to forty feet high notho-fagus, which in no way resembled the beech tree, of which they were supposed to be a cousin. The ground was flat under the trees, with little or no undergrowth; ideal for shelter from the wind but rather dank and almost swampy on the leaf mould.

Indians of these parts have a reputation for living in squalor. It was sunny between the hail showers, and as soon as the wind fell away the gnats came out, 'mosquitoes' Francisco had called them, though they didn't seem to be of the same family. Like small black flies they hovered in little clouds about our bodies, biting at any exposed part of our skin and leaving a small white lump that became intensely itchy. We had not encountered these flies before in anything like the numbers we found at the Indian camp, and I'm afraid we connected their presence, maybe quite falsely, with the filthy state of the place.

It was already seven o'clock in the evening when Richard and Krister returned after eight hours on the cliff. They were tired and wet but had reached the top and left the stores and fuel there. The climb had taken five hours and had not been without incident; their extremely heavy packs, made up of their own personal kit and tent as well as the rations and fuel, had caused them to slip badly on more than one occasion. The worst piece of news was that the 'hill 1189' (3,864 feet) as we came to call it, seemed a long way along the ridge from the top of the cliff, which was itself under snow and very cold.

We went to bed early that night.

I I

Towards 1189

IT WAS FOUR-FORTY-FIVE in the morning when I awoke. It had been a restless night; there was the worry about the climb and Marie Christine's position in the scheme, once or twice I had half woken to hear snuffling noises from some sort of animal close to the tent. Now it was nearly light and heavy drops of rain drummed intermittently on the orange tent cloth from the upper branches of the trees. It was another of those mornings when an early start was necessary but very uncomfortable. I just lay there for a few minutes, willing myself to get up and call the others. Marie Christine stirred and jack-knifed into a sitting position, eager as ever not to let the side down. I pulled on some clothes and crawled out of the tent. Sliding into the clammy orange waterproofs and tall wellingtons was miserable; there wasn't room for them inside the tent so we always kept them just inside the flap of the flysheet where they were always cold and damp. As I left I caught a glimpse of Marie Christine's hand reaching out of the tent for the black rubber bucket which we used to keep the cooking water: at least breakfast wouldn't be long in coming.

Krister is one of those characters who keep the alarm clock companies in business, he takes a great deal of rousing in the morning and it's as if each new day is the renewal of life after a long hibernation. Richard is much quicker, but on this particular morning he still felt tired after the strain of the previous day. Once I was sure they were both awake, I walked the few paces through the trees to the edge of the little river and looked out across the bay; everything was a uniform grey, the rain was falling steadily and the wind was gusty.

"Sorry, fellows, it's hopeless just now. Let's have breakfast in the Indian shelter at seven and decide on a move then," I said softly as I passed the two small tents. Grunts of approval were the only replies.

There wasn't much improvement by seven, but by ten I could wait no longer. Time was passing, rations were dwindling. We just had to get on with it.

The packs were too heavy, the heaviest I had ever carried, eighty pounds – maybe more. We set off in silence, the rain still plopping down from the branches high above. By this time we reached the little brook which runs through the end of the wood close to the foot of the cliff, our feet were already wet, not simply with water but with the inescapable slimy mire of the swamp there. The undergrowth grew thicker as we started the steep gradient, up a mossy bank towards a slight saddle, from where the main climb would begin. We were now in our usual single file: Richard, myself, Marie Christine and finally Krister. During that first few hundred yards which took us three-quarters of an hour, the weight of the pack seemed as if it were going to be just too much. The marker poles with their red plastic strips kept jamming under low branches and then the unfortunate carrier would have to take a few paces backward and crawl forward almost on his knees to see if he could clear under the obstacle at the second attempt.

It was all rather trying.

I had a severe attack of the 'Never agains' during that first three-quarters of an hour stretch. But by dint of great slipping and sliding and hauling, using branches and tussocks of grass for hand-holds, we eventually found ourselves at the bottom of the main cliff. Up above us it stretched, in a never-ending series of false crests, the only route we were capable of along the whole three mile face. We each had an ice axe, although only Richard had ever used one for any length of time before. Now we found them almost as useful as an extra hand. With the palm of the right hand clasped round the spade-like projection on one side of the T-piece, the nine-inch spike on the other side could be struck into the streaming moss or dirt to provide a fairly secure leverage.

We struggled up, zigzagging from one moss-covered ledge to another for an hour and a quarter. The heavy weights on our backs made for difficulty in manoeuvring. Marie Christine moved steadily and with cat-like assurance, never once slipping back down a slope as did the other three of us from time to time. She always ensured three of her four limbs had a firm hold before moving the fourth, and she stared with fixed concentration at the moss and rock before her face – never looking down, for fear of losing her nerve. I don't know which was the worse, her own fear of the climbing or my fear watching her climb.

It rained continuously and when we called a halt for lunch at twelve-fifteen, the mess tin was filled in no time from the steadily running beards of moss hanging down from a nearby rock-face.

"The real stars of this are the waterproof suits," Krister said, his beard and face streaming with rain. The suits are made of a PVC/cotton, and the combined anorak and trousers weigh a total 2 lb. 14 oz. This is heavy compared to the usual lightweight cagoule and overtrousers which might weigh less than 1 lb. 6 oz. We each had a lot of experience of walking in rain, and between the four of us we developed a tremendous regard for these Helly Hansen suits. Bought, I might add, on the open market without the makers even knowing we were going on an expedition.

The combined cocoa and chocolate Horlicks drink, saved from the unused rations of my unsuccessful round the world sailing trip of 1968, tasted wonderful. The biscuits and cheese gave us energy. But when we set off again we all complained of the cold, our hands seemed frozen and poor Krister fared worst of all, because his circulation wasn't very good in the first place.

The first drama came at two o'clock. Richard was doing sterling work in the lead as usual, threading his way along the same route as he had followed with Krister on the previous day. Every so often he would let out a shout of triumph and point to one of his own markers; such as two stones, one on top of the other. He was just checking along a ledge above and to the right of me, and I took the opportunity for a breather. I was standing on a steep soggy bank in Richard's footsteps. If he decided to continue on up and to the left, I should be ready and not have wasted a single pace. I was just waiting for him to confirm that we didn't have to go right when it happened.

The two footholds gave way simultaneously, but I didn't notice that at all. I just found myself suddenly shooting down the bank on my stomach; my face was very close to the moss which seemed to be passing in a blur. There was no way I could stop myself at this speed unless I was able to dig the sharp spike of the ice axe into the ground. This was unlikely to stop me at once, and I knew I wasn't far from where the bank dropped over an overhang to a rather long drop – enough to finish me. The slide continued, the weight of my pack pinning my stomach to the mossy bank. For some reason I didn't seem able to get my hands back from above my head to do anything with the ice axe. I had a curiously detached view of things, knowing that I was no longer in control; I felt hypnotised by the over-hang which I couldn't see, but which I knew wasn't far away. Quietly, suddenly I stopped. Both feet together had dug into a mossy rut and I wasn't even hurt. I struggled to get out, after first looking round carefully to see that I wasn't likely to free myself and fall straight over the edge.

I hadn't come very far down, but as I scrambled back up I could see three anxious-looking faces peering down at me.

"Johnny! Are you all right?" I could see Marie Christine was very close to tears.

"Oh yes – but I'm glad it's over." I tried to laugh, but my legs were shaking a bit.

"Well, let's keep going," I said, thinking that the sooner everyone got worrying about their own safety the sooner they would stop thinking about what might have happened to me.

Up we went, with Richard continually reassuring us that the worst was over and it wasn't much farther. The sheer weight of the packs was taking its toll, and the breaks became more frequent and longer. We were eating more than the day's supply of Kendal Mint Cake which everyone referred to as K.M.C. The air was getting colder and patches of snow lay in the gullies, but mercifully the rain was not coming down as hard and there were places where we could take our breaks out of the wind.

Spread out below us, we could see the whole bay, whenever the cloud allowed. From the formation of the main valley, down which both the glacier and the black rivers flowed to the sea, it looked as if until quite recently in geological time, a major glacier had been where Lago Munoz Gamero now lay. The woods in the delta formed by the two river mouths had 'rides' of smaller trees running through them, some without any vegetation. These looked as if they were the more recent courses of the ice. The whole area was littered with boulders of different sizes which had been dropped in their present positions by the melting ice. Similar boulders we could see riding along the top of the glacier ice away to our right. I couldn't help wondering just how small a distance a boulder might have moved in the course of my entire lifetime. Not much changed here.

Out in the bay itself there were two distinct shades of water entwined by the vagaries of the tide, one dark and clear, the other the pale milky green of the glacier water. Surrounding the bay and as far as the eye could see except to seaward, the snow-capped mountains stretched one after another until they became a white ring around the horizon. This great empty view heightened the feeling of isolation, which each of us felt to a greater or lesser extent.

Slower and slower we went, but we did keep on moving up. At last Richard shouted that he could see the cairn where the fuel and food was stored. It was dead ahead and the slope began to round off. Gone was the moss, or any sign of vegetation; in its place was only rock and snow. Marie Christine had done remarkably well, people usually can when there is no alternative, but now she was feeling exhausted after seven hours of constant effort. We stopped for a rest while Krister and Richard went on ahead to select a site for the camp. Around us two, the wind blew little clouds of whirling snow along the narrow corries at our feet. We could hear a stream bubbling along beneath the snow to our left and we made a mental note to avoid anything that looked very flat for fear that we might fall through thin ice into a lake. Soon the cold urged us to our feet and we followed along in the blue footsteps of the others.

The camp site was in deep snow on the top of the ridge, sheltered by a spine of jagged black rock. We were too tired to look around much and in any case the visibility was none too good. Everywhere but where we were looked a long way away.

Putting up the three tents took much longer than it would on a flat earth surface. First we had to stamp down a flat area of hard snow for each tent. This was not as easy as it seems, and we knew that if we didn't do it right, the occupants of the tent would find themselves on the skids during the night when the hard snow turned to ice. Marie Christine got a brew going in a crack in the rock, and kept warm by helping with the stamping.

The lightweight shovel now came into its own, clearing snow and cutting snow blocks for the shelter wall each tent needed, if there should be a storm.

It was nearly eight o'clock in the evening by the time we had the tents securely erected. In the process I suffered some damage. I was using my ice axe as the main tent guy peg for the windward end of our tent; as I lunged down on the point of the handle, the T-piece sank dutifully into the snow and the nine-inch spike gashed a great tear down the orange trouser. Luckily it missed the flesh of my leg, but all the same it was a depressing thing to happen in view of the soakings I would get in the future.

Once in the tent we warmed up with the heat of the stove. Richard did the same but Krister had no cooker and suffered in silence. Up in the snow we were in a new world; if we got too cold for too long then we would soon be in trouble. Self-reliance took on a new meaning. From here on everything we had must be made to last, no amount of masking tape could really repair the torn trousers and in really bad conditions they would start to let in the wet. We each fitted our crampons once more to our boots, to make sure there were no loose screws. The hot supper was never so welcome, and the half pint of scalding cocoa did wonders for morale.

After supper we turned our full attention to the problem of keeping warm during the coming night. We hadn't much equipment at our disposal; because we had to carry everything on our backs, there was no room for extra luxuries. Starting under the tent, we had a hard polished platform of packed snow, turned to a crust of ice and already showing us that it was angled slightly down on Marie Christine's side. The tent had a thin blue plastic groundsheet and there was immediate condensation on the inner side of this sheet when it was applied to the snow. We had a long narrow Karrimat each, made of close cell foam, and a broader one laid crosswise under our feet; the mats were scarcely a quarter of an inch thick but they had proved efficient at lower altitude. To reinforce the Karrimats we had nothing except our down sleeping-bags which we laid side by side with our feet pointing to the entrance of the tent. We slept in our clothes and wrapped our duvet jackets around the outside of our sleeping-bags. I have always believed that time spent in making sure the bed, whatever it may be, is as comfortable as possible is never wasted. There is not much worse than struggling about in misery in the small hours of the morning trying to make the best of a poor job. Once really cold it is very difficult to get warm again.

We both slept well, aided by exhaustion. By six o'clock I was taking a mug of good hot tea to the other two. Krister was all right but Richard had suffered serious subsidence of his tent, he had spent half the night miserably cold and wet. While Marie Christine made the breakfast I kept clear of our tent and tried to keep warm in the raw wind by bringing the stockpile of rations and fuel down from the cairn to the camp. All the same my feet were frozen by the time I crawled back into the tent for my porridge.

It took two and a half hours after breakfast before we actually moved off along the ridge on a bearing of 110° magnetic. We used the compass from the start in case visibility should suddenly worsen. In all our calculations with bearings we had to remember that the magnetic variation was 17° E in our part of Chile, whereas it is 9° W at home in Scotland. Wrongly applied this would give an error of 34°, and then it wouldn't be long before we walked over a cliff if visibility was poor.

The loads were heavier than on the day before, because we were now carrying some more food as well as everything else. We all wore our visors against snow blindness, and the labour of movement through soft snow soon caused them to mist up inside. The formation was the same single file, with Richard out in front bravely breaking the trail; I followed about ten paces later trying hard to place my feet in the blue footsteps which led up the misty screen of my snow visor.

For half an hour things seemed to be going quite well. We were so involved in the labour of the thing that we scarcely noticed the rapidly worsening weather.

I bumped suddenly into Richard. "Look, I can't see far enough ahead – there is no horizon – we could easily go straight over the edge!" he shouted against the wind. I lifted my visor and instantly the drifting horizontal snow bit at my face; the others closed right up. Out to our left, downwind I could just make out a reef of black rock jutting above the snow. Then it was gone. Conditions were now impossible. Even since Richard had spoken things had got twice as bad: the drifting snow doubled by falling snow. A billion white particles whirling before the roaring wind. A white-out. No horizon, nothing but a small world of white. It was extremely cold with the added wind chill.

"Well, you'd better do something! We might be here for a week!" I heard Richard shouting in my ear.

"Okay, follow me to the rocks I saw over on the left 020° M. Keep right close together but be ready to stop if I go over the edge," I shouted back.

My heart was in my mouth. I counted the even number of paces on my left foot . . . 2 – 4 – 6 . . . it was no more than 150.

At 130 the black shape loomed up in the snow. Cautiously I crept round to the sheltered side of the rocks; here the snow sloped away at a fairly steep angle and I signalled for the others to put their kit down and get on with digging a place for the tents. When Krister took off his pack he put it on the snow rather than the rock; then he turned to help Richard with his load. Suddenly he let out a great shout and shot off down the slope diving on to his escaping pack and skidding to a halt. After that everything was jammed in clefts in the rock, where it rapidly became encrusted with snow and ice. It looked like Scott's last camp.

It took the four of us two hours to get the tents up. No one wanted anything but an absolutely flat floor, for the idea of hurtling down the slope wrapped in a collapsed tent was uppermost in our minds. The business of holding a tent against the blizzard while poles and guys were positioned was a major job in itself. Everyone wanted to be using the shovel or stamping the snow, no one wanted to do the tent pegs or stand holding the tent. The cold was severe, particularly on our feet.

When at last the job was finished and we were in the tents drinking hot soup, then the doubts began to crowd in. Was this a normal day here? What would it be like two thousand feet higher? What was the slope we were sitting on?

The last question was answered first. At two o'clock the snow stopped falling and the wind dropped, visibility cleared. In front of our tents the snow fell away for a thousand feet into a valley with a lake. It was this lake which fed the great waterfall

which fell over the main cliff into the forest by the Indian camp
we had left on the previous day. We were sitting on a bulge in
the snow above the valley. Nothing and nobody wanted to go
far from the entrance of the tents. All the same I was quite
confident that we would be all right where we were, tucked in
under the rock. It was nasty material for dreams.

As the weather cleared so we all poked our heads out of the
tents to see what lay ahead. The ridge led along in the direction of
the ice-cap. 'Hill 1189' was set a little to the right of our path, it
looked more than 3,864 feet and made us wonder if we weren't
below three thousand feet ourselves. The contour lines were all
but invisible on my map.

"I reckon we'll have to go through that saddle to the left of
1189," I shouted to Richard. "Where the wind is still blowing
the snow."

"Yes, that's the way, but it looks as if the ridge may drop
sharply just before it reaches that saddle," he replied.

"Let's all have a cup of tea in our tent at three o'clock, then
we'll make a plan," I suggested and both of them agreed; then
there was the sound of zips as they closed down their tents to
keep in the heat.

I stayed looking out for a few minutes longer. Conditions
were just right for movement, but it would be pointless to move
half a mile and then have to go through the long business of
putting up the tents all over again. Better wait until morning
and concentrate on an early start. Over to the left of our ridge
I could see where the seven-mile glacier curved up from behind
another ridge which ran along the far side of the valley with
the lake in it, to our front. The glacier appeared to be covered
with snow at the upper end, but unfortunately I couldn't see
how it joined the ice-cap itself because this was hidden by
another mountain spur. From our position there was no way of
knowing whether or not there was an ice-fall, such as we had
seen at the head of other glaciers around the ice-cap. We
wouldn't be able to see this until we got past 1189.

Over tea Richard insisted that there must be no repetition of
today's performance. He and I should recce a route ahead in the
morning, at least as far as 1189, about one and a half miles
along the ridge. If this was all right, then we should move up
with the loads on the day after that. While we were on the

recce, Krister and Marie Christine could bring the stores and fuel up from the camp we had just left.

This sounded a most sensible plan and it was quickly agreed. The far side of the ice-cap was about eleven miles south-east of our present position. We had food and fuel enough for about fourteen days. Given good weather the project appeared well within our grasp.

Richard told us that when he had first got into his tent and taken off his boots, he had found his left foot badly frozen and without any feeling. He said that it had taken a long time to thaw but that it was now all right. Then, because he had slept so badly on the previous night, he said he had taken some Piriton tablets, which although primarily for allergic infection and insect bites, do also in fact cause drowsiness. Now he was feeling sleepy and felt the best thing he could do would be to get into his sleeping-bag for a few hours if we would wake him for supper. This we did.

Next morning reveille was at five, for Richard, Marie Christine and me; Krister was allowed a lie-in as he was not on the recce, and because three was an easier number than four in our tent for breakfast. It was a still clear day with sun and blue sky. Much like the best days of Alpine skiing weather. Richard had slept well and seemed in good heart.

After breakfast we set to and packed our kit. We agreed to take Richard's tent in case of an emergency, as well as the usual personal equipment that would be needed if we got caught out for the night, owing to a sudden change in the weather. He decided to collapse his tent on his own, and while he gathered the pegs the aluminium pole slipped out of the tent entrance and shot off down the slope and into the valley like a runaway ski. We couldn't see it after it went over the lip of the drop some thirty yards to our front.

The immediate result of this incident was that Richard was very upset and described it as a 'death blow'. He became increasingly pessimistic about the outcome of our attempt on the ice-cap, and even constant reassurance that Krister and Marie Christine would go down and look for the pole as a first priority, failed to cheer him.

We left the camp together at seven o'clock and set off along the ridge, just as Krister was emerging from his tent for breakfast.

At first the going was level, then after a few hundred yards the ridge fell steeply into a saddle before climbing even more sharply up a hill on the other side. The snow was frozen hard and we made quite good time, yet nothing seemed capable of bringing Richard out of his depression. When we reached half-way up the far side of the saddle we gained a point from where we could see clearly down into the valley where Richard's tent pole had disappeared. We scanned the most likely places with the little Zeiss monocular but there was no sign of the pole and Richard became silent. Across on the other side of the saddle we could see the remaining tents, perched high on the tip of the slope, and about a hundred yards to their front the slope was split by the big blue grin of a crevasse. From here the snow peeled off and avalanched into the valley below, whenever the weight became too much for the angle of the slope. It was an awesome sight.

Progress up to the top of the hill on which we were standing was aided by the snow conditions, which allowed our toes to dig steps, while at the same time preventing our feet from sinking below the frozen crust. We were approaching the point where we would need to be wearing crampons and roped together.

I was leading on the hill and so I was the first to gain the summit and see what lay before us. "That's a tough one," I called to Richard who was just getting to the point where he could see the next problem. A moment or two passed.

"Scrub it," he said, the two words sounding a death sentence on a year's work.

A couple of minutes passed in silence while I studied the steep fall to another saddle, then a tricky-looking zigzag climb on the other side leading up to the pass between 1189 and the lesser hill to its north-east. To the left of the saddle the ground fell sharply away to another valley almost at sea level. To the right it fell a long way down to a lake surrounded by cliffs.

Richard got out his camera and started to take photographs of the way we had come. Another five minutes passed. It was the trickiest piece of ground I had ever thought of crossing . . . but I'd come a long way. "Well, I'd like to try it," I said slowly.

"I can't agree. It's out," replied Richard flatly.

A difficult situation had now arisen. It had to be dealt with carefully. There was no point in having a shouting match here.

I left my pack and walked along the top of the slope leading down to the narrow edge of the saddle far below. It had the same blue crevasse features on it as the slope below our tents. The saddle was scarcely wide enough for a man to walk across and the climb on the far side was fraught with avalanche possibilities. But I still felt it would be possible to get down and up both sides with ropes. The snow features were so large that I didn't think a man's weight would make a great deal of difference either way . . .

"I reckon there's only about half an hour's weather left," Richard interrupted my thoughts; he had followed me along the ridge to tell me that we should return to the others. He turned and set off back to pick up his pack.

I waited a few minutes longer and marked out a site for a camp above the saddle before following in Richard's steps to my own pack.

"I wouldn't follow anyone across that, let alone lead it," Richard said as I stood looking again across the obstacle.

"I understand that, Richard, I respect your advice, but I want to do this. It's important to me." I replied with what I hoped was a level voice.

"That's the difference, isn't it? I climb because I enjoy it. For you it's something different. Well, there's only one thing I can do now – that is to go down to the Indian camp and wait for you there." He looked across the saddle once more. "It's brave but it's foolish. You'll get young Krister to have a go, he'll have a go at anything." Then he turned and started off down the hill towards the two little red tents.

I stayed a few minutes, looking and thinking. The sun still eluded the clouds and I felt a kind of elation that was in tune with the sunshine. Here I stood where no man had ever been, where a thousand years was but a yesterday. Out from under the swaying fringe of pettifogging modern life I had crept, looking for a simple private challenge. I had found it.

When we reached the little camp, the only sign of the others was a double set of footprints leading back in the direction of the cairns. We decided to follow them, first leaving off our packs; it was only nine-thirty and we had to keep warm somehow. The other two had put out the red markers every hundred paces or so, and as soon as we reached the top of the hill behind the camp, it was obvious from there that Krister and Marie Christine had gone off to look for the tent pole.

"We could get the stuff from the cairns," I suggested hopefully.

"Yes, I think we could manage it all in one load," Richard replied.

On our way back we saw the others coming back up from the valley. Krister held up the pole in triumph, and it glinted in the sun like some sacred olympic javelin.

"There's been a major disagreement on the next move," I said when we all met up on the ridge. "The best thing is to get back to our tent and all have a cup of tea together and discuss it." Everyone nodded rather tensely. Krister helped Richard put his tent up while Marie Christine made the tea. Soon we were all in our tent, Krister and Richard at the entrance end, Marie Christine and me at the other, with the mugs of steaming tea to warm us.

"Te dit Te de," Krister hummed a Swedish trumpet voluntary as he handed round pieces of mint cake he had hoarded. "Today is my sister Barbara's name day."

We all cheered and this did a lot to relieve the tension. Krister is nobody's fool.

"Well, the situation is simple. There's a very tricky saddle up there before you get to 1189. Richard says 'No' and I say 'Yes'. Richard feels he must go down the mountain and leave it to us."

I stopped talking and looked at the others. Nobody wanted to start.

"So if Richard goes down on his own in the morning, we three can get our kit together and have a go. I have marked out a camp site just above the saddle," I offered hopefully.

Marie Christine had clearly decided to keep quiet, but Krister came in and tried to keep the four of us together. I joined him and together we did our best to persuade Richard, for half an hour or more. Bit by bit, with the tea and the chat, Richard thawed out and admitted that he felt groggy and claustrophobic. The exposed position on the ridge, the emptiness of it all was upsetting him badly.

"I feel that if I stay up here, I may throw a real wobbler," he said. "The isolation and nervous strain of the whole show. It affects me far more than I ever would have thought."

There was no point in discussing the matter further. There was no bitterness, rather it was as if one of us had gone sick and was going to miss the best part of the trip. Richard went off to his tent for a sleep and the three of us planned our move forward. We'd go three in our tent, eighteen days rations, thirty refills of fuel for the cookers from the two outboard tanks. We cut our own weight down: Marie Christine cutting the handle off her beloved hair brush and sending the hot-water bottle down with Richard. I put my shaving kit in her wash bag and sent my own battered leather wash bag down with Richard too. I cut the three hundred-foot length of Kernmantel rope in half and rejected those pieces of climbing hardware that neither Krister nor I were familiar with.

At supper Richard was still determined to go down. He gave us the medical kit and the repair set for the cooker. Then he went off back to his tent with an old copy of *Time* magazine, the cover of which featured the wives of the two candidates for the U.S. Presidency, Nixon and McGovern, one of whom would by now have been elected. Krister stayed in our tent as a trial, he was in the middle with his head at the entrance end, Marie Christine and I were on either side with our heads at the other end.

There was a thaw, the wind veered to the north with a bit of east, and it started to whistle along the front of the reef of rock which had previously acted as our shelter. Now it hit the tents broadside. The floor had become a skating rink, and we three found ourselves hard pressed away from the wind. There was danger of the tents blowing down as the wind increased. The spectre of hurtling over the edge in a collapsed tent returned.

At two o'clock I heard Richard's voice like a raven's croak. "Is anyone there?"

"Yes, what's up?" I replied.

"All my pegs are out on the windward side. The snow's melted off the valances. I'll have to go out and fix it," he called again.

"Give us a yell if anything goes wrong," I shouted. There was no reply.

At three o'clock our tent collapsed at the entrance end. Krister and I groped about in the dark, finding the pin from the top of the tent pole which had broken off at the weld. The main worry was that our boots and waterproofs which were just inside the flysheet might blow away in the wind and disappear into the abyss. It was a bad spot to be in without boots and waterproofs. I hoped the wind wouldn't get stronger.

At four o'clock the light came. From somewhere in the rocks a startled bird set off a desperate trilling that sounded just as if someone had a radio full on and was winding the tuning knob up and down the wave band. Richard replied to my call. Still okay. I suggested we might get up and have breakfast, but there was no enthusiasm. The wind howled like a banshee through the tent.

At five o'clock our tent collapsed again. We managed to fix it and in doing so, Krister woke up enough to go along with the idea of getting up and having breakfast. Across at the other tent I could see Richard's back in a sitting position, holding the tent up from the inside in lieu of tent pegs.

At six o'clock it was tea and porridge for four. It had been 'just one of those nights'. I wondered if mountain tents really were the thing for the Patagonian Andes. Shipton's tents seemed to have been much heavier. I remembered the only previous time when I had been in this 'other world', on arctic trials with the Parachute Regiment near Hudson's Bay, Canada. Eighty-three degrees of frost Fahrenheit with the wind chill included. We'd had heavier tents there too.

We packed up most carefully. I sat in the tent to hold it down while the pegs were removed. We weren't going to let anything blow down the hill.

Richard had had an appalling night, he was packed and ready to go at eight-fifteen. It was a pretty tense farewell. He was going to wait four weeks at the Indian camp; if we didn't show up he would set off for home.

As he turned to go, he reminded Krister of their days together on the kibbutz. "If you don't show up on 4th January, Kris, I'll see you at the RV in the great banana field up there!" he said, nodding at the sky.

Marie Christine choked back her tears and said nothing about Rebecca, our small daughter. Suddenly he was gone. It was too cold to stand for more than a few seconds. We bent to the job of getting ready to move. Each with his own thoughts.

We were away at eight-thirty and within twenty minutes we

had to stop and repack Marie Christine's load, distributing six days' rations between Krister and myself. It was just too heavy for her to carry.

When we struggled up to the top of the hill overlooking the obstacle, it looked a lot less friendly than on the day before. Without the sparkle of the sun, it was easier to see in flat black and white. Marie Christine was silent while we all stood and looked but eventually it was she who broke the silence. "I'd rather put a pistol to my head – I'm sorry, Johnny," she said through her tears.

"Bloody hell!" I muttered through clenched teeth, all the tension of the past few days coming to the surface. I dropped my pack and stamped off down the ridge to look for a way round – and promptly fell into a snowdrift up to my waist. Krister stood by looking upset.

We couldn't possibly leave Marie Christine on the ridge alone. The saddle was out. Even my second line down the spur moving north-east was out because we couldn't see enough of it past the blue grins of the ice-fall.

"You know, I would give it a go," said Krister thoughtfully when I rejoined them by the packs. "It would be difficult, but I think it could be done. But it isn't any good going down this side with Marie Christine in case we get stuck and can't get up again."

"Why don't we go down to the Indian camp and try to get up the glacier?" asked Marie Christine.

"Well, we'll have to go down now anyway. I don't know about the glacier, we're running out of time and rations now," I replied miserably, picking up my pack and setting off back towards the Indian camp.

It was already ten o'clock and we had a long day ahead of us with heavy loads. By this time Richard was well on his way. He was carrying an extremely heavy load and had to stop fairly regularly. When he reached the cairns and began the descent of the cliff he noticed a pair of condors circling above him; they had never seen a lone man staggering along the top of the cliff before. Soon there were five condors, giant birds whose wing span stretched ten feet or more between the long feathers at each wing-tip. When Richard stopped for a few moments rest they took this as a sign of weakening and came in close, their feet hanging loose beneath them with talons ready to tear at the corpse. When the descent became especially steep, Richard decided to use his 150-foot coil of rope to lower his pack, and then to abseil down himself. The condors seemed to regard the rope as trailing entrails: they crowded in, snapping at one another in the air, in their eagerness to get at the dying flesh.

Perhaps it was the sense of competition produced by the presence of five birds, maybe it was only their natural behaviour, but they decided there was no need to wait for the crippled beast to actually die. Richard sat on his pack feeling more alone than he had ever felt in his life. His friends were miles away and going in the opposite direction, home was on the other side of the world, he spoke no Spanish and the nearest human several weeks away would speak no English. The great vultures were not even going to wait for him to die. Closer and closer they came, ugly bald heads turned in to stare coldly, assessing the meat. Suddenly he began to fight back, leaping to his feet he screamed abuse and waved his arms to show he was very much alive and kicking. He threw rocks, but the birds were too agile to be hit. Nevertheless they sheered off to a respectable distance while he continued his descent. Once in the trees they gave up, for by then there were three more tottering beasts high up on the side of the cliff and they were moving much more slowly than the man who travelled alone.

By the time we finally reached the trees ourselves, Richard had had a sleep and worked out a way of fuelling an outboard using the gear oil can in place of a regular fuel tank. He thought he was going crackers when he heard our voices. When we actually appeared, it was as if a great burden were replaced on his shoulders – for he knew we would want to try and go up another way and he knew we would want him to come with us as he was the only experienced climber among us. He also knew he had seen enough up there to know it wasn't for him.

That night I slept well, it had been a long time since I had really slept but at about two in the morning I was suddenly wide awake. Outside someone was digging. I felt the groundsheet of the tent; underneath was the unmistakable roughness of twigs and leaves. Smiling to myself, I rolled closer to the sleeping warmth of my wife and went back to sleep. There was no need to worry tonight, the tent was not blowing down and there could be no one digging the snow on to his tent valance outside.

We had breakfast for four in our tent next morning. Krister and I tried to persuade Richard to come with us on a three-man assault on the ice-cap using the glacier as the approach.

"Oh! Look," he replied, "it's like getting a reprieve from the electric chair and then being sent back again." His face looked haunted, almost tortured, but in the end he agreed to see Krister and myself through the glacier and up to the edge of the ice-cap. We were delighted, hoping he would warm to the idea as we got on with the planning.

"I woke up in the middle of the night thinking I was back up on the ridge again. I even thought I could hear digging," I laughed, trying to comfort Richard with the thought that we all felt the same dread of the place.

"I woke up lathered in sweat," was all he said.

We agreed that the three men would go up the glacier river that afternoon by boat and climb up on to a good place from where we could make a visual choice of which side of the glacier would be the best for us to go up the following day. Marie Christine was to stay in the Base Camp at the foot of the glacier on her own. This was a decision I did not reach lightly.

Richard and Krister went off to their tents to get ready for the trip up the glacier river, I had a look at the pile of equipment to decide what to take.

"Hey, John, come and look at this!" shouted Richard, his voice hoarse with excitement. I ran through the trees to his tent.

"Look! Digging – it must have been me **you heard!**" There all around the entrance to his tent the ground was scarred where the shovel had been stabbed into it. We looked at each other and shrugged. The heat was on.

12

Innocents on Ice

THE GLACIER RIVER was shallower than we thought. The fine chalk-like powder from the melted ice gave the water the appearance of slurry, we couldn't see down through it from the little Avon dinghy. Although the boat only sat three or four inches down in the water, the Seagull outboard had to be rather deeper to get a grip for its propeller, one sharp tap on a rock from the whirling blades and the shear spring would break, leaving us at the mercy of the racing current.

We rounded a bend and inched slowly up against some rapids, the noise of which must have helped to drown the sound from our engine.

"Look, a huemul – over there on the bank," Krister tapped my arm and pointed across the river. A dun-coloured animal about the size of a fat calf stood staring at us in amazement, it was our first sight of the elusive deer so rarely seen even by the natives of Patagonia. We drew nearer and it took fright, melting into the forest behind.

The river grew narrow and the current so powerful that we could only go against it by using full throttle on the motor. Ahead and all around us the water erupted in great boils where it was forced up from underwater obstructions. Once again we were worried the propeller might foul the rocks, so Krister and Richard kept testing the depth with their paddles, striking a rock every so often but never shallow enough to make me cut the motor.

At last we reached some rapids too powerful for our engine, where the river thundered through a cleft in the cliffs only twenty yards wide, then turned at right angles from the pool below. We motored into a small bay in the cliff itself and from there we managed to scramble up through some bushes to the grassy plain beyond. The ground here was a mass of huemul

slots and some of these led up towards a small hill which overlooked the foot of the glacier, it looked to be just the observation
point we needed. The sun came out and the wind eased.

We found a gently sloping slab of rock with a good view over
the tops of the Nothofagus trees. Spread out before us was the
lower half of the glacier; the upper half was obscured by cloud,
and in any case it turned to the right behind the shoulder of a
mountain at about the height of the cloud base. There was a
lake of milky water and icebergs at the bottom, where several
fish were dimpling the surface in pursuit of the afternoon
hatch of fly.

The margin of the lake was hard to define because much of
the ice was covered by gravel. Sharply pointed towers of ice
marching inexorably shoulder to shoulder towards the water at
the foot of the glacier, and now and then a creaking groan was
followed by a grumbling roar as one of these ice soldiers broke
from the serried ranks and splashed into the water.

While there was clearly no chance of our simply walking up
the middle of the glacier, there looked to be a good track of
gravel running up the northern or left-hand side of the river of
ice. Studied through the monocular, this route appeared very
much more comfortable than the ridge we had been on for the
past five days. Even Richard cheered up a little at the sight; we
decided we had seen enough to justify an attempt on the
following day, so we just lay back on the sun-warmed rock and
relaxed for half an hour. The view was wonderful and so was the
sun, but I couldn't help thinking it would have seemed a lot
better if we had just come down from a successful crossing of
the ice-cap.

We motored home without incident, collecting some more
berries for Marie Christine along the way. On balance it
seemed the best thing was to leave the Base Camp at its present
location; rather than carry out the original idea of boating up
the black river into Lago Munoz Gamero, and there setting up
a new camp by the lake, near to the glacier.

We had another bad night. Marie Christine woke up screaming and I sat up tearing at the zip of my sleeping-bag, convinced that we were back up on the ridge and the tent was
slipping down the slope on the snow. At breakfast next morning
even Krister admitted to a bad night of worry about the ice-cap.

Richard was silent, and I could tell he had lost any enthusiasm for the attempt which he might have gained at the observation point on the day before. The weather was hopeless with a gale raging across the bay beyond the trees of our camp; the two men went back to their tents to wait for an improvement but it looked as if any start was out for the day.

During the morning I tried to puzzle out the course of action most likely to result in the ice-cap actually getting crossed; at lunch when the others came into our tent, I stated my case to Richard.

"I've been thinking . . . it seems to me," I started lamely, "that the best plan is really for Krister and me to have a go on our own," I blurted out.

"That's what I've been thinking all morning – the dread of having to go up again. With me in this frame of mind, I'm hardly going to be optimistic," he replied calmly.

"What do you think, Krister?" I looked at the gentle Swede, sitting hunched up at the end of the tent.

"Well, it's a pity Richard doesn't want to come because we don't know what to do on the ice. But then this tent is more suitable for two. I think you and me go up and give it a spin," he said quietly.

"Okay. And leave the Base Camp here with Richard and Marie Christine?" I asked.

"Yes, I think so."

We decided to give up any thought of moving until next day, the valances of the tents were piled deep with hailstones which had filtered down through the trees.

It was still too windy next morning, but we packed sixteen days' rations and ate a huge lunch of curry with treble portion of biscuits and canned butter. A hurried goodbye to Marie Christine, leaving a lot unsaid, and then Krister and I pushed off in the little Avon. Within a few minutes the camp was lost to sight and I felt very homesick. Marie Christine and Richard would wait three weeks; if we weren't back by then, they would be so short of food that they would have to start for home with the other boat and motor.

We left our boat upside down and securely tied to a couple of trees near to but on the other side of the river from where we had left it on our visit to the observation point. The large smooth boulders were slippery and our heavy packs made it hard going through the small trees which grew in the bed of the old glacier. When eventually we came to the mountain between us and the northern bank of the glacier, we reaped the benefit of the extra large lunch and reached the saddle in just over an hour. It was only four o'clock and our goal looked deceptively close; we talked of pressing on up the side of the glacier and making camp for the night at a waterfall a couple of miles up.

But first we had to get down the mountain.

It took us an hour and a half to get down through the worst section of bushes and undergrowth we had encountered on the entire expedition. The bushes were to a height of ten to fifteen feet and they grew at an angle to the hillside, dictated by the prevailing wind and gravity. Our progress was slow, very slow. We took turns at leading and the swearing that went with leading. The bushes were so thick on the side of the mountain that we had to walk on them rather than the ground; every so often they gave way under the leader and he pitched forward, usually ending upside down in a hole or natural ditch. There the weight of his pack pinned him in that position, with feet waving impatiently at the sky. The other fellow was always too far back and too preoccupied with his own plight to make any useful contribution to the rescue. Only frantic work with the arms and much wriggling of the body brought everything to the same level, from which position the scramble could begin again.

When we finally emerged from the bushes sweating and cursing, it was on to a barrier of moraine some three-quarters of a mile in width. This had been deposited by the glacier, which had thus blocked itself off from the lake, Munoz Gamero, leaving an exit only round the other side of the mountain by means of the glacier river. This fertile barrier was covered with a number of small lakes, each surrounded by Nothofagus forest. The surface of the lakes was calm and thousands of small fish were rising for the midges, creating patterns of rings like heavy raindrops. Krister was leading and he found and followed the game trails through the low bushes which clung to the ground near the glacier. After a few hundred yards he stumbled to a halt, when a startled huemul fawn broke from cover right at his feet and then tottered ahead of him along the trail. It seemed frightened but all the same it didn't run far up the trail and we were able to walk right up to it. Krister sternly warned me not to touch its head lest, as the result of the human smell, its mother should desert it.

From where we stood we could see another place where the map was inaccurate. It was fortunate we had not chosen to go up the southern side of the glacier, because a long figure-of-eight-shaped lake flowed directly into the glacier lake on that side. What appeared as a river running into the ice of the glacier on the map, was in fact an impassable lake; we would have had to follow the lake's southern shore all the way until we came to the valley leading up to our old friend Hill 1189.

We camped for the night near the foot of the glacier, beside one of the little lakes on the moraine between the glacier and Lago Munoz Gamero. Marie Christine was sadly missed at supper: the dehydrated boeuf Stroganoff plus mushroom soup and farmhouse stew emerged as a curious dish. Plans were immediately laid to prohibit any such meal from being cooked again during the new ice-cap partnership. After swallowing the lumps like a boa-constrictor, I washed up (this indicates that I was not the cook!) and then went for a little walk up to a hillock overlooking the glacier. A pair of geese drummed down on to our lake but otherwise all was calm in the early dusk. The silent peace contrasted so much with the usual clamour of storm in this place, it provoked a time to think of many things.

I was cooking breakfast next morning so I got up at five-forty-five and took extra care that Krister would have no chance to complain about my cold porridge oats and tea. I practically polished each flake.

We set off in baking sun through the tumbled boulders and clinging bushes, sticking to the game trails where possible, making our own trails where necessary. The sweat poured off us and every time we stopped for breath, the flies gathered round. As we began the steady climb up along the side of the glacier, we came to an area of huge boulders all covered with a glorious golden rust of moss, then soon after that we found ourselves clambering across numerous rock falls. This was rather hazardous as the great chunks of rock were so delicately balanced on one another that at any moment they might tumble and so set off another avalanche above us. Occasionally we spotted little black birds about the size of a wren, which seemed to be nesting among the boulders; they hopped about on the rocks but seldom flew more than a few yards. There were some lovely rock chippings of different hues and textures, sometimes I'd pick one up to take home, but usually I'd drop it again within a minute or two; anxious not to increase my load.

Our route was clearly the regular path for both huemul and puma for we found ample evidence of their passage; somewhere up ahead there must be more than just rock and ice.

It was a long hard morning and by midday we had only just reached the place where we had suggested camping for the night before but that was when we had still been high up on the saddle above the awful bushes. Now we crossed a stream and emerged on to some flattish ground well above the glacier; on the left, to our horror, we saw a lake. This was not on the map, could it be that we were walking along a peninsula that would end in the glacier ice? We plodded on, the packs growing heavier by the minute. Surely we deserved some luck after all the setbacks?

"Oh hell! That's it, I'm afraid," I grimaced at Krister and he looked up at the sky for some deliverance. But all he got was the first smatterings of rain. Ahead the land ended in an ice cliff, the edge of the glacier itself. The only way forward was to retrace our steps and go round the landward shore of the lake.

Disconsolate we reached the stream again and decided to have lunch under a big overhanging boulder on an island in midstream. The rain came on heavier and heavier. Krister cut his cheese into tiny pieces and laid them in formation on his biscuits, he claimed they couldn't stick to his palate using this method. After eating his non-palate-sticking lunch he fell asleep. I felt rotten, the ice-cap seemed a thousand miles away and the rain was coming down in stair-rods. We must get on or we would just get bogged down where we were.

Out into the rain we went, sloshing along in the orange suits, our boots filling up with water as we struggled through the dripping moss at the margin of the lake. The sides were steep and in many places the bank had recently subsided into the water, with the result that there were trees and bushes floating among the pancakes of ice. Far above us and to our left a waterfall plunged down the mountain in a ribbon of white growing ever broader as it neared the lake. The wind was rising from the north-west once again and it slanted the rain against

Lunchbreak

The ice-fall – on the way up at last

our backs. All the icebergs, excluding those aground, had been blown to the north-western end of the lake by the balmy east wind of the morning sun, now they sailed like an armada back towards the east.

Luckily for me, Krister was quite cheerful after his little doze by the stream at lunch time, and he helped to keep me going until we reached the end of the lake. We put up our tent by the stream from the waterfall which we had seen on our way; then we crawled into our sleeping-bags, ate five biscuits and some cheese each and slept for a couple of hours. When I awoke it was with the kind of head pains which I knew come from dehydration; we had lost a lot of sweat in the morning and had nothing to drink. In heavy rain the ice-cold water from the stream had seemed unattractive at lunch time. While I waited for the cooker to heat the water I was filled with the gloomiest of thoughts. Damp and shivery, I felt horribly uncomfortable: that sort of suspended feeling when the only hope is that it will end. Krister snoozed on and so there wasn't even him to talk to, it wasn't fair to wake him until the supper was ready. The rain and wind beat away at the little tent. I tried thinking of the three principles of Ardmore: self-reliance, positive thinking and leaving things better than you found them. This at least made me smile, the living antithesis of all three.

After a big supper of curry with garlic and Marjoram washed down with a pint and a half of cocoa each, the world didn't seem such a bad place after all. We took care of the dehydration with a drink of salt and water as well. Outside the rain eased enough to let us get out for a good wash in the stream. All around our tent was the feeding ground for the huemul whose tracks we had seen on the way up; the geese and duck on the lake were the quarry of puma and fox. Across on the opposite side of the lake from the tent, the bank was three hundred yards of glacier ice cliff which occasionally avalanched into the lake. It appeared as if the glacier had originally formed the depression in which the lake lay, and then retreated, damming up one side. It was just a pity it wasn't on the map.

Next morning dawned cloudy but fine, Krister made a splendid breakfast at five-fifteen and we were on the move by eight o'clock. We both felt pretty fit and despite a lot of scrambling over the rocky lower slopes of the glacier valley, we were rather pleased with progress when we stopped for a rest at ten o'clock. We were sitting about three hundred feet above the glacier on a spur which ran down from the north. The Kendal Mint Cake (K.M.C.) tasted good; we could see well up the valley and it seemed a good time to plan our route to the ice-fall at the head of the glacier which was now some five miles away.

"I don't suppose we could try the ice," I mentioned casually, not really considering it seriously, after a lengthy discussion about the relative values of high- and low-level routes round the outside curve of the glacier.

"Well, it certainly would be days quicker," Krister replied half-heartedly.

"Tell you what then, let's go down and give it a spin. If we don't like it we can always get back on terra firma," I said brightly and so we got up and made for the glacier. Krister led the way down the ice and I could see him hefting Richard's ice axe with renewed interest; for ice axes, crampons and prussi-kers were completely new to us both. I tried to reassure myself with the thought that originally, before there were experts and handbooks on this sort of thing, someone had had to creep out on to the ice, and armed only with common sense, that someone had survived to tell the tale of how he did it. Along the way had come various inventions, four of which we now had (if you include the rope). Otherwise we were in the same position as that first pioneer. Richard would have been a great help, but the experience would be all the more rewarding if we made it on our own.

The last couple of hundred feet down to the edge of the ice was very steep, with crumbling brown rock and dust preceding us in powdery shoots. We were descending into a tight V for the ice rose just as steeply, although in something of a grey curve, up on to the top of the glacier. It took us fifty-five minutes to fit the crampons on to our boots, tie the rope round our waists and over our shoulders in the correct manner, and adjust the prussikers in readiness for use if one of us should fall down a crevasse. A lot of thought and a bit of adjustment went into this. Richard had shown us how to use the three prussik loops to climb up a vertical rope; the demonstration had been compre-hensive but brief and the sight of him hanging down from the branch of a tree in the Indian camp seemed far removed from the blue crevasses ahead of us.

I slid the sun visor over my face and the world went a little darker. Ice axe at the ready I took my first hesitant steps on the steep wall of dirty ice; to my great surprise the spiky crampons held me to the surface as if I were walking on flypaper. Up and up I strode. Krister followed twenty paces behind on the scarlet rope, several coils ready in his hand to belay round his ice axe if I should suddenly disappear into an abyss.

"This is grand!" I laughed, as we gained the smooth hard back of the glacier.

"Far easier than those rock avalanches," agreed Krister, peering through his goggles. Ahead, stretching like a gigantic airfield runway, the smooth river of ice stretched towards the ice-cap. There seemed to be nothing to it. The black rock buttresses in the ice-fall seemed no distance away, we'd soon be there. 'Grand oh, perfectly grand. A new dimension. What have I been doing all my life?' Such were my thoughts as I set a cracking pace up the gentle incline.

Lunch was eleven biscuits and eight Kraft cheese slices each, eaten squatting on our packs on the central spine of the glacier. We were on a smooth path which led through some badly twisted minarets of ice on either side. The rock buttress still looked very close – but no closer. Krister took the lead and as the afternoon wore on the spells of leading between breaks, narrowed from three-quarters of an hour to ten minutes. The ice opened up into deep but narrow crevasses for about half a mile; we approached the first few rather timidly, but soon we felt able to jump them quite freely, secure in the knowledge that the man at the back was ready to make a belay if the worst came to the worst.

Quite suddenly we reached the point where the ice became covered with snow, the crevasses were no longer visible but luckily the snow bridges held us without difficulty. It was in the soft snow that we found the going so difficult that we needed a break every ten minutes; deeper and deeper it became until at every step we seemed to sink to our knees in the stuff. The rock buttress in the ice-fall always looked only a few hundred yards away. The weather imperceptibly changed for the worse.

At half past three we decided to put the tent up on the

sheltered side of what appeared to be a large, low snow dune; we were just out of avalanche distance of the ice-fall by the rock buttress. It took us two hours to dig a level platform in the snow and erect our tiny dot of tent orange in that huge white waste-land, and by the time we had eaten and washed it was ten o'clock at night. Avalanches crashed down the ice-fall night and day, the greatest concentration I recorded was three in one minute. The cloud had been too low all day for us to see the top of the ice-fall and in spite of the ground covered we were far from relaxed as we turned in for the night. We were really feeling our inexperience.

Our first night on the ice was not very comfortable; we could almost feel our precious warmth leaking out through the ground sheet beneath us. Still, at least we weren't perched on the edge of an avalanche as we had been up on the ridge below 1189 – a camp now considerably farther from the ice-cap than was this one.

Early next morning, when we poked our heads out of the tent for the first time, the weather was calm and bright but the cloud base was right down and we couldn't see up the ice-fall any distance at all. There was nothing for it but to lie in our sleeping-bags and wait for the cloud to clear enough for us at least to see what we were doing.

Perhaps now for the first time we began to realise that for us the world had shrunk to just two people and a lot of snow. Previously we had either been on the move or too exhausted to think of much more than our discomfort and sleep. Two people was the wong number for the job in hand; if one of us fell down a crevasse and became unconscious there was no certainty that the other could pull him out. If one of us fell sick or was badly injured, the other couldn't carry him as well as the necessities of life in this cold wilderness. With three the situation would have been quite different, but we didn't have three. Life is short, opportunities must be grasped or let pass for ever. Krister and I had taken the opportunity and now we relied upon each other like brothers. The tiny patch of shelter under the orange tent was all there was. We had no communication with anyone else. Because of this, I found myself looking at the tall Swede through different eyes. I had admired the skilful way he had handled the boat out on the Pacific coast, his attention to detail, the high standard of personal pride he showed in his clothing and equipment. Now I found he was deeply considerate as well, being with him was a lot of fun because he never let things get him down. When we disagreed in the heat of a crisis, he was able to convey his feelings through a cheerful silence, instead of the sulking ill humour to which so many people, including myself, are prone to succumb. As an instructor at Ardmore he had worked hard on the three principles: self-reliance, positive thinking and leaving people and things better than you found them. Sadly I could see that he was able to interpret all three rather better than me, with the result that every minute of the day became an unspoken challenge for me to reach his standard. Win or lose I felt I was in for one of those priceless experiences in life, which in spite of all the cynicism still exist in plenty, but which just can't be bought.

13

Ice-Fall

AT ELEVEN O'CLOCK in the morning the grey cloud began to rise up the tumbled blue and white face of the ice-fall. The next act was about to begin.

Our tent was pitched on a rolling white plain of deep soft snow; the top of the glacier. To our front lay the ice-falls, two to our left and several more to our right; they were our only means of ascent to the ice-cap above. These ice-falls were bordered by buttresses of black rock jutting out from under the ice-cap itself; around and in some cases over these spurs, the ice-cap squeezed its surplus ice. The rock faces were unstable and frequent avalanches of crumbled rock ruled out our access to the ice-cap by this means.

The most obvious route was surely the shortest, the foot of the nearest ice-fall to our front was only about three hundred yards from the tent, perhaps fifteen minutes of strenuous walking through knee-deep snow. At one o'clock we set off with everything on our backs, in bright sunshine. The eight hundred to a thousand feet of ice-fall seemed not too great after all, and the thunder of the avalanches must not be allowed to put us off.

An hour later when we were well up an almost vertical snow slope and nearing the first of the crevasses, I noticed that I was missing the crampons on my left boot. With a sinking feeling in the pit of my stomach I called to Krister, who was leading, to stop. I suddenly felt naked, with only one crampon I would be like a stranded whale when we reached the ice. There was nothing for it but to go all the way back down again searching each left footstep for the missing spikes. I left Krister sitting on his pack and taking the opportunity to rub on still more glacier cream on the exposed skin around his balaclava and goggles.

Going down was easy without a pack and after a few paces I could see the difference between my right spiked footprint and my bald left boot-mark. A bit of Sherlock Holmes work led me to the conclusion that I could run down the slope and, as long as I could see the boot-mark I would know I hadn't yet reached where the crampon might lie hidden in the snow. I was almost back at the camp site when I saw the black nylon straps among our footprints. I had found it. Way up above, Krister responded to my triumphant brandishings with a happy wave and I started the long plod back feeling as if I had been reprieved. 'If I had taken the trouble to put the thing on properly in the first place, instead of goading Krister for his slowness we would have been well on our way by now,' I thought to myself.

By the time I rejoined Krister and my pack, I was in need of a rest and a piece of K.M.C. The mint refreshed me quickly as I refitted the crampon.

"The sun is going to burn us badly, I think we should put some of this biscuit wrapper under our goggles to protect our noses," Krister suggested, fitting the familiar blue plastic paper like a false beak on his nose. The glare was tremendous off the snow and I could feel the beginnings of sunburn, so I followed suit. We looked like creatures from outer space, it was a grand advertisement for Mackay's of Santiago – if there had been anyone there to see it.

We set off again and the slope soon became so steep we found ourselves slipping down on our stomachs in spite of the crampons. We were glad to be roped together; if we once really got going down it was a long way, and it was hard to see how we could escape injury or worse.

We reached the jumbled ice block safely at last. From the tent we had plotted a route which looked as if it might take us up to the top, without having to cross any really long crevasse.

Now we began to grope our way up. The leader firmly belayed to the follower's ice axe which was jammed right down in the snow. The scarlet rope was paid out by the follower as the leader inched forward, probing deep with the handle of his own ice axe. Right and left were yawning crevasses, whose blue depths appeared bottomless. The blocks were huge, and pieces the size of a house were frozen at crazy angles, ready to crash down when avalanche tremors or movement of the fall itself shattered the ice at their bases. We wove our way through and up, choosing the snow bridges to cross crevasses. More than once the bridge seemed firm enough to the probe of the ice axe, then as the leader moved cautiously across it would collapse. Quite suddenly he would find himself up to his armpits, his heart beating a little faster as he tried to wriggle clear without collapsing the rest of the bridge. It was tiring work.

We were about a quarter of the way up to the smooth lip at the top of the ice-fall, when we reached a crevasse some fifteen yards wide which ran right across the route we had planned from the tent. This huge crack had been in dead ground from below and so was out of sight from the tent. We walked along the side of the crevasse, there was no way down and up the other side because the sides were sheer and the bottom was out of sight in the blue haze below. At either end the crevasse simply ended in a cliff of ice.

"There's no way round here," I called from under my biscuit wrapper to Krister, who was behind me.

"No, it's too late to try another way. We must go down and try somewhere else tomorrow," his voice was full of disappointment.

"Okay, perhaps it was too much to expect anyway – after the progress we made yesterday," I said, trying to sound cheerful.

We got down quick enough, dancing in great strides through the deep snow once we were past the crevasses. Once on the snow plain at the bottom we turned right to walk towards the sheer rock wall which formed the eastern side of the glacier valley. About three hundred yards in from the corner, where the ice-fall was bounded by this rock wall, there was a sharp fang of dark brown rock which jutted out through the ice-fall itself; it looked as if we might get up along the side of this spur; the snow looked smooth enough, but some brown powdery stains across the route told of rock-falls.

In spite of our late start I found the tramp across the snow plain very tiring. My extra weight seemed to make me sink to my knees in places where Krister only went down to his ankles. Even when I was not leading, but simply placing my feet in the blue prints he made, I still found I sank through them. When in the lead I tried all manner of ways to keep going, from counting the paces of my left foot and always promising myself to give up at the next hundred, to thinking of places and things far away, like fitting out the new yacht I had ordered for Ardmore. At four o'clock we called a halt, knowing full well that it would take at least an hour and a half to get the tent up in a pre-dug space of ten feet by twelve feet by three feet.

It was already eight o'clock by the time we had finished our mince supper and washed away dehydration with a pint of cold cocoa each. Cooking took much longer now we had to melt snow, and iced cocoa seemed a good way of speeding up the drink . . . until after we'd had it and felt iced ourselves. We found the best way to make water was to fill the saucepan with snow, put the heater under it and keep jabbing through the snow with a spoon until it melted. At least the extra use of the cooker meant noise and heat, the noise almost masking the thunder of the avalanches outside. We managed to get a good wash in a quarter pint of water each, but shaving was becoming painful as the sun began to burn up our faces. Krister suffered badly where the sun had got him around the neck and he found any movement of his head uncomfortable.

Next morning we were up bright and early at five o'clock. I made a good breakfast of cold oats, baby's powdered milk, sugar and water. We washed down this elegant quasi-muesli with hot sweet tea. It was calm and sunny, conditions were just right for the ascent. Krister's sunburn was causing him a lot of pain but he kept it to himself. Today we were going to make it.

I led the way as soon as we had the tent down and had fitted the crampons and ropes, at Krister's pace this time. Perhaps it was the depth of snow which made me change my mind after fifty yards towards the rock spur, maybe it was fear. Anyway, I stopped and told Krister I saw a better way up through the ice-fall itself, without having to go right across the bottom of the spur. He said nothing and followed on. Soon he took over the lead, and we moved much faster up towards the crevasses.

The avalanches continued thick and strong, just as they had all night; the sound was something between an express train crashing and a coal lorry tipping its load over a cliff. Most of the avalanches came from farther to our right but frequently a whole section of the top of the ice-fall would peel away and rumble down on the huge blocks below. There had been some disturbance of the snow within fifty yards of our tent when we first looked round that morning.

My route went quite well, and it really looked as if we might be able to pick our way up and through, until we reached a steep snow slope running along the right-hand side of the brown rock spur. From there it would just be a question of whether or not we could get up the slope before the next rock fall came down. We took turns at the front with a thirty-foot length of rope leading back to ten coils of safety rope held in the left hand of the follower. Again we reached a point of no return, but this time we were not as easily put off; it was only ten o'clock in the morning and the weather still held fair, although it was thickening up over the mountains away to the north-west.

I led a traverse across in the direction of the rock spur, carefully threading our way through a maze of great tilted slabs of ice. Our path lay over a rubble of smaller ice blocks, the debris of previous avalanches. Slowly but surely we edged along, I found the whole performance becoming more and more of a nervous strain; the concentration required to probe the snow bridges and assess their strength began to make my legs tremble. Several times I fell through to my armpits, once the only escape was a forward roll down a steep slope.

During a break, when we were seated together on a sharp triangular block, with a flat enough top but crevasse sides, we saw a rock avalanche come down from the top of the valley wall near by. Most of the rocks came to a halt in a gully only a quarter of the way down; but one lump about half the size of a car vaulted this barrier and curved out into space. It seemed like we were watching something in slow motion, the rock fell smooth and noiseless, well clear of the wall. It hit the snow with a giant plume of snow like a whale's spout. Seconds later came the blubbery thump of impact. I looked across at Krister.

"Look, scouse, d'you want to have a go at leading this?"

"No thank you, you go on," he grinned softly.

"Well, look I'm bloody shattered, my nerves are in knots. If you don't want to lead I suggest we go down again and put up the tent. The weather's going."

"Okay, I'll lead back," he said simply.

Back we went. All that probing and balancing and leaping and collapsing all over again. Then we were back at square one putting the tent up again.

"There's only that ugly corner left now – what do you think?"

I asked. There was no reply. "Did you hear me? Why don't you say something," I said peevishly.

"I think it looks bad. So why say – it only makes it worse," he said quietly and pushed his ice axe deep into the snow as a peg for a guy rope. The first flakes of snow were falling and the tent was up.

"Well, that's all that's left – do you want to go up?" I asked rather irritably.

"Okay – so long as we don't hang about in the cocoa?"

"What cocoa?" My nerves still jangled. What the hell was he on about?

"Those brown streaks in the snow where the rock avalanches have come down – we have to go through that." The same unemphatic voice explained.

I smiled at my friend and got on with the business of crawling into the tent while he coiled up the rope.

"It ain't cocoa, you know, John," he laughed gently as I zipped up the flysheet.

There was a big avalanche while we had our small lunch – it was right where we had been climbing all morning.

Snow fell all afternoon and the wind tore at the tent. There was nothing for it but to wait for tomorrow and think about how we might get up through 'the cocoa'.

With us in the tent there was now a third person – Anxiety. While the blizzard raged outside we could only sit and wait, torn by the same doubts that plague all people at various times in life. It was like waiting before an exam, interview, dentist, doctor. Should we do it or should we not? If we didn't, then the opportunity would pass. This was the crunch, the final analysis. It didn't matter what we might have done in the past. What mattered now was whether or not we were prepared to go on. If we did go on and we succeeded, the prize was as sweet as any that life can provide: the warmth of achievement, an intensely private self-satisfaction that when it really mattered we had found what it took to go on and finish the job. Nothing more – but equally, nothing less. In spiritual terms it meant an intangible prize which not all the money in the world could win. It was everything and nothing.

These were warm feelings which welled up in conversation between the two of us. But when we woke in the night, feeling cold and alone, it was another voice we heard – Anxiety. As well as telling us that we hadn't even begun yet, and urging us to listen to the roar of the avalanches out there in the dark, the voice talked of family and responsibility. I thought of Marie Christine far below. It was always the first voice we heard in our heads when conversation died, our stomachs tied up in knots. A voice that spoke in dull flat tones of reality.

Next morning the snow and wind prevented any move. At four-forty-five Krister woke me up singing Santa Lucia, the 13th December is that saint's day and it is a great event in Sweden. One of his sisters had once been chosen to be Miss Santa Lucia in his home town of Sundsvall. At eighty-forty-five I poked my head out of the tent and looked down the glacier through the snowflakes towards the north-westerly wind: the sky was black with storm clouds. I crawled back into my sleeping-bag and Krister told me about his home in Sundsvall and all his brothers and sisters. At ten o'clock there was no change in the weather so I made the same breakfast as the previous day and then we tried to sleep again until lunch at twelve-thirty. The day dragged badly and the nagging voice of Anxiety droned on whenever we stopped talking to each other. The tent was running wet with condensation as well.

I read all through Marie Christine's miniature anthology of poems and two by William Blake seemed to fit the situation:

> *If you trap the moment before its ripe*
> *The tears of repentance you'll certainly wipe;*
> *but if you once let the ripe moment go*
> *You can never wipe off the tears of woe.*

and

> *Man was made for Joy and Woe;*
> *And when this we rightly know*
> *Thro' the World we safely go*
> *Joy and Woe are woven fine,*
> *A Clothing for the Soul divine;*
> *Under every grief and pine*
> *Runs a joy with silken twine.*

After another long night when sleep was hard to find, it was still snowing at five o'clock next morning – after twenty-nine hours. But by eight o'clock there were signs of an improvement in the sky to the north-west. Then began an agonising discussion as to whether or not we should give it a go.

At midday I led the way through deep snow towards 'ugly corner', hoping at every rise and bend to see some obstacle which would rule out any attempt for once and for all. When had I ever been so frightened? Up by the overhanging spur there were fresh cocoa stains across our path; it would only need a small stone to fall a couple of hundred feet on to my head and that would be that.

We reached the bottom of the slope up to the spur; it was an almost vertical snow-face but it was unbroken. The fresh snow enabled us to dig our crampons well in and by taking the lead in turns, it didn't seem long before we reached the worst area of crevasses. As usual getting on with the job was not nearly as harrowing as waiting for it to start.

We came to the inevitable cul-de-sac. This time the barrier was a wall of ice only twenty feet high above a ledge below which a crevasse fell away for another forty feet or so. We took off our packs, had a break and a few pieces of K.M.C.; then I stepped cautiously along the ice ledge to a point where it seemed there was a further small ledge a few feet higher. I got up on this and began to cut steps in the vertical ice. A few of the ice screws we had left up on the 1189 ridge would have been useful now, but we had nothing and the job was too much. Emptily I clambered down and rejoined Krister. The top of the wall was tantalisingly close, but it was just beyond us.

"I'll have a go over the top of this," Krister waved in the direction of some really rotten snow bridges in the middle of the crevasse.

"Okay – if you're sure." I shrugged. There was no other way as far as I could see. We put on our packs and I followed him, down, back, up and round to the bridges, ten coils of safety rope ever at the ready in my left hand. Ever so carefully he probed the snow, moving from place to place before making a firm attempt at a point where the crevasse was deep but relatively narrow. I stuck my ice axe, handle first, deep into the snow; as Krister moved up to the edge I gave him some slack on the coils wound round the axe head.

"Give me a good bit – I'm going to try and jump it," he called.

"Okay, hang on a sec!" and I eased a pool of scarlet rope on to the snow. He took two paces and leapt across, landing right on the edge. Part of the bridge collapsed but he was across. when he had a belay on the other side I had a go. I tried to take a half step in the middle and ended up on my face on the edge of the crevasse, my legs dangling in blue space below. The rope held firm and I crawled over the edge on my stomach.

The next stage was a steep and eminently unstable slope of snow leading to the cocoa rock itself.

"We really want to get going now – no stopping till we get clear of the rock," whispered Krister, in case even our voices should set off an avalanche. He led the way and we went up that slope at a cracking pace, almost running on all fours. We hardly noticed the weather because we were concentrating on the steep snow right under our noses, but blizzards were coming through with increasing regularity. For once the weather assumed only a secondary rôle.

Up we went, avalanches to right and left but nothing coming down on top of us. Krister kept on going, his time as a ski-instructor really helping now; he hardly slipped or made any mistake. Following him as hard as I could, the sweat poured down my cheeks and ran in rivulets into my mouth. My snow visor kept misting over despite the open ventilator flaps on either side. Sometimes we trod on fresh fallen brown rocks, flakes the size of dinner plates. We did not rest. More than once my foot, placed into Krister's blue print, plunged straight through into the void below and I fell forward like a stranded fish, to struggle back on to my feet again and push forward.

We were just emerging from the overhang of cocoa rock when there was a big avalanche high up to our left. A great section of snow peeled off from the upper end of the valley wall and swept down on to the saddle above us, some of it coming down the slope towards us like rivers of wet icing on a Christmas cake. Luckily it stopped before reaching us. We redoubled our efforts in case the vibration should set off something on cocoa rock.

At last we were above the level of the ice-fall and the slope slackened to a more gradual incline; although there were still plenty of enormous crevasses, they could be avoided by taking an irregular route. We were able to walk on two legs again, but we were both feeling pretty shattered. The climb up had taken five and a half hours and it was time we found somewhere to camp for the night. Visibility was poor and we were on a huge windswept curve of snow, there seemed to be no sheltered place available anywhere. Up ahead loomed a great black peak, bejewelled with ice. It seemed to be moving through the racing cloud like the bow of a warship. We were thinking of trying to find some shelter up near this sinister bulk when without warning the visibility went altogether. It was a replica of the white-out back on the 1189 ridge. Only this time we were exhausted after climbing for five and a half hours.

"Let's try up the hill a bit," Krister shouted in my ear. I nodded and got out the compass. For about ten minutes I led on a course of 100° M, then I ran out of nerve.

"This is bloody ridiculous – we might walk right over the top of the ridge – we'll have to dig in here!" I shouted.

"Okay. You stand still and let out thirty yards of rope. I'll run round in a circle, and if I don't disappear we should be safe," he yelled back.

We were okay it seemed, for the circus horse didn't fall over the edge of anything. But we were freezing up very quickly, the wind chill dropped the temperature right down and the drifting snow particles bit into our faces like hail. We quickly shook off our packs and competed with each other for the use of the shovel, for that was the warmest job. Stuck right on a bald windswept shoulder as we were, we had to dig a level platform deep into the snow. The surface was hard packed and we cut it carefully into big heavy blocks with the shovel, and then the other person lifted the blocks and made a powerful wall at the windward edge of the platform. Quite soon we were out of the wind and the whole idea of putting the tent up in such a dreadful position became something of a challenge. Krister was a tower of strength and a real expert at cutting snow blocks, born from years of clearing snow in Sundsvall. It was day seven of our partnership and we were going to make Camp 5 a real beaut.

It was getting on in the evening by the time we were satisfied that the tent would stand up to a hurricane, which the slope of the leading edge of the wall should lift over the top of us. The snow cleared and the wind dropped and in the late evening we were treated to magnificent views of the mountains in the north and east and the Pacific in the west. One by one the stars came out and things settled down for a clear and intensely cold night. The tent froze and our boots set dangerously solid under the flysheet, so we took them into the tent with us.

"Well, three days of fine weather will do it. It's four miles there and four miles back – we'll make it," Krister murmured as he ate the splendid curry he'd cooked for our supper.

"I hope to hell we can get back down that slope again," I replied, and he grinned back, saying nothing. Seven days had been like a whole lifetime, it was very reassuring being with him because he made so few mistakes and seemed completely at home in the snow.

It really was cold that night, much colder than anything we had encountered before. Once again we were grateful for the Damart Thermowear which we wore next to the skin. When I'd first seen this thermolactyl suit in Scotland, it didn't look as if it would be of much use because it looked so light. The long vest and pants could hardly weigh a few ounces and yet they kept us unobtrusively warm night and day.

Next morning we were up just after five. Miraculously it was still clear, so we ate a big breakfast, packed up our gear and set off across the ice-cap with all haste, leaving a marker stuck in the snow so we should easily find the camp site on our return. The snow was packed hard up here and our crampons bit in with a satisfying crunch and because we only sank in up to the soles of our boots we were able to achieve a sort of half trot on the level and downhill. This was the style for covering the ground, there had been nothing like it since we'd started the expedition.

Krister led the way, counting four hundred paces and then stopping for me to pluck a marker from the back of his pack and stick it in the snow. When we were moving, I followed thirty feet back, ten coils of safety rope in my left hand and the compass in my right. A wind sprang up from the north-west soon after we left Camp 5 and this helped to push us along our way. We were heading just a fraction east of due south, making for the glacier above Punta Rengo. From there we would be able to see down Canal Gajardo where it ran south towards Golfo Xaultegua; it was now a little over four weeks since we had motored down the channel on that balmy day in mid-November.

Our route lay between a high ridge, which rimmed the northern end of the ice-cap, and the stark black fang on its eastern border which we had seen so dramatically from Monte Inaccessible. We trotted along feeling achievement at every stride. When we stopped to put in a marker and have a bit of K.M.C., there was always our laughter to break the silence which had been there since the world began. The superb visibility, which had shown us so many familiar places like the Diadem Mts., Punta Laura, Cerro Atalaya, Monte Inaccessible, began to fail about half-way across. It began at our ankles, a whirling cloud of drifting snow, then gradually it drifted out off the edge of the ice-cap until it obscured everything below. We were still in sun, but it was as if we were running along on a giant mattress and I had to be careful with the compass.

By eleven-thirty we had reached the northern edge of the glacier which lay due north of Punta Rengo; visibility improved for ten minutes or less and we could see Canal Gajardo far below us. In front of us the head of the glacier was deeply crevassed, there was no reason to go farther.

"We made it!" shouted Krister, lifting his goggles to the top of his forehead with one hand and sticking out the other for me to shake it.

"I never thought we would do it, you know, not after we left 1189," he said.

I couldn't think of much to say except "Let's have lunch," and we moved down the slope about seventy-five yards until we were in the shelter of a group of ice pinnacles. Any one of these, had it been alone on the top of a mountain, would have earned the title of Cerro. While we ate double rations of cheese and biscuits, the wind drifted the snow into a white-out. It then became so cold that we couldn't wait any longer so we set off back along the way we had come.

We had turned for home. Shining like a beacon in my mind's eye was the old pot-bellied stove in the kitchen back at Ardmore. The wind had erased all signs of our footprints and fighting into the biting wind, bombarded by hard snow particles, was a different matter from our triumphant advance of the morning. We had the compass back bearing to go on, but the wind kept blowing the safety rope into a bow which acted as a sail to drag us off course. The markers were like old friends and we greeted them as such, for they loomed up ahead just as we were about to lose confidence in our direction. We could count them too, and so calculate our exact number of paces from the delightful camp site that we knew was waiting for us at the last flag.

Marker after marker came into view, each nodding its little red ribbon in the wind. Bowed sharply forward, we had to keep our heads down for most of the time to escape the wind-blown snow which filled the air like a blanket of flying needles. Every now and then we'd snatch a quick look up in search of the welcoming splash of red against a world of white.

Conditions eased when we reached half-way because our trail ran along the leeward side of the ice-cap. Out of the main wind force, which seemed to be dropping off again in any case, it became a sunny afternoon with a sprinkling of fluffy white clouds scudding across the blue sky. Wherever we looked the horizon was ringed by mountains, the dark green forest on their lower slopes paling to light grey rock ribbed with dazzling snow higher up. In all that great wilderness there was only one sign of man, a plume of grey smoke rolling lazily into the sky from Punta Laura far away to the east across the broad silver swathe of Skyring. Francisco was busy clearing the trees with fire again.

At our feet lay the incredibly ancient-looking Bahamonde Glacier, leading down to our original camp on the fiord below Monte Inaccessible, its surface compressed into vertical spikes of ice blackened by the refuse of countless rockfalls.

Heading for Camp 5, with only a couple of miles to go, we ran into the wind again. Now only a fresh breeze from a blue sky in the north-west, it seemed to cool us nicely as we trotted from flag to flag, our bodies working like machines in fine oil. This is the stuff of dreams. At last we rounded the final shoulder, below the ice-encrusted spur of black rock and there was the camp site, its marker motionless in the hot sun. Ten minutes later we were seated in the shelter of the snow walls grinning at each other like a couple of schoolboys who had just won a football match.

"We made it!" laughed Krister again. "What about going down the ice-fall now, in case the weather changes?"

"It's only two o'clock – we could. They have a saying in the Army that you are more likely to get killed on the way back from a patrol than on the way out," I said carefully. Now was a bad time for accidents, we had been going hard for eight hours;

flushed with success it would be easy to get over-confident. The ice-fall was the worst possible place for over-confidence.

"We could have a meal, rest an hour and then push on down. Make the most of the weather," Krister said, breaking into my thoughts.

"Yes, that's it," I replied, searching wearily for my pack and pulling out the trusty cooker.

We ate well, on cheese and biscuits washed down with draughts of melted snow cocoa. A pleasant lethargy seeped into our bones. The sun was surprisingly hot out of the wind, and Krister took off his shirt for a few minutes. It was the timelessness of the place which impressed me most, the enormous slowness of the way the snow was compressed to ice and squeezed over the ice fall to begin its long journey down the glacier below. I found myself looking at the sunburned back of my left hand . . . how would it look as a skeleton? Up here where a thousand years was but a yesterday, nothing lived. Now it had been crossed, a thin line of footprints across and back already eroding away with the wind. Something – or nothing?

"Come on, dreamy, let's hit the trail," said Krister, pulling on his shirt.

"Okay, but we really must take it carefully," I replied to myself really, because I knew he was a lot safer than me.

The wind had died away altogether now, there was just a baking breathless silence. The sun had plenty of burn and it still had six to seven hours to run before sinking into the Pacific far away to our left. As we neared the edge of the ice-fall the avalanches seemed more frequent than ever, as if the heat of the sun was making quick work of melting the ice glue around blocks all along the fall.

"We'll only whisper from now on," I said quietly as we stood looking for some sign of our route up on the previous day. It wasn't worth saying, but I couldn't help thinking of the effect the sun would be having on that critical snow bridge just below the cocoa.

"Okay, I'll lead. Going backwards on hands and knees. You belay me from above and then I'll take you in from below," Krister said slowly and carefully. We were both tired but we were going to concentrate on this like we'd never concentrated before.

The sun shone back off the snow so fiercely that it was as if we were not wearing the visors at all. All the cream we had rubbed on our faces and the backs of our hands ran off in sweat. Our noses burned even through the blue Mackay's biscuit wrappers. Avalanches sounded all the more sudden in the airless silence. We could hear ourselves gasping for breath as we struggled to maintain concentration, the tension involved in keeping balanced and placing our feet just so, was exhausting.

Quite soon we reached the critical snow bridge below the cocoa. It still stood, but the hole made first by Krister and then greatly enlarged by me, was now a yawning cavern with rounded edges.

"I'll jump back again – it should be easier downhill," whispered Krister. And so it was; he got cleanly across, I followed not quite so precisely, but there all the same.

We were now at the top of the steep snow slope, fifty yards away to our right was a similar slope more like a chute in the corner by the valley wall. This had been our original choice of route for the ascent from Camp 4 to cocoa rock, it avoided the crevasse with the most difficult snow bridge. However, we were glad we had come the way we had, three big avalanches had swept down that chute during the hour we were coming down. An experienced man would have seen the danger at a glance, but we hadn't.

Going fast down our own slope I began to realise I was very thirsty. Out of the corner of my eye I could see a beautiful little waterfall, cascading in a white ribbon down the black rock of the valley wall. It was only a couple of hundred yards from where we would reach the snow plain at the foot of the ice fall. 'It's all over now, let's go and have a victory drink,' I thought to myself.

We were just about at the bottom of the slope and I was going to suggest the idea to Krister, when it happened. An ugly rumble high up on the valley wall quickly grew to thunder and a spray of rock and dust temporarily obscured the waterfall from view. I didn't feel thirsty any more.

The snow was soggy at the plain and the short distance to Camp 4 took an awful long time. When we arrived it looked a sorry sight, rotten snow patched grey with dirt and yellowed at the edge with urine. Tired though we were, the work seemed light and our little tent soon blossomed again. We were light-headed with fatigue now and our limbs moved with that weighted ease that follows a hard day's work well done. The skin stretched tight across my cheeks; now I was nearing fitness again, the reserves of fat behind my hips had melted away over the weeks and I felt light and trim. In my head the crashing bars of Tchaikovsky's triumphant Fifth rang just as clearly as they sound impossible when life is not going well. For us it was unforgettable. Krister was singing quietly "Thanks for the memory . . ." Human vanity is a funny thing.

Supper was huge with spare rations, mince mixed with leek soup and thickened with potato and oats, garnished with garlic, marjoram and salt; then there was as much cocoa as we wanted. Sadly, we were much too excited to enjoy the meal and simply felt overfed with the unaccustomed size of the portions.

A great burden had been lifted from my shoulders and sleep came easily that night.

It was a good thing we had made it down the ice-fall in the afternoon because at five next morning it was snowing so thickly that we couldn't see more than twenty to thirty yards from the tent. At seven o'clock we had breakfast and decided to go down the glacier on a compass bearing, no matter what the weather, to save Marie Christine and Richard from worrying any more. It was day nine and we knew they had expected us back any time after day six.

When we set out at eleven o'clock the plan was to go all the way down to Camp 2, beside the unmapped lake on the north bank of the glacier. We both had a tremendous longing for clean clothes, and plodding along through the deep snow we fell into the trap of thinking it was all over. I kept my mind off the monotony by inventing a new challenge: to get back to London in time for the Boat Show, to see the new yacht I had ordered for Ardmore.

By lunch time we were off the snow and on the naked ice of the glacier, the weather worsened dramatically and we found ourselves in a white-out once again.

"Let's get in here," Krister called, and disappeared into a blue ice cave. The weather didn't let up in the short time it took to eat our cheese and biscuits, so we decided to 'get out and get on with it'. This was a poor idea, because it was so cold in the wind and the visibility was so bad, that we missed the narrow lane of smooth ice through the crevasses. Almost imperceptibly we found ourselves jumping crevasses each a little wider than the last, until we came to a dead end when we reached one that there was no crossing. We stopped for a large chunk of K.M.C. and took stock of our situation: it was obvious that we had strayed too far to the north. Back we went by the way we'd come, but not before I had slipped and nearly disappeared down a crevasse. I was saved by Krister's swift action with a belay, and I was able to lever myself back clear of the edge by pulling on the red rope.

When we reached the middle of the glacier, opposite the point where we had first got on to the ice an age before, it looked as if we might be able to keep going on down the glacier and get off below the lake. This would save us a good deal of time and distance on the morrow. It was tempting and after some discussion I agreed to Krister's urging to 'give it a spin'.

"Nothing if not a gambler," I said with a weary smile, it was already four-thirty and I was looking forward to putting up the tent.

An hour later we arrived back at the same spot after an abortive trip down to a point where we became long-jumpers. It needed only one of us to slip, and then injury was the minimum certainty. We were getting sloppy with fatigue.

"Gambler my arse," I shouted ruefully at Krister, as we plodded across to the exact spot where we had got on the ice six days before.

At six o'clock, for the last time, we took off the crampons and goggles which had become like extra limbs during our time on the ice. Again we were a little too casual and it was only luck that prevented an accident as we scrambled independently up the steep gritty slope away from the glacier. No sooner had we got the tent up on a grassy patch beside a stream, than the hailstones were beating a tattoo on the aluminium poles through the flysheet. Cooking was done in what seemed a flash with real water now instead of snow. Although very tired, I was filled with enthusiasm to get down to the Indian camp in the morning to tell the others we were safe. Krister felt the same, in spite of sore feet from leading all day, while I did the compass work badly at the back. The leader had to stamp each step into the snow while the second had only to follow in the prints.

Next morning we were away early, in spite of hail and a strong north-west wind. I did the leading as Krister's feet were still sore at the toes. I tried to follow the tracks of the huemul which nearly always led through the rocks and bushes in a way humans could follow. Sometimes I mistakenly followed the minor routes of the geese and these inevitably led to a bit of high ground from which they could watch out for fox and puma, a sort of cul-de-sac for humans. When we were only half-way along the lake, Krister almost tripped over a freshly killed goose, which must have been abandoned by its killer when we surprised it having breakfast.

It was another long weary day but our hearts were light and by four-thirty we were back where we had left the rubber dinghy ten days before. It was all a memory.

14

Homecoming

WE MOTORED QUICKLY down the glacier river and out into the bumpy water of the bay where the flood tide battled with the current from the river. It was half past five on Sunday afternoon, almost supper time, but there was no smoke drifting up through the trees of the Indian camp only a mile away.

Krister and I felt as if we were the bearers of a giant early Christmas present; we couldn't reach the camp quick enough to deliver the news that we were alive and well and had made it. The camp looked strangely quiet.

"What if they've already given us up and pushed off? They were very short of food, you know," I shouted anxiously to Krister above the motor.

"I bet they're there, they'll hear the motor any second now," he laughed.

Almost as he said this, I saw the little figure of my wife emerging from the trees farther up the bank of the river on which the Indian camp was built. My heart lifted. Suddenly she saw us and started jumping up and down, waving with joy; then she ran down the bank towards the camp to tell Richard.

Krister and I had rehearsed a way of letting the others know we had been successful as we approached in the boat. We cut the engine to quarter throttle and entered the river mouth only a hundred yards from the camp; Marie Christine and Richard were standing on the bank. Krister waved his right arm enthusiastically over his head, as if to signal the advance of a Grand Army; I raised both arms above my head, fingers outstretched. The result of this was that Marie Christine started to jump up and down again, and Richard's face became all smiles.

"I gave you up for dead when you didn't come back on day six," was the first thing she said, and I noticed that her brown

Krister on top

Hauling round the rapids

face looked thinner than I remembered it. Still we were back now and all was well.

After lovely hot tea I put up the tent, plagued again by the horrible black flies. Marie Christine transferred her belongings from Krister's tent which she had been using while he was up the ice with me. At last Krister and I were able to have a luxurious all-over wash in the aluminium wash bowl, then a celebration dinner of curried goose for four in our tent.

Over the bottle of Aguadiente, which Marie Christine had safeguarded during the whole expedition for this moment, the two Base Camp dwellers were told of what had happened in our absence.

Food was in very short supply, for we had all the best up on the ice-cap. They had made do with extra short rations rather than raid the stockpile on the Munoz Gamero river, in the belief that it might be needed later when we were travelling. Careful stalking by Richard had resulted in a goose shot with the ·22 rifle, the remains of which we were eating in the curry.

Because of the lack of food they had both moved about as little as possible, staying in their tents and reading for a large part of each day. The tiny one-man lightweight mountain tents were about forty yards apart and it was at night that Marie Christine heard most of the noises. She is well used to being on her own at Ardmore, which is four miles from the little coastal road that winds round our part of north-west Scotland; the winter gales there can be pretty scarey, even in a house with four foot walls of stone. The noises in the Indian camp were a little different though. As well as a background of distant avalanche thunder and wind in the treetops, there was always a scratching and snuffling of wild animals in the clearing. Time and again she looked at the clump of puma hair we had gathered and wondered if a puma really was frightened of a girl in a tent all on her own.

One morning at around eleven o'clock Richard could read no longer, and so he decided to take a breath of fresh air. He reached back over his head and carefully unzipped the flysheet of his tent, cautious to avoid any chance of a broken zip. He then rolled on to his stomach and from a lying position he could see through the trees to Marie Christine's tent. He blinked his eyes in amazement. Standing at the entrance of the tent in broad daylight was a large wolf. It was sniffing at the bottom of the zip on the flysheet. 'Has it eaten her already?' he thought illogically as he groped wildly for the rifle he kept alongside his sleeping-bag.

In a few seconds he took up the classical prone position on top of his sleeping-bag and slid the bolt quietly home on a ·22 high-velocity hollow-point in the breech.

He raised the rifle into his shoulder. Sight picture. Breath in. Breath out. First pressure on the trigger. SQUEEZE . . .

Nothing happened. Floods of panic. "Oh! I forgot to cock!" mutter, mutter. Wolf waits, patiently sniffing. Repeat procedure. Squeeze . . .

A shot rang out, coinciding with desperate screaming yelps only three feet from Marie Christine's ear. She sat up. Had she been shot? The yelping ran away. It wasn't her.

The sound of running footsteps. "It's a wolf, Marie Christine. I've shot it. We'll have to follow it," Richard's voice outside the tent.

"Okay I'm coming," she found the hatchet was already in her hand and within moments they were moving through the trees in cautious single file, Richard leading with rifle at the ready.

"There it is – on the right!" she whispered urgently. Richard swivelled and fired in one movement. The beast lay still. Possum . . .?

Richard re-loaded, told Marie Christine to stand back, walked up to the killer, placing the barrel to its head he put a round through its skull. He picked it up, four feet from the tip of its tail to its nose. A big fox.

The days went by in the Indian camp, with no news from the ice-cap save distant avalanches. Good weather, bad weather, good weather, bad weather. When day six came and went, conversation grew shorter and more stilted at their infrequent meetings. Each one silent with private thoughts of the present and future; it was a time for thinking, a time that would not be forgotten.

Marie Christine read what literature there was: a *Country Life* 1959, the *Army Nursing Guide*, Henry Cooper's autobiography, *Doctor on Everest*, *Bury My Heart at Wounded Knee*, *Aku Aku*, a recent copy of *Newsweek*.

'What if he doesn't come back?' she thought. 'Positive think-ing,' she thought. After day six she began work on a sketch and plan for a restaurant she would build in north-west Sutherland. When the books were all read, it helped to pass the time to day sixteen when thoughts would have to be put into action.

It wasn't much fun.

When I got back from the ice-cap we burned the plan for the restaurant together; the grass on the Patagonian adventurers' side of the hill is not always greener than that of the nine-to-five man at home.

The day after our return to the Indian camp was spent resting and planning the move up the black river and on up Lago Munoz Gamero. The weather was too bad to cross the bay. Our thoughts turned to Skyring – Christmas on a sheep farm; the scent of the fleshpots was in our nostrils. Next morning we were up early and in spite of gloomy skies and steady rain we set off to navigate the black river. It was a pleasant surprise to find the level of the water down in the river when we reached its mouth from across the bay; the slackening of the current was just enough to allow us to motor right up to the first portage at the rapids. Thus encouraged, we worked like mad and had our cheese and biscuit lunch at the stockpile, loaded up and then set off up the sinister black lake in a flat calm. The rain fell in a steady deluge, but when it eased its place was taken by a fresh northerly headwind which soon had the water slopping over our bows in familiar style.

I had looked up the glacier towards the ice-cap with a sort of friendly nostalgia as we passed it on our right. But I couldn't say the same about the outlook ahead of us down Munoz Gamero, it was bleak indeed; grim black mountains streaked with snow stood silent under leaden skies. The sudden piercing wind soon had us squirming miserably at the back of the dinghies. Marie Christine sang herself hoarse with Christmas carols in her attempts to take our minds off the dull monotonous ache of the cold in our bones. The wind made it look as if we might have to make for the shore and camp for the night, but such a dreary place spurred us on to reach the narrow channel which leads some fourteen miles east into Estero Excelsior. We knew the channel would be sheltered from the wind and might even offer a wind at our backs.

It wasn't simply the channel which was the incentive. The Admiralty Pilot read: "Estero Excelsior is an arm, about three miles long, extending from the north-western end of Seno Skyring; it has a very narrow entrance, obstructed by submerged rocks which barely allow the passage of small craft." Francisco had told us of this 'very narrow entrance' and called it Paso Del Indios (Pass of the Indians), apparently this was the route they used to come down from the northern waters around Puerto Natales. In fact Francisco said he used to gather giant mussels himself at one time from Lago Munoz Gamero, string them and send them for sale in Punta Arenas.

There was only one snag in all this information: Munoz Gamero is a freshwater lake, we knew that because we were floating along on it. There were no giant mussels in fresh water. Estero Excelsior must therefore also be a freshwater lake if it were part of Munoz Gamero. Therefore the 'very narrow entrance' must also be a very rapid river because it would have to fall the same height only over a much shorter distance, as the black river at the southern end of Lago Munoz Gamero. Still the printed word of the British Empire and local information should not be taken lightly, so we motored on into the long channel feeling desperately cold, but with a spark of hope that in some way we might avoid another portage of all our kit down to Seno Skyring.

The freshwater lake seemed depressingly dead in comparison with the sea. There was no weed and no sign of fish, the birds were few and always seemed far away, as if going somewhere else. The shoreline was rocky and without kelp beds to act as markers we had to be on the watch for shallows and submerged rocks. The dark green forest grew in tangled profusion right to the water's edge, interspersed here and there with roaring white torrents from the mountain peaks which glowered among the grey clouds above. The narrow channel wound on and on, each bend luring us to the next. Afternoon turned to evening and at the hourly refuelling stops we inspired one another to keep going until we reached Seno Skyring.

The weather began to lift a bit, and with it a movement started to keep motoring all night, right down Seno Skyring to the Estancia (sheep station) to make the most of the possible good weather. Any hopes of this faded when we neared the southern end of Estuario Excelsior at nine o'clock. We came to a headland with a channel running on either side towards Seno Skyring; from the map we chose to go down the right one as it offered the best chance of a clear passage into the sea. Sadly we came to a dead end in a sort of lagoon, backed by thick undergrowth leading up a gentle incline on to a low saddle; beyond this must lie Seno Skyring.

While we were motoring gently round the lagoon, looking for a camp site which afforded both shelter and easy access to the saddle above, we surprised a full-grown huemul. It must have been asleep beside the lake, for it stood up and stared at us with a puzzled expression in its big limpid eyes that looked as if it thought it was still dreaming. We cut the engines and drifted right on to the pebble beach to within ten yards of the deer which then began to look more curious than frightened at our approach. We felt too cold and tired to go up and try stroking it, so after a few moments we paddled off the beach and started up the engines once more. The sudden noise of the starting frightened the huemul and it trotted off into the bushes, while we headed for our camp site.

The portage across to Seno Skyring next day went well and we had everything done by three in the afternoon, thanks to sunny weather and a good route chosen by Richard. We left a stockpile of rations and equipment for Francisco to collect for himself at a later date; or for the Indians who were supposed to pass this way, although we saw no sign of anyone's having ever been there before us.

Anxious to press on and with Christmas bells jingling in our ears, we set off for Isla Rucas, cutting first across into the shelter of the eastern shores of Seno Skyring. The weather began to deteriorate rapidly and the sea was soon whipped to white; because of this we hopped from the shelter of one island to another and refuelled, so as always to have the tanks as full as possible in case of emergency. We were rafted together in the lee of one of these islands, half-way across Skyring, with Richard holding on to a trailing branch from an overhanging tree to keep us still. I had just passed the yellow fuel can to Krister, when a huge killer whale surfaced quarter of a mile away along the course we had just followed. It was much bigger than those we had seen at the narrows.

"Look at the size of its fin – it's like a black flag-pole," gasped Marie Christine as it surfaced again.

"Perhaps it was attracted by the sound of our engine," suggested Krister, for it appeared to be cruising round in search of something.

"I reckon we shouldn't start the motors until it's gone," I said and everyone nodded. Every time it came up its black spiky fin would roll from side to side as if it made the creature top heavy.

Ten minutes passed before we were satisfied that it had stopped circling and was making its way north-west along the opposite side of the island from us. The weather was blowing up all the time and we were anxious to reach the eastern shore of Skyring before it became too bad for us to move, so we set off again. If the whale appeared again it would serve us right, I thought, but it didn't.

Severe williwaws began descending Monte Olvidado at about ten-minute intervals, sending sheets of whirling spray high into the air as they came spinning across the surface of the Sound. Monte Olvidado was curiously granted the same spot height of 1189 metres as the mountains above the ridge where we had camped on the way to the ice-cap; the memory of which sent shudders down our backs. It was our first experience of running before a big wind in the little boats and we soon found ourselves surfing as the wave crests broke under us; while this was exhilarating it needed a little getting used to. Once or twice the engines stuttered when the spray reached the carburettors and we were rather relieved when at last we shot out of the gale into the sheltered waters of Isla Rucas. It was like coming home again; we felt a childish eagerness to speak to someone other than ourselves.

We landed first at the little woodcutters' lean-to, where Silva and the two boys had been staying when we were last here; but there was no sign of anyone now, in fact it looked as if they had abandoned the place some time before. Rather sadly we returned to the boats and motored on down the channel for ten minutes until we reached Francisco's little log cabin; but here again there was no sign of our old friend. The house had been tidied up rather dramatically, in expectation of our arrival and there was plenty of firewood cut and stacked by the fire, so we settled down for the luxury of our first night under a roof since we had left this house forty-four days before.

The sight of human dwellings had such an effect on us when we arrived out of the storm that evening that we wanted to hang on to them; next day while the storm raged on out on Skyring, we were quite happy to just laze about the cabin and listen to the wind and rain tearing impotently at the tin roof. Marie Christine who had rather dreaded the spiders and mice before, acted now as if she was in the Hilton. In between the violent squalls, the atmosphere on the sheltered beach in front of the little wooden house was quite like an English summer. Pale green weed, of a fluffy kind we had not seen before, lay just offshore; it seemed to highlight the extreme clarity of the water and framed the mother of pearl which reflected from empty mussel shells on the bottom. The bushes we had left drab brown in early November were now transformed to a fresh green. The air was full of a delicious smell from beds of mint which had run wild on the patches of ground cleared and then left to lie fallow by the industrious Francisco. Bright-eyed Patagonian cinclodes, rather larger than wheatears, hopped along the beach looking for the tiny crustacea which is their principal food; if we came too close they screeched the alarm "P-i-r-r-r!" There was plenty of evidence that the ashy-headed geese had been resting along the shore continuously since we were last at Rucas. The onions and carrots which Marie Christine and I had helped Francisco to plant were now thrusting their heads eagerly through the soil, and the crude paling fence had managed to keep the sheep at bay in our absence.

Next morning the weather was a little better and we decided to chance a run down the channel inside the protection of the islands, south-east in the direction of Punta Laura. If we managed to round the point which had thwarted us for four days in October, then we should be able to reach Senor Vasquez's place for the night.

It was sheltered in the channel, and we had the benefit of a tail wind. We were sad to see Francisco's cabin disappear from sight, but soon our attention was distracted by the many steamer duck sheltering behind the islands from the rough weather out in the sound. Although the mountains along the shore now had much less snow on them than we remembered from before, it seemed as cold as ever in the dinghies. When we reached Punta Spoerer, after crossing Fiordo Pero we found ourselves running downwind along the front of the Diadem Mountains which had a fresh mantle of snow from the storm of the previous day.

Gradually we could see Punta Laura rising over the horizon ahead, and inevitably as we drew clear of the shelter afforded by Isla Larga, so the north-west wind had a longer run at us. Quite suddenly it seemed, the waves grew much larger and steeper and we were riding a sea much larger than anything we had tried before. The reason for this was simple: we were running before the wind. Surfing along on the crests was easy compared to holding the boat into the wind, as we found out soon enough when I tried to circle round the other boat during a refuelling session. Fortunately we decided to refuel well before Punta Laura itself, so as to ensure plenty in the tanks when we reached the point; and this was done before we were completely clear of the lee of Isla Larga. Even so quite a bit of fuel was spilled during the crew acrobatics involved in filling the tank while at the same time trying to keep the stern well clear of the water – one good wave over the back would have swamped the boat.

The bottleneck in Seno Skyring formed by the projection of Punta Laura across the sound towards Isla Grande and Isla Torre, is a stretch of water incongruously named Canal Euston. We knew it could be rough, and it was.

"These dinghies are used by the Royal Lifeboat Institute," I shouted to my rather white-faced wife as we rode up and down the walls of water, across in the other boat I could see from the green of Richard's face that he was going to be seasick.

The trip down to the point took rather longer than I had calculated; perhaps the steep seas made it look as if we were moving faster than we really were. In the event I cast anxious glances at my trusty Rolex; the fuel time was running dangerously near to zero. There could be no stopping now, certainly we were close to the shore, no more than a hundred yards, but the shore was a line of black cliffs up which the sea sent great gouts of spray like serpent's tongues. Engine failure now, would mean being driven downwind right across Skyring on to a distant storm-tossed shore which showed as an unbroken white line, even from where we were.

With spluttering carburettors we shot past the end of Punta

Laura with only a few spoonfuls of fuel slopping about in the tanks. For a few seconds we turned sharp left and ran broadside to the seas and then we felt the immediate benefit of the shelter. Five minutes later we refilled the empty tanks and motored slowly past the bay heading towards the hot springs; then we ate our lunch of cheese, biscuits and for a great treat the cooking raisins so jealously guarded by Marie Christine throughout the expedition. Thus fortified we reach Isla Unicornio in under an hour, but the sight of one of the dogs with its rotting ear dangling down its face on a strip of flesh turned us against landing to greet Fresia and Alexandro who waved cheerfully from their little beach at our approach. We pushed on, and after a close shave when our engine was drowned in a squall we landed below Senor Vasquez's house at Dynover. Here again we were sorely disappointed to find no people, although the calendar had been crossed off for the day, 22nd December, and there were unwashed cups and plates on the table.

So far we had seen two Alacalufe Indians, with whom we had had no conversation. After nearly three months away from any news, in a country fraught with economic and political problems we were anxious to bring ourselves up to date on the current situation.

Where had everyone gone? The easy answer was Christmas, but what if there had been another revolution? Why had that plane flown over us four times at Portaluppi on 23rd November? Could the communist regime have become so tired of American economic pressures that they were really hostile to gringoes, perhaps as a gesture of alignment with North Vietnam? What had happened in Vietnam? Who was the new U.S. President? How was the striking going at home? These were the sort of questions that we asked one another, but mainly we wondered where everyone had gone. Francisco had assured us that Silva would be at Rucas in case we should light emergency fires on the western shores of Skyring; Vasquez had assured us that there was always someone at his place and specifically over Christmas.

The reassurance we felt at seeing the old iron stove in Vasquez's kitchen, with the name, Carron, Dover, stamped on the front was not enough to keep us waiting about next morning. We left at eight o'clock sharp in calm grey weather and soon crossed the bay that had been so troublesome in October when we had first noticed the damage to one of the motors. The first refuelling point was on the beach where Calisto and Alexandro had camped while we stayed with Sergeo.

"Let's miss out Sergeo and cut straight across to those islands," said Krister enthusiastically and I looked at the other two to see what they felt. The weather was deteriorating and it promised to be a rough ride.

"There's a cut through the island, isn't there?" asked Richard, because we were now off the 2·7 miles to 1 inch map, and only had my section of faded photocopy paper of the southern end of South America at 16 miles to 1 inch. It was more like a page from an atlas and it was hardly a navigational chart.

"Well, I can remember the channel was very much disguised by the land from both sides. We'd have to approach the cut from memory, and if we don't guess right, it's on to the rocks in this wind," I said.

"Give it a spin," laughed Krister, careless of fear as ever.

"Yeah, always a gambler," I joked meaningfully at the Swede. "Christmas is only a sales curve, let's give it a bang." Suddenly and stupidly I was tired of all the hanging around and wanted to be gone. I'd been cautious for too long.

We pushed off from the beach and a dolphin followed us out into the wind. From the start it was clear we couldn't make it on one tank of fuel, in other words it was more than three to four miles and for much of the way we would be one to two miles from the nearest shore.

It soon became clear that the weather was going to have one last go at catching us. The wind rose sharply to gale force and the surface of the sea covered with streaks of foam. I couldn't really believe that we should be back in the same perilous situation as the previous day, but here we were rolling along on an even bigger sea heading straight towards a rocky headland. Somewhere, we had to guess correctly for we wouldn't see it until the last minute, was the narrow channel which split the headland, making the tip of it an island.

"You fill the tank with the airborne mug and I'll lean forward on the cargo," I shouted to Marie Christine, after we had been going nearly an hour. She took off her gloves and started to prepare for the crucial business of refuelling in a gale.

"Don't worry about how much you spill – just don't let the motor stop," I called again when she was ready with the half-full jerrycan and the aluminium pint mug. She nodded back with an anxious look on her face.

"Okay?" I yelled. She nodded again, so I handed her the tiller and crawled forward on to the cargo.

The boat continued to career along, the overtaking waves lifting the stern first, then rushing us forward on a carpet of hissing white surf before dropping us again into a trough. The motors stood up to the treatment very well indeed, helped by the flexibility of the boats which ensured that the propellers never came too close to the surface. The problem with refuelling was to prevent the extra weight in the stern from causing either the boat or the engine to be flooded. It was really rather a desperate operation in the circumstances, and Marie Christine's heart stopped when fuel spilling from the tank caused the carburettor to choke and the engine to stop for an agonising moment, before coughing back to life again. Over in the other boat they had the red plastic funnel, and so they tackled the problem differently. First they filled the funnel holding a finger underneath to prevent leakage, and then one of them held it over the tank at arm's length before releasing the fuel into the filler hole in the top of the tank.

We were some fifteen minutes from the rocks of the headland by the time refuelling was successfully completed to give us at least a further forty-five minutes' running time. The sea was worsening all the time and looking across at the other boat, we could easily have been riding a fairground roller coaster. The boats were no longer steering a straight course but swinging from side to side as they followed the dictates of each sea as it rushed up from behind. It was at this point that those in the other boat had a brainstorm and 'remembered' the hidden channel to be well to the left of our present heading! I felt none too sure of my own judgment, when they started to wave their arms in a most demonstrative fashion for us to head further left.

We could not afford to be wrong. There could be no running broadside to this sea, let alone turning back if we saw not a channel but an unbroken line of surf in the last hundred yards or so.

I decided to stick to my own memory, and so I waved just as frantically at the other boat to follow me. They did.

Marie Christine said nothing. I just kept heading for the rocks, hoping on hope that I was right. The spray clawed emptily up into the sky above the rocks, slowed, hung for a second, and then shot horizontally towards the land in the grip of the gale.

Nearer and nearer we came. Still no sign of a channel. I began to think about how to get Marie Christine safely ashore if we hit.

"There it is," we both shouted together, eyes shining with laughter and relief. Two hundred yards right ahead, barely twenty-five yards wide, there it was, a sharp turn to the right. Then suddenly we were through, the others following, dodging the kelp beds and past a rock sculptured by the waves to look just like an eagle.

On the sheltered side of the island we found a pretty little bungalow with a white cement chimney. Plenty of geese but again no people.

We paused for a few biscuits and cheese, and joked half-heartedly about our luck, before setting off on the last leg of our journey to Estancia Skyring; it was about three or four miles down the lee shore in calm waters, and we would be there. No one felt hungry for the biscuits and cheese now, we wanted to meet people again.

It seemed to take ages. First we passed outside the single row of spiky black rocks, which with cormorants perched on their tops, looked like the lower jaw of some giant prehistoric crocodile. Then we left the area of rolling bright green grassland and passed alongside a large dark green forest. The mountains had pulled back into the distance now and those ahead, without snow, looked mere hills. The whole country was opening up into flatland, far different from the narrow steep place which had been our home for the last three months.

"Look there's the bridge over the river," cried Marie Christine, excited to recognise how near we were to the sheep farm. I smiled, remembering the sense of anticlimax I had felt when we first arrived at this bridge and found it cluttered with litter and the banks fouled with nylon fishing lines hanging in festoons from the trees. 'It's just going to be a tame dirty national park,'

I had thought then. Luckily I had been very wrong. The litter had ended at that bridge, and for us now the litter of humanity began again.

A few minutes later we pulled up on the beach in front of the smart red buildings of the Estancia Skyring. At first there was still no sign of people, but then we saw faces pressed up against the window panes in the cookhouse. Soon they came running out to shake our hands all round in greeting, and we were escorted as triumphantly towards the cookhouse as if we had just landed from the moon.

The summer hol was over.

We were in the mutton again!

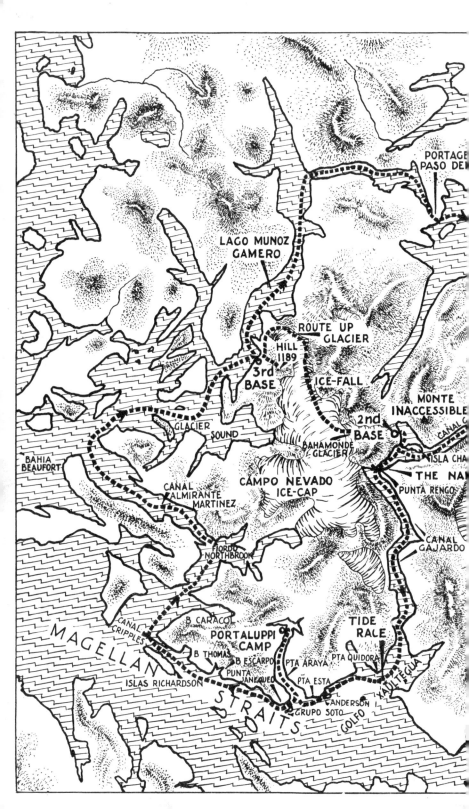